# HOPE REALIZED

A DAILY MEDITATION JOURNAL FOR
HEALING, GROWTH AND TRANSFORMATION

## DIANNE A. ALLEN

Copyright © 2018 Dianne A. Allen, MA

All rights reserved. No part of this book may be used or reproduced by any means, graphic, electronic, or mechanical, including photocopying, recoding, taping or by any information storage retrieval system without the written permission of the publisher except in the case of brief quotations embodied in critical articles and reviews.
Because of the dynamic nature of the internet, any web addresses or links contained in this book may have changed since publication and may no longer be valid. Any people depicted herein are fiction and are not representing any specific person.

Cover design by Shake Creative, Tampa, FL
Interior design by Richard Jibaja

ISBN-13: 978-0-9995778-2-0
Library of Congress Control Number: 2018910528

*At the moment of commitment, the entire Universe conspires to assist you.*
— **Johann Wolfgang von Goethe**

This book is dedicated to the courageous individuals I have had the honor to guide over the last 30 years and everyone who is searching and seeking for answers and solutions to life's challenges.

# Contents

Introduction .................................................................. 6

Acknowledgments ........................................................ 7

Using This Book ........................................................... 8

Daily Meditations ...................................................... 10

Journal Pages .......................................................... 381

Contributors ............................................................ 384

About the Author .................................................... 389

# Introduction

This book comes to you from my heart and my sincere desire to ignite the authentic power deep within your being. My style is conversational. I tell personal stories, use personal examples as well as offer ideas of the collective. I understand that we are all connected and that the pronoun in this setting is not the point. Yes, I change between first, second and third person often.

I wrote this book with the vision of inspiring you as you move along your journey. Sometimes we all need a little focus and inspiration to help us with taking right action. There are daily applications and places to journal your ideas and progress. You may use the book or another journal. Be sure you have a nice writing instrument as well. I find that I write more when the instrument is nice. Many of my clients report the same. By writing a little each day, you will be able to see your personal journey of transformation.

Being inspired each day sets the stage for a life of purpose with a vision that comes into reality. I trust that the words and ideas will inspire, awaken, challenge and affirm you and your journey. The thinkers quoted are both historical and contemporary. You know, great thinkers are alive and well these days.

There are many stories mentioned. If you find yourself in one of them, this is meant to remind you that you are not alone. None of the stories depicts a singular person and I have always changed an aspect of the story to demonstrate our connection rather than to single out a particular person. When you think I am speaking to you, think about the others who are having the same sentiment!

There are several contemporary thinkers featured among the greats as you read their quotes. I have placed a ** after the names of those I know personally and contacted to contribute a quote or two. Take the time to go to the contributors' section to learn more about these amazing people. Let them know you found their quotes in the book!

# Acknowledgements

No work is done alone. This project has taken hours of dedication. I would like to honor and thank my colleagues and professional friends for all your amazing ideas and contributions. You have supported my work and this text in a multitude of ways.

My canine friend, Maggie, has been by my side while I worked, and she never complained. Her faithful service is reflective of my desire to serve our world.

A special thank you to each contributor who shared their quotes from their work. Your contributions have made this work richer and thought provoking. I am honored to know you.

My work has taken me on an amazing journey that continues. I have met fascinating people along my road. Sharing journeys together inspires me every day. I acknowledge each person for your unique contribution to life.

Thank you to those who have cheered me one during the process of this writing. Vince and Maryellen and the many others. Your support and encouragement kept me going!

I offer a humble thank you to Our Creator for the Divine inspiration that keeps burning within my soul. When I wanted to stop or give up, that Divine spark kept urging me forward.

To you the reader, I offer sincere gratitude and humble thanksgiving. It is a privilege to share ideas and you choosing this book is a great honor for me. I acknowledge you for your presence in my life, known and unknown.

Thank you, thank you, thank you.

# Using This Book

You will be the last one to see your changes. Being in the middle of the change, writing as you go, will show you your inner and outer progress. Look back only to see how far you've come, not to move there!

Be encouraging with yourself. If you forget a day or two, pick up the book and move forward. The days are numbered from 1 through 366. You are covered for a leap year and an extra day for the others. You can start any time and end any time.

If an idea or concept inspires you and you do further work and transformation in that area, do it and then return to the book. Your life is fluid and has a flow. Being rigid all the time does not always serve your highest good. Trust that you are on purpose with a purpose and you can't help but be right on time.

In my experience, we all resonate a bit differently even when we agree about something. The best time to start is *now*. Each day has a word of the day. Do three things with the word of the day. 1. Notice how the word in all its meaning shows up in your life today. 2. Notice where bringing the word into a situation can benefit and do so. 3. Teach the concept and idea to someone.

Each day also has a quote from a thinker. I find it useful in my transformation joourney to honor the views and ideas of others. Using critical thinking, I examine the quote and discern how it is useful for me in my life. Some of the quotes are from current day thinkers. If you see a (**) after their name, see the contributors section for more information about each one. Let them know you found their quotes in the book! Next comes a reading. It is short and often containing expanded ideas. I do not expect us all to agree. I do expect us to use our ability to read and see where alignment is and then to deepen our personal life by adding more depth from others.

Next is a daily application that offers a sort of homework for the day. This guide is meant to be with you throughout the day, not forgotten after reading only to be checked off the to do list. You may apply the information in a different manner and that is perfect. The idea is to apply the information in an inspired fashion. Taking action anchors the information and ideas more deeply.

Lastly, on each day there is a space for journaling any ideas, thoughts, comments. This is important to your journey. Written goals, input and feedback set the stage for your success and fulfillment. If you are reading the eBook, I suggest you have a dedicated journal for your use as you read each day.

I recommend that you take some quiet time following reading to sit with the ideas and contemplate them. I do not expect us all to agree with every comment and quote. They are more designed to keep you thinking. Use your skills for your transformation and to live your vision.

Enjoy the readings. Feel free to visit my website for more information or contact me with ideas or questions. www.visionsapplied.com

# The Beginning...

Any thoughts you have as you embark? Write or sketch them.

## Day 1
# STEPS

*Fortunate are those who take the first steps.*
~ Paulo Coelho

We grow and transform by taking steps and passing through different stages. The best way to move forward is to follow your inner guidance system. If you are feeling disconnected from your own inner guidance, it is helpful to engage the support and guidance from another who is walking the path yet is further on the path. This can be a mentor, sponsor, colleague, friend or another trusted other. It is best to have support and guidance from others outside of your family.

Consider yourself among the few who are taking steps for your benefit and welfare. All too often, I encounter people who are not taking steps to support their health and transformation. They are choosing, knowingly and unknowingly to be stagnant. Their quality of life becomes diminished.

You are fortunate because you are taking the first steps by reading this book along with your other daily actions for your transformation and healing. Keep stepping. You are supported in ways you know not of at this point. Within a few months you will begin to see and feel your deeper self emerging in a whole new way. Keep your journal and celebrate your growth!

**Daily Application:** Reflect on your life and the steps you are wanting to take today. Tell your story and honor your journey. Allow yourself to live life vibrantly. Breathe deeply and say yes to the richness of your life. Take some time to honor you and your willingness to move forward.

**Personal Reflections:** _____
_____
_____
_____
_____
_____

## Day 2
# COURAGE

*Courage is what it takes to stand up and speak; courage is also what it takes to sit down and listen.*

~Winston Churchill

Courage comes in the face of fear and other distractions. All those who are considered courageous overcome obstacles and get the job done no matter what they are feeling. As I reflect on the times I have used courage in difficult situations, I see that my actions were easier when I spent time in quiet each morning. Sometimes you are asked to act in courageous ways in response to threatening events that could harm another or yourself. You are a courageous being.

Winston Churchill has a good point. Courage is the ability to both stand up and speak as much as it is the ability to sit down and listen. Courage is your strength in fearful or challenging circumstances.

Reflect on the courage you demonstrate. You are not on the road of transformation by accident. You are here on purpose with a purpose. This is a time for you to celebrate the courage you possess.

**Daily Application:** Honor the courage that resides in you. Bring courage to light at the right time in the right way. Ponder ways you can support courage in others.

**Personal Reflections:** _____
_____
_____
_____
_____
_____

## Day 3
# FUN

*It's kind of fun to do the impossible.*
*~Walt Disney*

Fun used to be a frivolous word when I was growing up. Some of the other kids were made fun of for being full of fun. I was rewarded for being the serious, "grown-up" as a child. I look back now and say "Wow!"

Once I heard that it was never too late to have a happy childhood. I came to realize the higher Truth of this quote that I heard as I traveled through my younger serious days. How could anyone as serious as I have a happy, fun time I wondered? As I learned to lighten up, I was uncomfortable at first. When a bad thing happened, I kept making changes that served my creative and happy sides. What a difference some fun makes.

Yes, being focused and serious is great and often required. Also, fun, enjoyment and joy are required for a perfect balance. Too far on either side and things can get rather sketchy. Now, today, give yourself permission to begin to move toward a healthy balance and have FUN.

**Daily Application:** Today, enjoy fun that is creative, healthy and enlivening. Remind yourself that all is well.

**Personal Reflections:** _____
_____
_____
_____
_____
_____

## Day 4
# TOLERANCE

*Certainly, tolerance and acceptance were at the forefront of my music.*
*~ Bruce Springsteen*

Tolerance means different things to different folks. Tolerance, I believe, is an important part of our personal development. Tolerance allows us to explore and experience things that we might otherwise avoid in judgment. Contempt prior to investigation and a lack of tolerance has kept many people from reaching great heights. Many are still stuck and cannot see that intolerance keeps them isolated and alone on many levels.

For some, tolerance means indifference. For others it means that exploring new avenues because of initially being tolerant of something previously outside of known concepts and ideas is a desirable way of being in the world.

Tolerance alongside acceptance brings you to great awareness and offers you inspiration. Next time you are exposed to something new and different, allow tolerance and acceptance to help you remain open minded. See where you can go from there. Bruce did.

**Daily Application**: Sing your own song, dance to your own drummer. Be tolerant throughout the day in your interactions. Journal you own ideas of tolerance and acceptance.

**Personal Reflections:** _____
_____
_____
_____
_____

## Day 5
# FAITH

*Now faith is the substance of things hoped for and the evidence of things not seen.*

*~Hebrews 11:1*

In what do you have faith? You have faith if your drive a car. You must have faith that the other motorists will not cross the line and hit you. You have faith when you sit in a chair. Faith that the chair will hold you, right?

Faith is a practical way to approach the world. Faith is the substance that gives us evidence of what cannot be seen. This reminds me of the wind. You cannot see the wind yet there is evidence as it blows by seeing things move and feeling the wind on your skin.

In what do you have faith? I have faith in people, in myself and in the awesome power of nature. Whatever you have faith in multiplies and is drawn to you as each day unfolds. Faith is the substance from which you bring your ideas to life.

**Daily Application:** Ponder your faith in your ideas and inspiration as part of your unseen that is coming into visibility. Write your insights below or in your journal.

**Personal Reflections:** _____

_____
_____
_____
_____
_____

## Day 6
# JOY

*Joy is your natural state.*
*~ Michael Bernard Beckwith*

Joy is often interchanged with happiness conceptually. I see them as different experiences. In my life, I have been in a state of joy yet not necessarily happy. Joy, I believe, runs deep within your being as the connection to all that is within as well as without. Happy is a feeling when a temporal experience elevates your mood and makes you smile or laugh. These ideas can coincide yet may not happen simultaneously.

How joyful is your life day to day? When was the last time you slowed down and allowed your deep joy within to show up and brighten your day? Is your joy thermostat set on high? If joy is in fact your natural state, then everything that is not joy is an altered state. Imagine how your world would be if more people connected with the deep joy within. Today is a good day to let Joy come out of hiding.

**Daily Application:** Spend some time in quiet reflection. Breathe fully and allow your inner essence and energy to rise to your awareness. Color your world today with joyful thoughts, words and actions. As you go to sleep, smile and offer gratitude for the wellspring of joy within you.

**Personal Reflections:** _____
_____
_____
_____
_____
_____

## Day 7
## ACTION

*Your actions speak so loudly that I cannot hear what you are saying.*
~ Ralph Waldo Emerson

Taking action is central to our lives. Even inaction is an action by default. Your actions are the effect of the cause that first started in your thinking and belief systems. It is often easy to determine your motives and beliefs as you reflect on your actions. Paying attention to your words being aligned with your actions makes for powerful leadership.

Some of your beliefs are nonverbal or unconscious and therefore may seem elusive. By taking right action and paying attention, you have the opportunity to gain great insight and wisdom. Taking action is often what sets leaders apart from the masses. Many people tend to talk about taking action yet do not actually take the action. Are you an action taker? As the saying goes, *don't talk about it, be about it.* Have fun taking action. Feel your own personal power.

**Daily Application:** Take time and notice your actions. How are they serving the greater good for yourself and others? Notice any of your actions that could be changed to serve you better. Notice the actions that are effective in your life.

**Personal Reflections:** _____
_____
_____
_____
_____
_____

## Day 8
# BLISS

*Follow your bliss and the universe will open doors where there were only walls.*

~ Joseph Campbell

Bliss is a powerful word that reminds you that you are here for a mighty purpose. Your purpose is always found in your bliss. Our society has taught that stifling or even denying your bliss in favor of struggle in life is a noble act. This idea is outdated. I believe that now is the time to truly follow your bliss. Be ready to walk through the open doors and enjoy the journey.

By following your bliss, you create opportunities for a better world. Your bliss or heart's desire is no accident. It is meant to be created and brought into this world by you. It is for you to do like no other person. I have noticed that each person's bliss is uniquely theirs. Your bliss is for you and only you to manifest and bring forth. This is a form of liberation that you can breathe into and say yes.

**Daily Application:** Spend some quiet time alone and allow your heart to open. Listen within to your message regarding the next right action for your personal bliss. Take notes and then do the next right thing.

**Personal Reflections:** _____
_____
_____
_____
_____

## Day 9
# EASE

*Being at ease with not knowing is crucial for answers to come to you.*
*~ Eckhart Tolle*

I remember tubing down a slow river while in college. It was simple and easy. I look back and remember not having to do anything outside of enjoying the ride with my friends and steering clear of obstacles. Learning how to go about an activity with a sense of ease; fully invested in the activity yet unattached to the process and outcome to allow the flow to be unimpeded. I did not know what was around the bend or when we would arrive at the pick-up spot. The answers came organically as we progressed.

To live in ease does not mean that there are no challenges. It simply means that you handle challenges differently than when you are rigid and controlling. Ease is a process. Ease takes practice. Ease is here for each person. It is perfectly okay to skip and be joyful as you ease through live. Life is always happening; you have the opportunity to choose how you navigate your river. Today, I choose ease. What do you choose?

**Daily Application:** Give yourself the opportunity today to move a little slower and see how some parts of your life are more vibrant. Observe life's happening from a place of ease and flow. Relax often, breathe in calm. Reflect on your life's pace. Adjust as you see fit.

**Personal Reflections:** _____
_____
_____
_____
_____
_____

## Day 10
# ORDER

*The world is not to be put into order. The world is order. It is for us to put ourselves in unison with this order.*

~ Henry Miller

To have order is a necessary aspect of living a healthy life. Order may seem like a restricting concept yet order is the other side of Zeal in spiritual practice. Order is the quality within each of us that supports our creativity. Zeal is the enthusiasm in practice. Order balances enthusiasm with rhythm and consistency. I remember as a child hearing to have things in order before leaving home. Today, it appears that a sense of disorder is often the case and some folks even appear to choose disorder over order. I choose a sense of order within which allows for a fuller flow of life on all levels.

Order is vital to a well-rounded and meaningful life. How is the order in your life? How does enthusiasm and order dance in your world? Are you able to maintain a sense of order within even when there is less order in your environment?

**Daily Application:** Take time today to assess the order in your life. Are there any areas that could use additional order? Are there any areas that are overly rigid and could use some zeal? Spend time today focusing on the balanced flow of order and zeal. Note any insights.

**Personal Reflections:** _____
_____
_____
_____
_____
_____

## Day 11
# PASSION

*There is no passion to be found playing small – in settling for a life that is less than the one you are capable of living.*

~ Nelson Mandela

Passion is a word of power and focus. You might first think of physical passion. Passion exists in all areas of life. Spiritual passion, for me, is the fuel for passionate thoughts, words and actions. In what do you have passion? If you are not sure, spend a couple of days and document your daily actions and ideas. The things you spend much of your time involved with is your passion.

If you realize that your daily time is more involved in things that you would not describe as your passion, you might be in a distraction loop. Today, I invite you to take action to get into alignment with your passion and heart's desire. Your life is meant to be full and vibrant. Distraction and fear can steal your passion and enthusiasm. Playing small does not serve you. Choose passion.

**Daily Application:** Move your body with joy and passion. Dance, exercise or simply jump around for a short time. By breaking up your routine, you free yourself. See passion in your daily thoughts and actions. Smile and keep focused on your dreams.

**Personal Reflections:** _____
_____
_____
_____
_____
_____

## Day 12
# GRATITUDE

*Gratitude is not only the greatest of virtues, but the parent of all the others.*
*~ Cicero*

Gratitude is the foundation of a content and successful life. People who live from a place of gratitude are typically happier. Gratitude comes in several forms. Gratitude for the desirable things and events is the gratitude that is typically referenced. Many people struggle with this type of gratitude and this is called entitlement or simply being ungrateful. Gratitude in the face of undesirable circumstances is a way of gratitude that can elude you. This does not mean to be grateful for the undesirable situations rather it means to have a grateful heart amid struggle.

It is your grateful heart that will be the key to your transcendence through the difficulty. The third gratitude demonstration is being grateful just gratitude's sake. Simply holding an open heart and mind in gratitude; not being grateful for anything; yet being grateful from the inside out. I invite you to honor your ability to hold gratitude in your heart.

**Daily Application:** Today, be still and look within your heart and notice all that you are grateful for in your life. Notice the things you most take for granted, like being able to read this book, having eyes to see and a sound mind. Start writing a list and continue the list until you have 100 entries without repeats. Share your gratitude and it will multiply.

**Personal Reflections:** _____
_____
_____
_____
_____
_____

# Day 13
# WORTH

*If you are respectful by habit, constantly honoring the worthy, four things increase: long life, beauty, happiness, strength.*

*~ Buddha*

All people have inherent worth and value. All beings are enough at their core. Do you honor your value and worth as a human being? Or is your worth tied to some external person, place or event? If you were raised in a culture of unworthiness, then seeing and believing your own worth may be difficult at times. You are worthy just because you are you.

Your worth and value is not dependent on your actions. All people have great value deep within. Too many people are letting grief, fear, pain and anger discolor their true essence. You are more than your actions. Knowing your value is a healthy way to live. Some may say that knowing your worth could be a sign of pride or being conceded. Knowing your inherent value is part of your worth and is not prideful. Pride comes from shame or the belief in inherent unworthiness. Thus, pride is the antithesis of knowing your true value and worth.

**Daily Application:** Write yourself a letter expressing gratitude and appreciation for your inherent worth. Be sincere and honest. After some time, read the letter aloud to yourself while looking in the mirror. Note your emotional responses. Affirm your value and others' value as well.

**Personal Reflections:** _____
_____
_____
_____
_____
_____

## Day 14
# VISION

*Vision without action is merely a dream. Action without vision just passes the time. Vision with action can change the world.*

*~ Joel A. Barker*

Vision is necessary for living a productive and fulfilled life. As Joel Barker states above, vision with action can change the world. All throughout history, people with a vision acted and things changed. Some changes we would agree are for the enhancement of humanity. Some changes may be questionable. Yet the constant remains: Having vision AND acting are the key ingredients to movement in your life, in our culture and our world. Every day I have the honor of helping people with their personal clarity of vision and action for their life.

Hamster wheels and rocking chairs are great for action yet there is no vision. Leaders are in touch with their vision while remaining open and flexible in actions. What is your vision? Do you share your vision clearly with others? How about your actions? Do your actions align with your vision? Is what you do throughout the day furthering your vision or are you acting without vision and thereby merely passing time?

**Daily Application:** Take some time today and focus on your inner vision. Connect with what makes your heart sing. Now hold your vision in the forefront of your mind throughout the day. Ask yourself frequently: "Is what I am doing getting me where I say I want to go?" Adjust your actions accordingly.

**Personal Reflections:** _____
_____
_____
_____
_____

## Day 15
# RENEWAL

*Love that does not renew itself every day becomes a habit and in turn a slavery.*

~ Kahlil Gibran

Each day you are born anew. Will your day be fresh, young and clean or are you carrying yesterday's burdens into today? Renewal of your love is necessary to remain free and out of inner bondage. When you do not renew yourself each day in a meaningful manner, you become susceptible to resentments and feeling out of sorts.

Renewal comes in many forms from spending time in nature to a bubble bath to enjoying a good book or even spending dedicated time on creative pursuits. There is no wrong way to renew yet you must determine and use the renewal methods that work best for you. I enjoy spending time in nature, under an oak tree or walking on the beach and listening to the surf. You may want to examine your life and add renewal into those stagnant areas. Stagnant areas can spoil your overall outlook and energy. Allow your inner spark to shine the light so you can be continually renewed. Keeping the renewal flame alive, you become free.

**Daily Application:** Take at least 20 minutes and quiet yourself within while breathing deeply. Drink plenty of pure water. Spend time in nature and be grateful. Journal some renewal actions, post for use later.

**Personal Reflections:** _____
_____
_____
_____
_____
_____

## Day 16
# CREDIT

*If you worry about who is going to get credit, you don't get much work done.*

~ Dorothy Height

To be of service while maintaining your sense of self is vital for a healthy and productive life. Shifting your mentality from the getting mentality to a giving mentality promises amazing life altering awareness and experience. You have most likely heard it said that when you volunteer your time, you will receive a greater reward than those who received your assistance. In my experience, this is true. "How can I be of service?" is often the best question to ask yourself to begin to change and focus on service. This is not about service others give you or not, it is about your offering service to others. This means that you begin to seek opportunities to serve others in respectful ways. Service freely offered keeps your joy alive.

Always looking for the credit and a "me first" consciousness creates a grid lock as well as resentments. Be quick in giving credit and slow to receive credit. You will see more progress toward your vision. Your leadership credibility will soar.

**Daily Application:** Seek at least 2 opportunities to be of service today. Choose actions that will truly change your heart as well as the other person's heart. Holding a door and being present for a friend without them having to ask are all ways to serve. Journal your thoughts and feelings.

**Personal Reflections:** _____
_____
_____
_____
_____
_____

## Day 17
# HARMONY

*Happiness is when what you think, what you say, and what you do are in harmony.*

~ *Mahatma Gandhi*

Have you ever been captivated by a beautiful harmony? The coming together of notes that is truly inspiring. To harmonize takes talent, attentiveness and a focus that makes the beauty possible. There is a powerful harmony when your thoughts, words and actions come together and flow beautifully into the world. Your inner harmony is reflected in your alignment of thought, word and deed.

How about harmony in nature? The harmony of the movement of the waves, the wind as it refreshes the evening air, the local ecosystem that has many seen and unseen aspects. To thrive in nature as in music and other areas, you want to identify and function within the flow and harmony. To achieve life's harmony, you bring together the key components with focus and precise action as seen in nature. This is radiant beauty emanating from you in ways that transcend words. Allow your inner harmony to emerge.

**Daily Application:** Notice harmony in motion. Where there is disharmony, focus your thoughts, words and actions to move toward increased harmony. Journal your thoughts.

**Personal Reflections:** _____
_____
_____
_____
_____
_____

## Day 18
## EQUILIBRIUM

*Chance throws peculiar conditions in everyone's way. If we apply intelligence, patience and special vision, we are rewarded with new creative breakthroughs.*

*~ Walter Bradford Cannon*

I like to think of life as being in a sort of equilibrium as differentiated from being in balance. Every time I think of balance, I think of the scales of justice with seem to be unidimensional. When I think of equilibrium, I think of an ocean drum with all the individual beads within representing an aspect of responsibility in life. As the drum moves, all the aspects remain yet they shift orientation. For me, this more closely illustrates how life unfolds. What if everything was fluid and could be rearranged and re-prioritized easily? Would your life flow better?

Every day, I take the time to honor the beauty and simplicity of living in the flow of life. May you be patient and intelligent as you focus on your vision while dealing with the interesting challenges of life.

**Daily Application:** Today, identify the many facets and responsibilities in your life. Allow these aspects to move freely and notice how they interact with one another. By living in the flow, you can remain powerfully connected to the greater power of the Universe and Nature.

**Personal Reflections:** _____
_____
_____
_____
_____
_____

## Day 19
# MISSION

*To succeed in your mission, you must have single-minded devotion to your goal.*

*~ A.P.J. Abdul Kalam*

You have a mission that is uniquely yours. Your heart's desire is meant to come alive through you. Everyone has a personal mission and you will know that mission when you see it coming forth in service to our world. When you try to ignore your mission, it will keep appearing in various ways until you pay attention. Knowing your mission allows you to focus your thoughts, words and actions toward your higher purpose and vision.

Single minded devotion to your goal helps you make progress and ultimately experience your personal mission. When you allow distractions to get in the way, you will eventually become frustrated because you will think that your mission has no value when really, you allowed distractions to cloud your focus.

What is your mission? Do you have single-minded devotion to your goal of living your mission? Today is a good day to restore your focus from any distractions that may be lingering.

**Daily Application:** Write your personal mission statement. Feel your inner connection to your mission as you read it aloud. Take at least 2 action steps toward expression of your mission.

**Personal Reflections:** _____
_____
_____
_____
_____
_____

## Day 20
# LOVE

*Let there be spaces in your togetherness.*
*~Kahlil Gibran*

Love is defined and expressed in a myriad of ways. This word and the emotion it evokes ranges from angry or sad to joyful or heavenly. Love is both a verb and a noun. Love is the ability and the willingness to allow another to do what is right for themselves without any insistence they satisfy you. Anything short of this is a form of manipulation. Love is also endearment.

Love is the fuel for a commitment that bonds people with other people, pets, ideas, beliefs and things. Love is the motivator for much of human behavior – including war or other unrest, having babies and getting married. When attached to another person or ideal, love can also be what creates amazing experiences.

There are many ways to identify and express love. Does love and the expression of love enhance your freedom? How do you know you are loved? Is it easy for you to receive love? Some say that love hurts. I think it is the agendas and attachments that hurt.

**Daily Application:** Take time to observe love in action in your life. Observe how attachment affects love. Choose to express love toward yourself and others.

**Personal Reflections:** _____
_____
_____
_____
_____
_____

## Day 21
# HONOR

*Who sows virtue reaps honor.*
*~ Leonardo da Vinci*

When you sow virtue in your world, the entire Universe benefits. Your bringing goodness into any situation is honorable. Da Vinci was a wise creative who brought much good and virtue into the world. His legacy continues today because of his virtue and desire to allow his creative vision to come alive.

Do you think he was planning to create a lasting legacy? Or do you think he was just following his vision and the legacy was born out of his commitment to his calling? Da Vinci, like many others, honored their vision and inner spark of goodness. By allowing it to come through, everyone is blessed and the legacy is born and remains alive.

How are you honoring your goodness and virtue? Are you sowing goodness while honoring your gifts and talents? What are you honoring about your contribution? Allow your goodness to emerge and share your talents. You are an original masterpiece. Start signing autographs.

**Daily Application:** Today, honor all your contributions. Remember that smiling and gentle assistance and encouragement for others is contribution. Every prayer, blessing and kind thought or word is a contribution to your own sense of wellbeing and inner peace.

**Personal Reflections:** _____
_____
_____
_____
_____
_____

## Day 22
# INTUITIVE FLASHES

*Before you speak, it is necessary for you to listen, for God speaks in the silence of the heart.*

~ Mother Teresa

Everyone has intuitive ability. Some are more open and aware of this ability than others. Some people have a keen intuitive ability. They have the natural *intuition muscle* much like natural born athletes. Intuitive flashes are those inspired ideas and amazing thoughts that seem to come out of nowhere. Often, they answer a question you have been pondering or they shed light on any situation of event.

Pay attention to these flashes; document them for your future use. Sometimes they flash into your consciousness for a future purpose. Trying to figure them out or otherwise analyze these flashes can be frustrating as they do not follow typical logical thought process. I suggest noticing, observing then documenting and using the flashes for your betterment. Offer gratitude for your ability and gift. By noticing these bright ideas that pop in, you will have solutions to challenges and questions in a more effortless manner.

**Daily Application:** Take the time to document the intuitive flashes you have today. Use the inspired ideas for your highest good. Save the ones that seem different for your future. Enjoy your ability to listen in the silence.

**Personal Reflections:** _____
_____
_____
_____
_____
_____

## Day 23
# DIVINITY

*Meditation is a way for nourishing and blossoming the divinity within you.*
*~ Amit Ray*

Meditation comes in many forms yet they all awaken us to the divinity within. Everyone has the spark and some allow it to become bright. Meditation is the way to fan the flames of your personal inner spark. People often resist the word or idea because of a belief system or unfounded fear that stops their beauty from emerging. What are your thoughts on the divinity within you?

    Meditation is the loving embrace of your being in the inner stillness and quiet. Your mind becomes still and you are open to guidance and connection that is not available as readily when you are moving fast and distracted. Some people mediate by sitting still, some use yoga, some exercise and others use music. There is no wrong way, there is your way.

    The divine spark within you is wanting to shine brightly. It is your choice how to allow your divinity to come forth. Nourish your inner light and allow your beauty to blossom from within much like a beautiful rose.

**Daily Application:** Today, take some time in quiet and relax. Allow your divine inner spark to shine a bit brighter. Honor where it leads by seeing what it is shining light on within you. Honor your inner spark by acting in alignment with your divine inspiration.

**Personal Reflections:** _____
_____
_____
_____
_____

## Day 24
# EMERGENCE

*All changes, even the most longed for, have their melancholy; for what we leave behind us is a part of ourselves; we must die to one life before we can enter another.*

~ Anatole France

We are all constantly emerging. Every day you are born anew and you must release yesterday to enter today fully alive and present. In Western culture, we are taught to hold onto resentments from the past. This yields a melancholy and heaviness that blocks the emergence of our true calling and purpose. Yes, you must be willing to release the story and the attachments therein. If you have built your identity around the story, releasing it will be more difficult as that part of yourself may die so you can enter your new life.

You may say you want positive changes in your life. Are you willing to allow those changes to emerge by releasing your attachments to what once was? Your inner self is always inviting you to be free of the bonds of yesterday. It is perfectly OK to honor your feelings of melancholy or fear while taking the steps to release the old. The old must die so you are free to move into your new day.

**Daily Application:** Journal your commitment to allowing your true mission and inner calling to emerge. In the evening, take the time to let go of anything in the past that you are holding on to that is blocking your happiness and emerging Joy.

**Personal Reflections:** _____
_____
_____
_____
_____

## Day 25
# GENTLENESS

*Nothing is so strong as gentleness. Nothing is so gentle as real strength.*
*~ Ralph W. Sockman*

Looking at a small plant emerging through the soil you see the tender new life standing strong yet it feels so gentle and soft. The plant is strong to break through. I think of the same gentleness and strength when I think of a butterfly emerging from its chrysalis. Strong and gentle at the same time.

When you mistake gentleness for weakness, you are missing the true value of gentleness. Gentle people have a quiet inner strength. Your gentleness is a powerful gift that enables you to transcend obstacles much like the plant and the butterfly. Your sense of perseverance and focus yield great results. Now is the time to embrace your own gentleness and know with conviction that your strength is part of this gentleness. Release any perceived need to put on the façade of being strong which comes from a place of perceived weakness. Your gentleness is the root of authentic strength.

**Daily Application:** Today take some quiet time and connect with the gentleness of your inner self. Now, notice how your authentic strength can be present while expressing your true gentleness as you move through your day. Notice gentle strength in others and honor them silently or share with them. Remind yourself that true gentleness yields great results.

**Personal Reflections:** _____
_____
_____
_____
_____
_____

## Day 26
# EXPANSION

*Your ego tells you that you were wronged and it validates your separation. Your Higher Self tells you that you were blessed and it validates your expansion.*

~ Alaric Hutchinson

You are meant to expand and evolve as you grow through your life. You are not the same person now that you were years ago, or even yesterday for that matter. Your ego can keep you feeling separate and alone, isolated if you will. This part of your psyche looks for separation and confirms your differences from others. This often leads to misunderstandings and can lead to self-righteousness. This way of living is not pretty.

Your Higher Self knows better. It reminds you that the separation is an illusion and that as you expand, you see that even those wrongs were actually blessings because your Higher Self could take the pain and transmute it into a blessing. When you hold on to the pain and discord, you block the power of the Universe from moving through the situation to promote you further in life.

Your ego is not your amigo my friends. It serves you well for some linear problem solving and other tasks. It cannot always be believed. This is particularly true when you are being held down on any level. Your Higher Self knows better. Listen to your inner still voice. It will show you how to emerge from your pain like a phoenix.

**Daily Application:** In your quiet time this morning, listen to your Higher Self. Take actions for your life expansion. Put yourself in position to receive your blessings. If you feel wronged in some way, ask your Higher Self to help you see your blessings.

**Personal Reflections:** _____
_____
_____
_____
_____

## Day 27
# HELP

*Life's most persistent and urgent question is: "What are you doing for others?"*

~ Dr. Martin Luther King, Jr.

What are you doing for others? In some circles, you may hear comments about helping people to get out of their own head. You are most likely a helper or giver type person if you are reading this book. Dr. Martin Luther King, Jr. has a valid point. It is urgent that we approach life by serving and assisting others. This is a way of life, a consciousness if you will. Helpers are those who are focused on serving. This does not mean to help others in a needy, clingy way so you can be the martyr and remind them of your goodness. That is manipulation and not the goal at all.

When you do for another expecting a return from them, you ae missing the point. The Universal Law reminds us that we are blessed in abundance. The key here is to go beyond your limited thinking and remember that the blessing can come from anywhere and may never come from those you served. You are blessed by helping another. You receive immediately through your action and you receive in the long run as well. As I see it, helping and serving others is the way to go.

**Daily Application:** Help another today without expectation or agenda for future return. Let go and allow the Universe to bless you. Take care of yourself and help others. You can do this.

**Personal Reflections:** _____
_____
_____
_____
_____
_____

## Day 28
# NURTURING

*Find out what your gift is and nurture it.*
~ Katy Perry

Nurturing can be challenging to many. Do you nurture yourself on a regular basis? Many of the people I work with struggle with nurturing themselves. Yet without nurturing, you become depleted and often exhausted and tired. This is no way to travel through life.

Your gifts are beautiful seeds within you that only you can nurture and bring forth the fruits. No one can do it for you and no one can take your place. It is your personal responsibility to explore your gifts and nurture them into the beautiful gift for your life.

The more you nurture and care for your gifts, the more you are inspired to share the radiant luster and beauty that is emerging through you. You have amazing gifts, nurture them and share them.

**Daily Application:** Today, journal or draw your gifts emerging. What do they look like and how do you feel when you let them emerge? Share your gifts with another. Nurture your gifts by taking good care of you.

**Personal Reflections:** _____
_____
_____
_____
_____
_____

## Day 29
# LAUGHTER

*The human race has only one really effective weapon and that is laughter.*
*~ Mark Twain*

Laughter is an amazing healing power. Laughter awakens creativity, reduces stress and allows you to experience a richer life. I have had times in my life when laughter seemed to elude me. Whether it was a result of stress, depression or fear based pressure, my life was lacking depth and fullness during those times. When everything within is either shut down or serious; your daily life becomes 2 dimensional and flat. This is obviously not the goal. As I was able to laugh again, I came to life in new and amazing ways.

Laughter is the elixir that frees you from the bondage of false beliefs, self-importance, fears or pain. Laughter connects you to the inner you. Laughter brings you together with others. A good laugh can bring relief and healing to those stuck parts of you. Laughter is good. Laughter is good for you, like a great vacation.

**Daily Application:** Laugh today for at least 5 minutes. Notice the inner freedom that develops. Create beauty in your life from that freed space. Enjoy.

**Personal Reflections:** _____
_____
_____
_____
_____
_____

## Day 30
# DELIGHT

*The true delight is in the finding out rather than in the knowing.*
*~ Isaac Asimov*

I love my Ah ha moments and epiphanies. When I learn something or find out the answer to a question, I am delighted. Isaac Asimov hit the nail on the head with this quote. After the epiphany, you know the content. That knowing eventually becomes part of your autobiography and the delight wanes.

Are you investing time each day in learning and expanding your awareness? This is how you can experience delight each day. Every day that you experience delight, you have the honor of connecting to your inner Joy. A happy life is a string of happy days. Delight adds to each day to uplift it and create authentic Joy and happiness for you.

Be curious. Explore. Ask questions. Learn something new every day. Share your ideas and knowledge with others who are curious and delight in their *finding out*. There are many ways to experience delight in your day. Be open. light wanes.

**Daily Application:** Today, go out with the focus to find answers to your inner questions. Pay attention to your delight when you have that ah ha as you receive the answers. Notice your visceral experience of delight. Take a moment and honor your experience. Note your delight below. Create delight every day.

**Personal Reflections:** _____
_____
_____
_____
_____
_____

## Day 31
# ABUNDANCE

*Not what we have but what we enjoy, constitutes our abundance.*

*~ Epicurus*

Abundance is a big word in that it has many meanings within our society. It can mean dollars, relationships, experiences, wealth and other combinations. It seems that each person has their own inner construct of abundance. For Epicurus, it is not in the having that we are abundant, it is in the enjoying. This makes sense to me.

You can have many things and yet not truly possess them. Enjoyment of things is true abundance. What are some things you enjoy that you do not personally own? I enjoy racing sailboats. I sail on other people's boats. The pure joy I experience is true abundance for me. What are some things that you enjoy that you do personally own? What experiences do you enjoy? All your enjoyment constitutes your abundance. Seek to enjoy more by being open and your abundance will increase from the inside out.

**Daily Application:** Enjoy today. Pay particular attention to your abundant opportunities to enjoy your life. Make enjoyment your focus and then feel your abundance. By changing your focus, you can create abundance on many levels.

**Personal Reflections:** _____
_____
_____
_____
_____
_____

## Day 32
# CONTRIBUTION

*Each of us is a unique strand in the intricate web of life and here to make a contribution.*

~ Deepak Chopra

Each day we have the opportunity to offer our time or talent to others. When you freely give, and are able to also freely receive, you transcend many obstacles. Contribution begins with receiving from others and one's self or Spirit. Contribution continues and grows as you share your talents and abilities with the world. Benefits of contributing include: a sense of peace, inner harmony, increased immune system response, decreased stress and anxiety and an overall sense of well-being.

As you reflect on your own contributions, take time apart and honor your willingness and ability to freely offer your special gifts. Remember that only you can contribute what is yours to offer. No one else can contribute what you are uniquely called to contribute. Looking for contribution from others that is not theirs to give will set you up for disappointment.

**Daily Application:** Choose how you will contribute to your family, friends or group. Share some of your talents freely. Decide to take daily action in this area of contribution.

**Personal Reflections:** _____
_____
_____
_____
_____
_____

## Day 33
# TENDERNESS

*Tenderness is greater proof of love than the most passionate of vows.*
~ Marlene Dietrich

I know a woman who is so beautifully tender with other beings. Her voice is soft and her hands are gentle. I have witnessed her great courage and strength in navigating this human experience. Her voice has a melody that nurtures, supports and uplifts. When I think of tenderness, I think of this woman.

In an insensitive world, it is often a challenge to experience and witness real tenderness. Tenderness, for me, reflects an inner knowing of the connectedness of all life: being gentle with all creatures, including the self. Sensitive people can have a difficult time with expressing their tenderness in a not so tender world. Remember the small seedling pushing through the soil? It does not lose its tenderness yet it is strong enough to withstand the seeming restrictions of the soil. The soil ends up being the perfect place of rest and sustenance that the tender sprout needs to grow. Today, reflect on the strength that underlies real tenderness. Honor that place within you.

**Daily Application:** Be tender with you today. Think loving and supportive thoughts about you to you. Be tender with others. Choose boundaries that are supportive.

**Personal Reflections:** _____
_____
_____
_____
_____
_____

## Day 34
# LEARNING

*A man only learns in two ways, one by reading, and the other by association with smarter people.*

~ Will Rogers

I have heard it said that life is like a school; we are given tests and as we pass them, we get to move forward. This is one way to see things. Some say that everything is a learning experience. How do you learn? Do you learn from your mistakes? Do learn from others' mistakes? Are you a learner that doesn't necessarily need a mistake to learn anything?

When I was younger, I read all the time. My first book I loved to read was the dictionary followed by the encyclopedia. My mother instilled reading and the love of learning from an early age. I wonder if she ever heard this quote.

Learning comes in a myriad of ways. From formal education settings complete with tests and papers to life learning. All learning has value. All learning helps us grow as people. I even think that people who don't like to learn are learning. It is kind of like gravity to me, whether you focus on it or not, it remains present. Who will pay attention and take the lessons forward?

**Daily Application:** Today, notice what you learn and the many ways you learn things. Spend time acknowledging your gifts and talents in learning. Learn something new and teach it to another. Keep it going.

**Personal Reflections:** _____
_____
_____
_____
_____

## Day 35
# PEACE

*Peace comes from within. Do not seek it without.*
*~ Gautama Buddha*

Peace begins within each one of us. I have found that every time I am looking to someone or something else to give me peace that I was looking in the wrong place. Peace, real Peace, lives within my heart. Peace is an inner state of well-being. In my work, I have spoken with many people who have mislabeled Peace with boredom. These are two different experiences. For those who struggle with the proper label, I have noticed a certain affinity for chaos and drama in their lives. These are those folks who must have had a lot happening and many things with time demands in order feel productive and alive.

Peace is not merely the absence of chaos; rather it is the experience of a deep harmony and calm. We can act while experiencing peace. In fact, many great actions happen while the person is feeling peaceful on the inside. When you begin to see peace as an inside out radiance of your essence, you begin to see the outward expression of peace in your world. It is time for us to cultivate the expression of peace by allowing it to emerge through us each day.

**Daily Application:** Take time today and take several long slow deep breaths with full exhales followed by deep inhales. Feel your heart slow. Choose peace today and remember that it all begins with you.

**Personal Reflections:** _____
_____
_____
_____
_____
_____

## Day 36
# FREEDOM

*Freedom lies in being bold.*
*~ Robert Frost*

Another word for freedom is redemption. When we are freed from the bondage of our own limited thoughts and behavior patterns, we are redeemed in many ways. Freedom seems to be one of those principles that many seem to think is a good idea yet can never quite reach it. So, I see many people become distracted from their journey because of unbelief and a kind of apathy that causes them to give up on some level.

I have heard that some think freedom is simply a construct. My belief is that freedom is an inside job. You can be free and be in an outer prison. Elie Wiesel was bold and he remained free inside while enduring the unthinkable. Your boldness can be internal or external, either way you are free.

It is time for you to be bold in living your life's purpose and to do the good you want to do in the world. It is time to say yes to that inner knowing and move forward, offering your gifts with a bold assurance. You are free to be your authentic self.

**Daily Application:** Express your gifts today in a bold manner. Let your light shine and stand on your desire to be a beneficial presence. Know you are supported in living your vision. Journal your experience and share your inspiration with others.

**Personal Reflections:** _____
_____
_____
_____
_____
_____

## Day 37
# TRANSITION

*Step back in perspective, open your heart and welcome transition into a new phase of life.*

~ Linda Rawson

Sometimes the hallways of transition can be very challenging and scary. Transition can also be thrilling and uplifting. The human experience of transition varies. Some of my life transitions have been scary and others a beautiful, gentle ride. The common thread is that every transition afforded me the opportunity to experience all of life from an expanded vantage point. Transitions have been most difficult when I was holding onto what was no longer good for me. Transitions have been gentler when I was ready and conscious about the transition.

I believe, after many years, that each transition affords us the opportunity to choose how our lives will continue to unfold. Hurrying the change or trying to hold on seems futile because the universe is moving whether you like it or not. The only constant is movement from one time and space to another; it is simply that we don't really pay attention until the resistance creates enough pain. I have learned to slow my mind and body by deliberately breathing. Long slow deep breaths, and then allow the flow of my life to be gentle. I have made friends with transition.

**Daily Application:** As you make small and larger transitions today. Notice the energy needed to switch thinking, movement and speaking. Notice how much easier transitions are when you practice nonattachment from the outcome.

**Personal Reflections:** _____
_____
_____
_____
_____

## Day 38
# OUTRAGEOUS

*Nothing is impossible, the word itself says I'm possible!*
~ *Audrey Hepburn*

I love this quote by Audrey Hepburn. In many ways, she was outrageous in her time. In what ways are you outrageous in your time? To be outrageous is to step outside of the box of what others think you are going to do or be. I have seen some who take this idea to a point of vulgarity or too far which begins to put a different meaning on the idea. Outrageousness for today is about stepping out of your box and taking a stand!

Do you ever have any self-doubt? Well, to be outrageous is to move past the doubt into possibilities. What if you could achieve everything you think and believe with focused, smart action? That would make much of your ideas and hard work go together for a greater outcome.

To be outrageous is to step outside of the comfort zone smallness and grow into your greatness by believing in yourself. It may seem outrageous on some levels and remember that you are possible.

**Daily Application:** Use the mantra "I'm possible" in its various forms throughout the day. Take note of the many doors it opens in your mind, words and actions. Be outrageous and break one of your self-imposed restricting behaviors and step outside for some fresh air. Note your experience below. You'll be glad you did.

**Personal Reflections:** _____
_____
_____
_____
_____

## Day 39
# RELAXATION

*If a man insisted always on being serious, and never allowed himself a bit of fun and relaxation, he would go mad or become unstable without knowing it.*

~Herodotus

Healthy people learn that relaxation and taking a Sabbath regularly is essential to a vital and powerful life. Breathing and how you breathe tells you so much about your relaxation level. During your hurried day, you may notice that you are breathing shallowly from your chest. You may even be holding your breath from time to time. This is not conducive to relaxation; in fact, it hinders your ability to relax. Herodotus appears to be on point and applicable for today's world and he was writing centuries ago. Relaxation must be universal issue.

Relaxation offers you the chance to collect your ideas, vision and energy needed to strive for and attain your goals and desires. Relaxation affords you the time and space to be inspired and to rest as to also maintain mental clarity and focus. To relax, you do not have to go away to some place far from humanity though that is an option. Relaxation well used is practiced throughout the day. Breathing on purpose with an intention of allowing your entire being to decompress and simply be.

**Daily Application:** Take several minutes at least 3 times today to stop and breathe. Give yourself times to decompress and relax. Before retiring for the night, reflect on any changes you noticed in your day today. Rest in peace and relaxation tonight.

**Personal Reflections:** _____
_____
_____
_____
_____
_____

## Day 40
# UNIQUENESS

*Be uniquely you. Stand Out. Be colorful. The world needs your prismatic soul!*

*~ Amy Leigh Mercree*

Some say that no one is unique. I say we are all unique and we are connected by our common human and spiritual bonds. In our personalities we are unique, in our individuality we are all connected. As I say to my clients: "Everything effects everything". Because of our connection to each other, I believe it is important to be our unique selves while honoring the beauty in others.

Nothing great was achieved by playing small and hiding. Your uniqueness is meant to shine and bring light and goodness to the world. How are you letting your prismatic soul come out and play? Standing out can take you into uncharted territory and at the same time with your focus on the highest good, you can be that beneficial presence for you and others.

Think about a time when you wanted to stand out yet you held back. Remember the discord and heaviness of stifling your gifts? Now, think about a time when you risked stepping up for something important to you. I'll bet your uniqueness helped remind you of your goodness and power to create the life you desire.

**Daily Application:** Today, stand out and be your unique self. Let your light shine through your smile and your eyes. Offer colorful good to others and be blessed in return. Express your soul colors.

**Personal Reflections:** _____
_____
_____
_____
_____

## Day 41
# PRACTICALITY

*The leader has to be practical and a realist, yet must talk the language of the visionary and the idealist.*

~ Eric Hoffer

Visionaries often dislike being practical. I remember times when I was told to be practical and I cringed inside. As I grew into leadership roles over the last couple decades, I had to learn to be practical and more of a realist. This does not mean that my visionary skills and my idealism has gone away or that I am squashing these parts of me. With experience and knowledge, you learn to balance your visionary self with the practical self. Yes, both can mutually co-exist.

Where is your comfort zone? Realist? Idealist? Are you the practical person or the visionary? All these are great and each one you resonate with demonstrates to you the exact power and multifaceted beauty of who you are. You are not unidimensional. Be practical as you make decisions while also allowing your visionary self to navigate. Eric Hoffer has a point to be able to be practical while also speaking the language of the visionary. If you are the visionary leader, learn to speak practically and appeal to the realists so they will support getting the vision to come alive. That's what Disney has done.

**Daily Application:** Take some quiet time and honor the parts of you that are included in the visionary and the realist arenas. Notice how they currently show up in your life. Take some time to bring your varied assets together for your unique leadership style. Notice the words you use. Any adjustments needed?

**Personal Reflections:** _____
_____
_____
_____
_____
_____

## Day 42
# SUCCESS

*A successful man is one who can lay a firm foundation with the bricks that others have thrown at him.*

*~ David Brinkley*

There are many different operational definitions of success. David Brinkley has one idea that is interesting. If you are a person of influence or a free thinker, chances are bricks have been thrown at you. Well, lay your foundation and use them as your walkway.

In our society, victimhood is rampant and litigiousness the norm. Maybe an effective way to keep moving forward is to lay that firm foundation and keep going, eyes set on achieving your vision for the good. Most people who set out to make a difference are met with skepticism and often bricks are thrown in an effort to stop them. The brick throwers are small minded folks. Sometimes you throw bricks at yourself. Those times are important and they show you where your blocks are to your own success. Sometimes you are the biggest brick thrower. You are a leader in your own right. See what great foundation you can create from the bricks.

We, like David Brinkley, have had bricks thrown at us. Are you going to let others stop you from fulfilling your mission? Today is the day to walk upon your foundation and use any bricks for your stepping stones.

**Daily Application:** Meditate on the word "Success". Understand and feel its meaning in your life. In what ways have you avoided or sabotaged your success. Does envy get in your way? Take the bricks and make your foundation.

**Personal Reflections:** _____
_____
_____
_____
_____
_____

## Day 43
# REASSURANCE

*Ask before asking advice or reassurance.*
~ Marshall B. Rosenberg

Reassurance is often an important part of relationships. We all could use some reassurance. You may seek it from family, friends, colleagues or mentors. There are times when past clients have called me to "say hi" and it seems that their undisclosed motive was to get reassurance and maybe some advice. They didn't ask for either, they simply asked to speak to me.

When you want advice or reassurance, ask the listener in the beginning of the conversation. This is the most respectful approach. I listen with different ears. I can be your friend, mentor, minister, counselor, colleague, consultant or teacher. Each role has different ears. By engaging with me without being clear about your needs, you may not get what you are seeking. And maybe you won't feel heard. If you want business advice and you call me to "chat", that is a mismatch.

Practice asking the listener for what you want so both of you are clear and you can end the conversation successfully with both of you feeling heard and respected. Reassurance is an emotional experience and without asking for this type of response, you may not get it if the listener thinks you want advice or just a listening ear.

**Daily Application:** Notice the many ways you ask for what you want from others. Are you as clear as you would like to be? Who offers reassurance to you when you need it? Thank them in a unique way today for being an important person in your life.

**Personal Reflections:** _____
_____
_____
_____
_____
_____

## Day 44
# VITALITY

*When we connect with our personal authenticity and truth, the vitality that is triggered becomes an eternal spring of regenerative passion that continues to expand our experience.*

~ Heidi Reagan

I love the word vitality. It brings energy and joy to me to think about the power we all possess in our breath. You are a vital being. Your presence matters. Your being authentic brings your natural life force to the forefront. I remember times when I was not authentic and I'll bet you can remember times when you weren't as well. Your vitality suffered due to the disconnection from your life force. Mine did too.

To continue to expand, your vitality must have an avenue to express and that avenue is your authenticity. The more authentic you are, the younger you feel. Your inner light radiates and your world expands. Think of the times when you felt *really* alive. I'll bet your natural authenticity was obvious. Through your living your truth, you were energized naturally. You were experiencing your inner vitality in expression.

Your presence is vital and your vitality emerging into the world is necessary for the growth and progress. Take a few deep breaths and relax. Now, let your light shine!

**Daily Application:** Notice your energy level. Are you experiencing your vitality right now? Now, take a few long, deep breaths and feel your life force raise. This is your vitality in expression. Today, express your authentic self and notice how your energy elevates. Spread your Joy.

**Personal Reflections:** _____
_____
_____
_____
_____

## Day 45
# PARTNERSHIP

*Here's good advice for practice: go into partnership with nature; she does more than half the work and asks none of the fee.*
~ Martin H. Fischer

Partnership is often thought of between people yet partnership with nature is a vital element in our thriving on Earth. Nature lives with an elegant simplicity that transcends the two-dimensional linear time. Nature knows her seasons and she gets everything accomplished without hurrying. Nature moves forward with rhythm and flow in a circular type, seasonal manner. Maybe we have something to learn from her.

How would your life be different if you honored the seasons of life and you released the need to control or hurry the process? Going into a true partnership with nature means that she is working on your behalf, in cooperation with you and she freely gives to you. You simply need to do your part along with receiving her gifts and support.

You are not in this world alone and you do not have to push to make it. You must take right action and allow your partnerships to serve you or release them. Allow nature to be included in your partnerships and you will be richly rewarded.

**Daily Application:** Spend at least 30 minutes in nature today. For some time, focus on being grateful for your natural surroundings and for the seasons. What season is it in nature as you read this? What can you learn from nature today? Now, let the truth emerge in you and share your insights with another.

**Personal Reflections:** _____
_____
_____
_____
_____
_____

## Day 46
# WISDOM

*Turn your wounds into wisdom.*
~ Oprah Winfrey

All of us have wounds of some sort. There are physical wounds, emotional wounds, mental wounds, spiritual wounds and social wounds. How are you addressing your wounds? Or are you attempting to stuff them and pretend they are not impacting your life? Buried wounds are often the cause of physical illness and dis-ease.

Turning your wounds into wisdom as Oprah suggests is a transformational way to approach your pain. By extracting the lesson and releasing the painful charge of the emotion, you are placed in the driver's seat as to how you move forward. Any perceived victimhood disappears and your authentic strength emerges.

Wisdom is the result of taking your knowledge and experience and using both to create the life you desire. You make better choices and your overall happiness and satisfaction levels rise. The wisdom you develop is a gift for you and for those you impact. You are not in a vacuum; your wisdom or lack thereof is felt all around you without a word being said.

**Daily Application:** In your quiet time, reflect on the wounds that you have healed and turned into wisdom. Also reflect on the wounds that are not yet turned into wisdom. Offer gratitude for your life experience and honor your wisdom. Share some of your wisdom today. Let your wisdom touch another's heart.

**Personal Reflections:** _____
_____
_____
_____
_____
_____

## Day 47
# FRIENDSHIP

*There is nothing on this earth more to be prized than true friendship.*
~ Thomas Aquinas

What does friendship mean to you? I notice that some people use the word frequently while others make qualifications when using the word. Friendship means different things to different people. Who are your friends? Are you happy with your expression of friendship with others?

I have some clients who have shared that when they are stressed or in pain that they come out of their personal alignment regarding their friends. They have shared that they often take their friends for granted and never really think about the investment and power of true friendship.

Because true friendship takes investment on both people's part, it is a real prize or reward for your investment. Authentic connection and the power of a good friend cannot be replaced with things. Be sure to invest in the people in your life. Allow them to invest in you.

**Daily Application:** Take some time today to express your gratitude to your true friends. Allow your friends to give into your life. Pay particular attention to the power of the bond with those true friends. Now, celebrate your investment.

**Personal Reflections:** _____
_____
_____
_____
_____

## Day 48
# CONVICTION

*One with the Earth*
*With the sky*
*One with everything in life*
*I believe it will start*
*With conviction of the heart.*

*~ Kenny Loggins \*\**


What is your conviction? To hold a belief firmly is how visionary leaders are able to lead effectively. Kenny shares that he firmly believes in living from his heart. It is vital to know your convictions and have the ability to articulate them effectively. Many people try to lead from their intellect and their results tend to lack connection and passion. Leading with your heart yields deeper soul connection and a richer life.

As you have heard me say: "Everything effects everything". We are all essentially one in spirit, yet we have our individual personalities. When you remember to lead with your heart and allow your intellect to be the perfect navigator, you become happier and more fulfilled. It all starts with leading from the inside out, leading with your heart. What is your heart saying? Are you listening? Take the time to connect to the artful masterpiece that you are and start signing autographs!

**Daily Application:** Focus on your heart center and allow your energy to emerge through your heart and into the world. Bring to mind your convictions or beliefs and journal what is most important. Allow yourself to become even more aligned with your beliefs.

**Personal Reflections:** _____
_____
_____
_____
_____

# Day 49
# BREATH

*If you want to conquer the anxiety of life, live in the moment, live the breath.*

~ Amit Ray

Many people come to me and want help with anxiety. The first order of business is usually to work on breathing. When the brain is oxygen deficient it sends emergency signals to make the body breathe to sustain life. Theses emergency signals are a form of anxiety. It is not the mental illness that is often medicated.

Anxiety from not breathing is fixed by breathing. Full deep breaths allow the body to settle and receive vital nutrients and even proper hydration. When your body is in emergency stage from a lack of air, it only does the minimal to sustain life. Always remember that air is your friend.

Holding your breath is a form of medication for emotional pain. Look within and be willing to heal what is stopping your breath. When you are moderating pain of some type, your breath is shallow. To reduce the anxiety of life, breathe deeply.

**Daily Application:** Breathe deeply and enjoy your breath. Lay flat and place a book on your belly. Now breathe deeply and make the book rise and fall. Notice how being oxygenated really feels! Live in each moment with a full breath and you will experience transformation.

**Personal Reflections:** _____
_____
_____
_____
_____
_____

## Day 50
# INTELLIGENCE

*The brighter you are the more you have to learn.*
~Don Herold

Intelligence is a vital part of your success and joy. Your intellectual or linear intelligence is wonderful in solving linear challenges in life. Using the well-known scientific method that you learned in elementary school is useful and necessary in many aspects of your day. To be able to solve problems and figure out solutions to challenges is part of your intelligence. No matter how intelligent you are, there is always more to learn. The moment you think you have learned all there is marks the moment that you place yourself at a disadvantage.

Emotional intelligence is lesser known yet critically impactful in your relationships and major life decisions. Think for a moment of decisions that you did not feel right about but acted from your intellect only. You might notice that some of the decisions were not your best. By aligning your intellectual and emotional intelligence, you can make effective and responsible decisions that lead to powerful and successful actions.

**Daily Application:** Today, notice the many opportunities for emotional intelligence to support your goals and desires. Teach this to another and journal some of your thoughts.

**Personal Reflections:** _____
_____
_____
_____
_____
_____

## Day 51
# CONNECTION

*We are like islands in the sea, separate on the surface but connected in the deep.*

*~ William James*

We are all connected by an invisible yet powerful force. We all feel it in different ways yet we all feel the connection. You have felt it if you picked up your phone and it rang and you knew who was calling. You have felt it in the connection of loved ones when you know something is happening without being there. We see it in our pets when they respond to our vibe without us even saying anything. Everything is connected to everything.

Our individuality and personalities may be varied and quite different, yet we remain connected in the deep. Our Earth is the core and the Heavens are the energy and we are fueled and supported by both. All the same. The differences in our personalities is how we use the power within us to create our experiences. Some don't believe we are all connected yet that does not make it so.

**Daily Application:** As you go through today, notice your connection to others. Can you feel their presence? Are you open or closed to connecting? What serves you best? Notice how your presence in the room changes things. Journal.

**Personal Reflections:** _____
_____
_____
_____
_____
_____

## Day 52
# AWE

*He who can no longer pause to wonder and stand rapt in awe, is as good as dead: his eyes are closed.*

~ Albert Einstein

Open your eyes. I mean *really* open them. See the beauty of nature and the elegance of the Universe swirling all around. You are a vital part of this world on multiple levels. You have the birthright to co-create an amazing life and to be able to serve and inspire others.

Many people marvel at the full moon. This connection is real and powerful. This is awe. Once you begin to move too fast and you pass by the moments to wonder, you are as good as dead as Einstein would say. I call this state *sleep-walking*. Many folks walk around oblivious to the amazing happenings and microcosms all around them. What is your awe level?

The more I stop and experience wonder, the happier and more satisfied I am with life. External events pale at the power of wonder and awe. For me, awe is most prevalent on the beach, sailing, in nature, in my dog's eyes, connecting with friends and the satisfaction following a great time together. There are many more. What keeps your wonder and awe alive?

**Daily Application:** Put on your curious eyes today. Open them wider and expand your world by taking in things with more wonder and awareness. Notice the vibrancy. What do you see? Share this with another.

**Personal Reflections:** _____
_____
_____
_____
_____
_____

## Day 53
# ENLIGHTENMENT

*Really, the only thing that makes sense is to strive for greater collective enlightenment.*

~ Elon Musk

Enlightenment, for me, is a daily focus as I walk around and do whatever I do. We all have a bright light within. The question is: "how dim have you dialed down that dimmer switch?" I meet some who seem to have the dimmer switch down very low. They are often fearful, angry, depressed or just plain walking around like they are sleep walking.

Are your eyes brightened by your inner life force? Are you taking steps every day to continue to brighten your light, fan the flames so to speak? I believe that we are all meant to seek and walk toward a brighter inner light that then reflects a brighter outer world. Each one of us is uniquely responsible for your inner light and for letting that light shine into the world.

The more the merrier. As the collective brighten their light, the more harmonious and joyful our world will be. It must be so. Ever notice how serene a group of people meditating are while in that collective? What can you do today to become more enlightened which certainly adds to the collective?

**Daily Application:** Invest some time in your personal enlightenment today. Do something that transcends simple cognitive information. Use your breath to brighten your inner fire. Meditate and allow your inner beauty to more fully emerge. Take an action toward your own enlightenment today and share. Enjoy.

**Personal Reflections:** _____
_____
_____
_____
_____
_____

## Day 54
# COOPERATION

*The only thing that will redeem mankind is cooperation.*
~ Bertrand Russell

Do you think mankind needs to be redeemed? Many would say yes. Cooperation is a vital part in successfully co-existing with others. Whether family, friends, work, community or countries, cooperation is a cornerstone for getting along. Cooperation is powerful.

Much of the discord in my life has been because of me or the other not cooperating with the process. This does not necessarily mean agreement or persuasion. To be more effective and move toward increased harmony, I must cooperate with the process. When I am met with a lack of cooperation from others, then I use my cooperative focus to discern how to move forward, being careful not to squander my vitality.

Are you generally cooperative? Are you the one who is always challenging and struggles to get along with others? Maybe you are both at different times. To cooperate does not mean to compromise your personal integrity or authenticity. Cooperation is meant to help your stay in alignment while engaging with others.

**Daily Application:** Notice your cooperation levels (inner and outer) today. Where is the resistance? How can you shift inner stress that is cause by resistance to? Journal your thoughts as you become more aware.

**Personal Reflections:** _____
_____
_____
_____
_____
_____

## Day 55
# IMAGINATION

*Imagination is the highest kite one can fly.*
~ Lauren Bacall

Imagination is one of your beautiful gifts. This is one of my favorites. If you can imagine it, then you can achieve it with focus, persistent action and believing in yourself and the outcome. Sadly, many people carry the baggage of not being worthy or the disbelief in their ability or power to achieve what they can see, so they look at others with envy or jealousy and they stop. This saddens me so much.

I firmly believe that if you can imagine something for your life or the world, then you are uniquely equipped to walk that road to fulfillment. You are not meant to do it alone. Your imagination may spark another who has other resources and together the beautiful vision comes to life.

The inventors and the fore runners in many industries have keen imaginations. They are looking for how their inspire ideas can come to pass, not saying to themselves that it won't happen. Their answer is often "Yes, how?" rather than a pessimistic deflection. Do you use your imagination in your life? Take the perspective of the kite, high above the situation and see things anew.

**Daily Application:** Journal some of your imaginings. Write and/or draw what you see in your imagination. Now ask, "how?" note the answer and be open. Today, notice your inspired ideas and how they all come together. Create a plan and say yes.

**Personal Reflections:** _____
_____
_____
_____
_____
_____

## Day 56
# ORIGINALITY

*Originality is the best form of rebellion.*
*~ Mike Sasso*

I had a friend who gave me a button that said: "Rebel with a cause". At the time, I thought he was commenting on me being a rebel or maverick. I wasn't sure how to respond except that he was jovial so I knew he admired this quality in me. Later, he mentioned my originality as the inspiration for the pin. I never thought of myself as original. Now, years later, I see my originality more fully. He could see and appreciate qualities in me as original that I could not yet see.

We are all original and unique in who we are and what we offer. How we express and use our originality is where rebellion can be used to serve a greater good. Many admired thought leaders use their originality to facilitate personal and social change. This is a form of rebellion. Not all rebellion is problematic.

You are an original, one of a kind. You possess awesome and powerful talents, ideas and gifts. Let your inner light emerge and shine. Be a rebel by bringing your light into the world. Your original light is a blessing that, when shining, changes things for the better. Now, that's the higher rebellion.

**Daily Application:** Spend some quiet time to go within and connect to your originality. How can you express this in an enlightened manner? Express yourself. Note your feelings.

**Personal Reflections:** _____
_____
_____
_____
_____

## Day 57
# SYNERGY

*Synergy is better than my way or your way. It's our way.*
~ Stephen Covey

Come together. The Beatles had the idea, right? It is in our coming together that we create and experience amazing results in life. Two heads are better than one, right? Or: "Wherever two or more are gathered, there I AM in the midst of them." Synergy is noted in many forms and throughout history.

Though Stephen Covey speaks about business, this message is important to all individuals as well. We are not in this alone and we require the connection with others to thrive. Acknowledging synergy in our relations brings a greater impact regarding harmony, productivity and satisfaction. As our *way* catapults you forward, you will be rejoicing that you chose to engage with others.

I use synergy in my workshops and speaking to audiences. I know that as we all engage; the outcome will be better than I imagine and it always does transcend my vision for the result. Synergy plays a large part in the power of in-person experiences.

**Daily Application:** Practice seizing opportunities for synergy today. Notice how outcomes and ideas change and enhance outcomes. Trust that each person brings forth their originality and best. Now, write about your experience.

**Personal Reflections:** _____

_____
_____
_____
_____
_____

## Day 58
# ENERGY

*Create your unique ripple, with no thought of where it might end. Yes, you are that vast.*
~ Sharon Rosen **

We all need fuel. Food for the body and ideas and vision for the mind. Our souls' energy comes from connection to our Source within and without. Energy is a natural part of life. Energy comes from light, wind and water. As you vision and plan your day, make sure you include enough energy!

You are an energy being, producing energy all the time. Is your energy uplifting and transformative or is it heavy and stifling? Your unique way and energy gift to the world changes things and goes out ad infinitum. Imagine your energy print permanently imprinted in our Universe. Are you creating and leaving the imprint of your highest vision?

You, like me, are best served by being attentive to our energy levels and using our energy for a profitable outcome. Busyness can look good and use energy and still you must ask if you are using your energy for the highest good of all concerned. You can raise your energy simply by changing your breath. You can calm your energy with your breath as well. How are you energizing yourself? Are you paying attention to your own vastness?

**Daily Application:** How is your energy level today? Remember you must properly fuel your body. Use your breath to raise and lower your energy and see how easy this is to accomplish. Now, change your breath to match your energy levels to what you are doing. Journal your results.

**Personal Reflections:** _____
_____
_____
_____
_____

# Day 59
# FLY

*You gotta want success like a caterpillar wants to fly... stretch, grow and change.*

~ Dave Kauffman **

Many people love to fly. Many people are afraid of flying. Which one are you? Are you willing to stretch beyond what you think you can do so you can fly? Do you want to become more than who you are today? To fly, you must be willing to put out the effort, you have to want it.

Just like an airplane takes off into the wind, so too you must stretch and grow into and through the resistance to take off and fly. Your wanting success is the beginning that sets you up on the run way. You must also learn and gain momentum and trust to lift off and fly.

When you have a vision or goal and you are struggling with achieving your vision, ask yourself if the goal is really yours or is it just a good idea. Achieving success from the inside out works much better than taking on a good idea and hoping you can fly. The growth on your journey will lead you to flight.

**Daily Application:** In your quiet time today, remind yourself what success means to you and what flying in your vision looks like. Then take some growth actions and stretch. Document your focused actions and take flight.

**Personal Reflections:** _____
_____
_____
_____
_____
_____

## Day 60
# RESPECT

*Respect yourself and others will respect you.*
~ *Confucius*

Confucius shared this wisdom many years ago. It holds true today. Do you really respect yourself? I mean *really*, deep within your being. Do you respect yourself? Many of my clients might say they respect themselves yet deep within they have doubt and some disrespectful words to say about themselves. They are hard on themselves and this often leads to inner disrespect. You get what you put out into the world. Any self-disrespect is mirrored back through others just as respect is mirrored back through others.

Many of my clients who struggle with addictions share that they struggle to respect themselves again after a time of disrespect. How do you re-orient yourself when you get away from your inner integrity? How do you know you respect yourself? Do you have any hidden places where you disrespect yourself?

Respect has many levels. What does it mean to you personally? How do you know you are respecting yourself and others? Where is your line crossing over to disrespect? How do you act respectfully toward yourself?

**Daily Application:** Today, pay particular attention to your level of self-respect. Are you satisfied with how you treat yourself? Do three respectful actions and note the response that comes your way. Journal your results and share respect freely.

**Personal Reflections:** _____
_____
_____
_____
_____

## Day 61
# LIFE

*The tragedy of life is what dies in man while he lives.*
~ Albert Schweitzer

Addiction progressively takes away the vitality of your life. As I look around, it is obvious that our society has become an addict. My definition of addiction is that you cannot get enough of what you don't want. This includes inner addictions to fear, pain, power, self-pity as well as outer addictions to substances and people. Addiction isolates people from the life sustaining connection with others and deteriorates existence. When you are engaging in the "having fun" of your addiction, you may believe your own lies. The problem remains that the pain of your isolation and progressive life challenges creeps into your mind when you are alone. Thus, you end up with sleepless nights because you are living a lie.

The fun that you are convincing yourself that you are having is really an addiction to the distraction that is zapping your life energy, vision and motivation. If you truly want to live, free and vital, you must stand up to your addictions and call them out for the lies that they are. Then you can live by higher standards and motives. Your life becomes easier and less painful.

**Daily Application:** Take a few long, slow deep breaths. Allow the conscious stress to dissolve for a moment and say yes to life. See yourself letting go of the need to distract yourself from the beauty of your life. Decide to use your courage to confront the lies you are telling yourself so you can be free to live the life you have imagined.

**Personal Reflections:** _____

_____
_____
_____
_____

## Day 62
# HOME

*We are all just walking each other home.*
*~ Ram Dass*

Home is where your heart is, right? Ram Dass is speaking of our spiritual home. In other words, he is saying that the journey here on Earth is where we are all walking home to Spirit together. Just as young school kids walked each other home, so too we area walking each other home in the higher sense. I love this visualization of people, young and innocent, walking each other home. Sometimes the walk is happy with skipping and running and sometimes slower because of sadness. Still, we are all walking each other home.

Who is walking with you? Do you feel at home with them? When you think of *home*, what do you see and feel? Your home ought to be a safe place where you can relax and be your authentic self. Do you experience safety now in your life? Aggression is prevalent in today's world and we all need a safe place to rest. This is home.

**Daily Application:** Spend time in your safe spot and exhale fully. Allow your breathing to relax and decompress from the stress all around. Care for your home. Offer gratitude for your home and safety in your life. Support others in creating a safe home.

**Personal Reflections:** _____
_____
_____
_____
_____
_____

## Day 63
# INVOLVEMENT

*Without your involvement, you can't succeed. With your involvement, you can't fail.*
~ APJ Abdul Kalam

Have you ever had a time when you were uninterested in being involved with others, especially at work or social situations? Are you involved in your life? Is there enthusiasm and excitement in the air? When you are authentically involved, fears lose their power and real passion emerges.

Consider now your involvement in your vocational and/or personal life. How often are you on *remote control* or *automatic pilot* so to speak; blindly going about your day without really paying attention? These times can be ones where your actual involvement is diminished. When you are passionate, you are truly involved and are part of the magnificence of life.

To be involved in your life involves paying attention to your inner landscape as well. From inner involvement comes authentic involvement with others. When you are involved from your soul out, you have the opportunity to experience excitement on a daily basis. Get involved!

**Daily Application:** As you go about your day today, take time frequently to stop and check your own inner involvement level. Are you engaged fully in your life? Places where you are not involved give you the opportunity to re-engage with your life's purpose and thus reconnect with your inner joy.

**Personal Reflections:** _____
_____
_____
_____
_____
_____

## Day 64
# TRUST

*Trust yourself. Create the kind of self that you will be happy to live with all your life. Make the most of yourself by fanning the tiny, inner sparks of possibility into flames of achievement.*

*~ Golda Meir*

Trust can be thought of as consistency over time. If you are consistently ten minutes late every time you are to meet someone, it won't be long and those whom you are meeting will begin to adjust their timing by 10 minutes. Then if you decide to be timelier without telling them, you will then be waiting those 10 minutes as the others have been trained by you to be 10 minutes later than the appointed time. Many people are easily trained and conditioned to accommodate others' habits.

Often trust is viewed from the vantage point of one person trusting another in a safe and consistent manner. When one person disrupts the *trust* then there tends to be harsh emotions that can cause pain. Yet *trust* is a neutral word. It is much more than if another does what they say or they hold a confidence; it includes consistent behaviors and words over time. I can trust you to be friendly and joyful if that is your pattern just the same as I can trust your angry or hurtful words and actions if that is your pattern. Either way, it is trust. In what ways are you trustworthy?

**Daily Application:** Pay attention to the consistent thoughts, words and actions that you experience. Do they accurately represent the type of trust you desire to have associated with your name? Spend time today honoring the process of creating and building trust.

**Personal Reflections:** _____
_____
_____
_____
_____

## Day 65
# PERFORMANCE

*An ant on the move does more than a dozing ox.*

*~ Lao-tzu*

Performance requires action. The ant will outperform the ox if the ox snoozes. People who perform are consistently acting. The secret is that there is no secret. Focused action yields powerful results. Are you on the move or are you over thinking or procrastinating, using a good excuse to not perform?

Ants work together and they can accomplish major tasks for their world. I once watched a few ants carry away a dead wasp. They moved it across the sidewalk with pace. They were on a mission. Think of the good you could do by taking focused action in tandem with others of like mind. Your performance would be much greater than going about the task alone which can foster procrastination, distraction and overwhelm. One ant couldn't have completed the task alone. Even in tasks that appear solitary, there are others involved.

Act and focus on up-leveling your performance by engaging others. Release distractions and the need to overthink. Your rhythm soon yields body memory and action becomes second nature. This is how your performance excels.

**Daily Application:** Notice today your performance and the actions that make it possible. Notice where you are like the dosing ox. Wake that part of you up. Do an honest appraisal of your performance. In your quiet time, release the need to hold on to the blocks. Take action.

**Personal Reflections:** _____

_____

_____

_____

_____

## Day 66
# PRAYER

*If the only prayer you said in your whole life was, 'thank you', that would suffice.*
*~ Meister Eckhart*

There are several different types of prayer. It is often said that gratitude is the highest form of prayer. Offering gratitude for gratitude's sake, without expectation opens your heart to receive. I think this idea makes the practice of prayer user friendly. More than a gratitude journal, focus your ongoing thoughts of *being* the gratitude rather than having gratitude.

Every thought is its own prayer and every prayer is answered. By holding thoughts of gratitude, you remain open to receive your blessings. Your life has a sense of ease, even when things are challenging. Keeping your prayer life simple and focus on gratitude rather than acquiring, you will possess much more than you imagine. Start with being grateful for your breath. No need to get it right, prayer comes from your heart. Open your heart with gratitude. That is all that is needed. The rest is great yet not more important than an open heart.

**Daily Application:** Hold gratitude in your mind throughout the day. Remind yourself that being truly grateful opens your heart and the power of prayer emerges. How is today different in your prayer life? Honor your journey and smile.

**Personal Reflections:** _____
_____
_____
_____
_____

## Day 67
# LETTING GO

*When you have faults, do not fear to abandon them.*
*~ Confucius*

You are not stuck. Your faults can be released. In letting go, you are free. I'll bet you can name some of your faults rather quickly. This message is about releasing them rather than using them as a name plate and hiding behind them. It is OK to let go of what does not serve your greater good. Letting go of the fear based parts of you brings freedom to your life.

Every time I let go of a blockage or perceived fault, I experience freedom. When I look back over my life, I can see clearly how releasing old faults has freed me to be a better person. I am able today to be of better service than earlier in my life, not because of wanting to serve more now but because of having cleared out the inner junk by letting go.

What could you let go of today? How can abandoning some of your faults help you live your heart's desire. Today is a good day to free yourself.

**Daily Application:** Reflect on some of your faults that have been in your way and causing you pain or discord. Now, take a few deep breaths. Imagine letting these faults go. How will you feel. What changes when you are free of the fault? Journal, let go and fill your inner world with Love and Gratitude.

**Personal Reflections:** _____
_____
_____
_____
_____
_____

## Day 68
# OPTIMISM

*In what feels like an endless winter, squawks fill the air, bringing me back to the truth of impending spring.*
~ Sharon Rosen **

Optimists tend to live longer. Are you someone who can find the positive spin, make it yours and then see the world anew? Some people call themselves optimists yet see the negative side in secret and speak positive words, thinking that makes them optimistic. It does not. Being out of alignment causes many problems and the first lesson is to be sure you are aligned and in integrity with regard to your life outlook.

Optimists look for the good. They experience the more positive experience rather than a lesser experience. Let the light in and allow the natural goodness to cascade all over you and your world. Some of my clients struggle with optimism. They often have an underlying fear or belief that keeps them hostage to what could go wrong. Reframing your ideas and beliefs can give freedom for a new way. It only takes a small crack and you can be on your way to a new outlook that is bright and amazing. Are you naturally optimistic? How do you approach life challenges?

**Daily Application:** Journal your thoughts in the morning. Notice your internal dialogue and beliefs as you go through your day. In the evening, journal your insights and awareness about how you approach challenges and your life in general. Do you have optimism?

**Personal Reflections:** _____
_____
_____
_____
_____
_____

## Day 69
# HALF MEASURES

*An ounce of action is worth a ton of theory.*
*~ Ralph Waldo Emerson*

Half measures avail you nothing of substance. In fact, half measures often yield no return on your investment or could even yield a loss. Many people who have life experience can recount numerous times when they pulled back and the result was not so great.

When approaching your life, are you using the full scale and many instruments or are you playing along with a kazoo? If you hold your breath often or you have anxiety and fears, then you may be plagued with a half measure experience. You are meant to live out loud in high definition and with surround sound. You are the composer of your life and you get to choose your experience.

What does your symphony sound like? Are you thrilled? What changes would you make? Remember, your life is not a dress rehearsal, it is the live performance.

**Daily Application:** Today, take some quiet time to assess the sound and rhythm of your personal symphony. Make changes that suit your vision. Now, incorporate the changes and journal your results. Keep tuning until you establish the desired groove.

**Personal Reflections:** _____
_____
_____
_____
_____
_____

## Day 70
# VICTORY

*We seek victory- not over any nation or people – but over ignorance, poverty, disease, and human degradation whenever they may be found.*

*~ Franklin Delano Roosevelt*

FDR was an inspired leader. He saw many things differently than the majority. His idea of victory applies today. It seems that human ignorance and fear cause much of the world's poverty and strife. Cures for diseases are squashed due to fear of financial loss by big Pharma. Groups of people destroy their own neighborhoods with lateral violence.

I think that when you limit your understanding of victory, you risk being caught in a trap of self-created poverty. Poverty of thought and poverty in the material realm. Really, if you have poverty of thought, you are in prison and being victorious will elude you.

Victory is less about control and domination and more about being free of ignorance and all forms of dis-ease. Many of the people I work with invest time and energy in exposing their inner ignorance so they can free themselves from an inner bondage they did not know they had running in the background of their life. Moving away from existential fear makes you victorious. Spread the word.

**Daily Application:** In what areas do you claim victory? Where is there still work to be done? Everyone has some work to do so use your inner awareness to direct your next actions toward your personal victory. Use your victory to inspire and motivate others.

**Personal Reflections:** _____
_____
_____
_____
_____

## Day 71
# CARE

*Self-care means giving yourself permission to pause.*
*~ Cecilia Tran*

Caring for yourself if a requirement for your growth and transformation. Too often, you can be distracted by caring or focusing on others when it is most important for you to focus on you. Self-care is often overlooked yet it is the source of your ongoing fuel of growth.

In order to truly care for you, pause every once in a while. I was speaking with a friend recently to was lamenting about being so busy and feeling the need to keep pushing to make things work. He was not aware of the negative price he was paying for this belief and actions. I suggested that he take time to pause, even for a few hours. You are healthier and more productive when you give yourself permission to pause.

**Daily Application:** Every time pausing or resting comes up today, notice your emotions and your actions. Are you using a pause to support your self-care? Journal about your relationship with caring for you. Be open to making changes in your relationship with yourself by pausing and focusing on caring for you. Journal your ideas and observations.

**Personal Reflections:** _____
_____
_____
_____
_____
_____

## Day 72
# MODESTY

*A superior man is modest in his speech but exceeds in his actions.*
*~ Confucius*

Modesty is a word that I do not hear often these days. I think it is because its meaning is not fully understood and people think it is a sign of weakness. It is a sign of great strength. Many think it means to be unexceptional which is being interpreted as unimportant. Modesty is about being unassuming yet living in your personal power. As you raise your consciousness and become aware of how modesty serves, you will certainly see the world differently.

I believe Confucius was encouraging people to under promise and over deliver; to use our current language. Be modest means to not brag and then not deliver. People who over promise and under deliver are allowing their ego and old shame based beliefs to cause problems.

By being modest and then over delivering, you rise above the drone of bragging and self-aggrandizing words and actions. Your actions speak for you and yet you remain authentic and modest. This is a powerful and admirable combination.

**Daily Application:** Notice any temptations today to over speak or exaggerate. Pay attention to how often your actions exceed your speech. Journal any insights and ideas about your personal modesty.

**Personal Reflections:** _____
_____
_____
_____
_____
_____

## Day 73
# CREATIVITY

*Creativity takes courage.*

~ Henri Matisse

Creativity shows up in many forms. By realizing that you are a unique creation, you free yourself from the fear associated with competition. When you are authentically you, you are perfectly unique. Your creativity emerges through you in ways others will be drawn to naturally. You stand out because of being uniquely you in an authentic manner.

No two artistic creations or pieces of music can compete with one another. They are simply creativity in action. All perfect in their own way. Without creativity, your life would be lived in black and white with little depth.

These days, superficiality is taking a back seat to authenticity. Each one of us is unique and therefore one of a kind. It is this inherent uniqueness that can allow for great creative things to happen. Where in your life are you stifling your creativity due to competition and trying to be like the others in order to win? You have already won. Now go be your creative, unique self.

**Daily Application:** Is a perceived threat of the competition stifling your creativity? Are you misusing your creativity while focusing on others? Go within today and allow your personal creativity to be known to you and follow that path. Feel the freedom and go for it.

**Personal Reflections:** _____
_____
_____
_____
_____
_____

## Day 74
# FACTS

*Facts do not cease to exist because they are ignored.*
*~ Aldous Huxley*

Putting your head in the sand is a most dangerous practice. Ignoring facts is a way of putting your head in the sand. As I look around today, I notice the consequences of anger, rage, fear, grief and guilt that comes because of ignoring facts. Information must always be checked out and discerned as to validity and at the same time ignoring facts or other information does not change them.

Facts are different than truths. A fact is a piece of information. A truth is a belief that is accepted as true. Facts are information and ignoring them does not make them disappear. Many of my clients find themselves in interesting circumstances because they ignored the facts.

Are you ignoring a fact in your life? Many health problems result in ignoring the fact of the symptom. Many relationship struggles come because of ignoring a fact or facts, pretending they will go away. I believe that we all would be healthier and happier if we would just pay attention to the facts and then make discerned decisions.

**Daily Application:** Today, take some time and ask yourself if there are any facts that you are ignoring. If there are, evaluate what actions you can take that will promote your personal integrity and help you move forward in your life.

**Personal Reflections:** _____

_____
_____
_____
_____

## Day 75
# SPIRITUALITY

*For me, spirituality is best summed up in being a positive and creative person.*

~ Leo Booth

Leo makes a great point here. Many people think that spirituality and religion are synonymous. They are not. Spirituality means to be set free while religion means to bind or constrict. They both have different meanings and different functions. Leo is a creative and uplifting soul. This is one of the reasons why I love this quote. When you Say Yes to your inherent value and creativity, you are free to be a positive, beneficial influence.

By allowing your spiritual light to shine more brightly each day, you become a mighty force for Good. Have you ever noticed that when you are open to higher ideals that you have an inner peace? Well, Spirituality and developing deeper connections with your Higher Self and the Universe yields more creativity and Joy. Remember that you are inherently a spiritual being and Joy is your natural state. Any upset or pain that comes from the misuse of religion cannot hold down your inner beauty. Heal the old pain and rise in your spiritual glory.

**Daily Application:** Notice any place where you are holding religious misunderstandings against your spiritual nature. Now, become willing to heal the old pain. Spend quiet time and listen to the still small voice within, it will show you the way to your freedom. Journal your messages.

**Personal Reflections:** _____
_____
_____
_____
_____

## Day 76
# GIFT

*What you think is holding you back or is your greatest problem is your greatest gift and opportunity.*
~ Raymond Hinst **


Do you have any idea about the things that are holding you back? You most likely have goals and a vision for your future. There are opportunities and possibilities all around you. Often, the very things that you think are holding you back are actually your gifts trying to emerge. When you suppress your natural gifts, they have to show up somehow.

Within your greatest challenges are the opportunities and possibilities that are for you to discover. You may think the things holding you back are your liabilities when actually they are your gifts that are not being properly utilized so they appear to be a problem.

Have you ever noticed that after you solve a substantial life challenge that you can see your gifts more clearly? Well, notice your gifts within your opportunities and use your setbacks as set ups for a bright future!

**Daily Application:** Be still for some time and reflect on what you think is holding you back. Journal the things that come to mind. Now, ask yourself what opportunity and gifts are hidden in the challenges. Note your answers and take action to let your gifts seize the opportunities in front of you.

**Personal Reflections:** _____
_____
_____
_____
_____
_____

## Day 77
# LIMIT

*Every man is a damn fool for at least five minutes every day; wisdom consists in not exceeding the limit.*

~ Elbert Hubbard

Know your limits. We all can be that fool. I'll bet you thought of a few instances as you read the quote. Remember the times when you were wise and you automatically set limits with yourself that worked out? The more you pay attention to healthy limits, the wiser you become.

The fool is the one who is the jester and can herald in a new beginning of some sort. Are you ever the fool and then doors seem to open for you? Being the jester for an extended period risks not being taken seriously. Know your limits.

Limits serve to help you remain focused. I had a client who enjoyed the attention of being goofy, like the fool. He got a lot of mileage from his antics. When he decided to become serious about his vocation and work, he struggled with why no one took him seriously. He was smart and knowledgeable in the subject yet his goofing around worked against him. He exceeded his daily limit over time. Are your limits clear? Do you honor them?

**Daily Application:** After your quiet time, journal some of your personal limits that you want to be more mindful of today. Food intake, jokes in a work setting, goofing off rather than focusing on a project, you name it. Give yourself a short limit for the distraction and then refocus. Note your success in the evening.

**Personal Reflections:** _____
_____
_____
_____
_____
_____

## Day 78
# ACCEPTANCE

*Acceptance looks like a passive state, but in reality it brings something entirely new into this world. That peace, a subtle energy vibration, is consciousness.*

~ Eckhart Tolle

Acceptance is the answer to the questions that I ask most frequently. When I find myself asking "why?" or wanting an explanation, I find that acceptance is a vital part of my inner peace. The more freely I accept, which doesn't necessarily mean I condone or agree, I am free to make intelligent decisions regarding words and actions.

If you wish to experience an enhanced experience of inner peace and calm, take a few deep breaths starting with a full exhale. Slow your breathing and allow your body to relax. Connect with yourself for just a moment and remember who you are as a beautiful, talented, spiritual being. Now, speak words of acceptance to yourself or out loud. "I accept _____ fully and unconditionally." After repeating this a few times, move forward into the remainder of the day.

Remember that increased levels of acceptance yield increased health on all levels. You are worth the investment. The energy vibration of acceptance will give you peace and an elevating consciousness.

**Daily Application:** Notice 3 times today when you can practice acceptance rather than focusing on your personal agenda. Notice the outcomes of the situations. Give thanks for your free will to make the choice to accept rather than fight life.

**Personal Reflections:** _____
_____
_____
_____
_____
_____

## Day 79
# PRESENT

*We do not heal the past by dwelling there; we heal the past by fully living in the present.*

*~ Marianne Williamson*

I created my career. This quote inspires me. I have many clients who suffer great depression, frustration and grief because they are trying to desperately fit into a career or job that is not meant for them. This feeds low self-esteem and doubt. How is it that smart and talented people are reduced to tears over not fitting into something that isn't even meant for them in the first place? The perceived limits around you can cause inner strife. It is time to create.

You are a creative and amazing person. If you look around and nothing seems to fit, create a career for yourself. Your vocation comes from your soul's calling or heart's desire. Follow the urgings and the perfect career will show up because you created it from the inside out. You do not have to suffer in a place you do not fit in any longer.

Choose your career path. Create opportunities. Be your authentic self. Dance to your own drum. Do good. Serve others. Be willing to receive support and direction from others. Seek a mentor.

**Daily Application:** Use part of your quiet time today and assess your career and your satisfaction. Are you living your purpose? Are there changes that you want to make? Write down your vision and any changes. Be willing to follow directions. Journal your ideas and actions. Schedule a feedback day for a progress report.

**Personal Reflections:** _____
_____
_____
_____
_____
_____

## Day 80
# DISCIPLINE

*Self-respect is the fruit of discipline; the sense of dignity grows with the ability to say no to oneself.*

~ Abraham Heschel

Having discipline is vital for a happy and successful life. There are two important ways to experience discipline. The first is to have discipline. This is when you have the self-respect to say no to yourself and to do what is right for you even when tempted otherwise. To have discipline is the cornerstone of being focused and on purpose. Consistent action that is in alignment is most often how discipline shows up in your life.

The second is to be disciplined. This is when you may be off course and the discipline is an invitation to get back on course. Sometimes this comes from others and at times from yourself. In both scenarios, self-respect and a sense of dignity are important aspects of discipline. I have some visionary friends of mine who struggle with the idea of discipline because they want to be free-spirited. I say that because of being disciplined, I am able to express my free spirit more authentically. Sometimes saying no to myself is hard yet it is worth my effort. How is your self-discipline?

**Daily Application:** Pay attention to your discipline today. Is it primarily from within or do you rely on others for your disciplined structure? Ask yourself where you can improve saying no. Notice any resistance and then practice doing what is right anyway. Write your experience including your feelings

**Personal Reflections:** _____
_____
_____
_____
_____

## Day 81
# HUNGER

*Your calling is where your deep gladness and the world's deep hunger meet.*
*~ Frederick Buechner*

It is not always about what you can do, it is about what you are called to do. When you are living in the flow of your calling or vision, you experience a joy and gladness that transcends words. Everyone I have spoken to reports that when they are following their calling, they are in a flow that is life changing.

The important thing to remember is that your calling is needed in this world. It is uniquely yours and only you can bring it forward into reality. Often, when I begin to share freely my inner ideas and thoughts, the listener comments about the power of my ideas and more importantly that they touch them in a way that feeds their soul. This is such an honor for me.

It is vital to remember that living in your calling is how the world is fed with important and vital information, ideas and energy. There are people hungry for what you are serving. Serve them freely, you will prosper in ways you cannot yet imagine.

**Daily Application:** Journal what brings about your experience of deep gladness. Now, journal ways you can serve and feed the hunger of those searching and seeking for what you are bringing forth. Claim your calling and journal your commitment.

**Personal Reflections:** _____
_____
_____
_____
_____
_____

## Day 82
# IDENTITY

*Never be bullied into silence. never allow yourself to be made a victim. Accept no one's definition of your life, but define yourself.*

~ Harvey Fierstein

How you define yourself sets the stage for your experience. If you see yourself as a victim, then things will look that way. Being bullied into silence does not serve you or anyone else. This quote from Harvey Fierstein hits home for many people who have been bullied into silence.

How other people define you does not make it accurate or true. Your identity is essential to your life and you are ever evolving. Thus, your identity shifts and changes on some levels over time. Being bullied into silence for any reason is abuse. Accepting another's definition of you is also not OK.

Stand with your inner knowingness and personal authority. See how things change as you are aligned with your definition of you. Some of the gifted, professional adults that I work with have been bullied and are struggling with sharing their true identities and becoming free. It is a process if you have been bullied to set yourself free. I am honored to work with people who are on their personal road to freedom.

**Daily Application:** Take some time to journal about your life and your identity within your life and your many roles. Be aware of any bullies and remain clear of their tactics. Remember you are free to be you and you define yourself, not anyone else. Journal some of your thoughts.

**Personal Reflections:** _____
_____
_____
_____
_____
_____

## Day 83
# CONTROL

*Control what you can control.*
*~ Dave Moore* \*\*

Often, I witness folks attempting to control things outside of their sphere of influence. When going for a job interview or a business meeting, prepare to the best of your ability. After fully preparing, no matter how things turn out, you will always know that you did your best and you will not look back with a bunch of should haves hanging over your head. You are responsible for controlling what is in your control in any situation and that is YOU.

Distinguished Leaders are known for putting in hard, focused work when others are out playing. The hard work pays off and others may say it is luck when the success is really coming from diligence, focus and action. To excel at any endeavor, you must focus on the goal and be willing to make sacrifices along the way in order to achieve the goal. Ask any notable athlete or musician and they will be able to recount for you the sacrifices and the hard work that has gone into their superior performance. Always remember to control what you can control.

**Daily Application:** Notice the many things that you are tempted to attempt to control. Notice how many of these things are outside of you and therefore out of your control Now, notice your actions. Are you acting in a manner that you will be happy with tomorrow and in years to come? Is what you are doing taking you toward your larger goal?

**Personal Reflections:** _____
_____
_____
_____
_____

## Day 84
# AMBITION

*The indispensable first step to getting the things you want in life is this: decide what you want.*

~ Ben Stein


To decide means that you cut out all other possibilities. You are focused upon your goal. Having clarity about what you want is vital to being able to focus on the goal. Ambition is maintained by clarity of focus and the ability to act upon your goals and desires. What do you want for your life? Do you have the ambition to make it happen?

When I decided to write this book, I had ambition. I still have ambition to write this book even though the project has taken longer than I imagined. Still, the decision has been made and my ambition has carried the project forward. Have you decided what you want?

If you have things you want in life, making specific, actionable decisions makes your success more likely. With ambition, you will meet of exceed your personal expectations. You must first make the best decision about what you want.


**Daily Application:** Take some time to see what you want then also take the time to check in with your inner ambition to get the project through to completion. Write or draw the goal and the projected path. Now create an anchor to help you stay focused.


**Personal Reflections:** _____
_____
_____
_____
_____

## Day 85
# CONTINUITY

*Continuity does not rule out fresh approaches to fresh situations.*
~ Dean Rusk

Distractions abound. We can be seduced into many different directions at once each day. There is an ever-flowing continuity that's inviting you into a safe place of gratitude and peace. You must be willing to release the frenetic distractions and impulsive behaviors. The continuity of life flows much like an easy flowing river with some rapids yet overall peaceful and purposeful. The river flows with continuity and it nourishes the plants and wildlife that live along the banks of the river. Imagining a river without continuity seems funny or odd, right?

In sailing, when the air flow detaches from the sail due to incorrect angles to the wind, the boast slows down and could even stall. Continuity of wind flow across the sail is essential. Our approaches must remain fresh for each situation.

You are meant to live in a flow or continuity. Being disjointed or disconnected in any way is detrimental to your overall well-being. Focus on establishing continuity and maintain this flow in a manner that serves your growth and development. Distractions can impede your journey if you allow them. Returning to continuity after any disruption is an important of health on all levels.

**Daily Application:** Notice the impact of continuity today. Allow yourself to interrupt distractions with a calm assurance. Allow confidence to arise from a sense of continuity in your daily routine. Notice your fresh approaches to situations today.

**Personal Reflections:** _____
_____
_____
_____
_____

## Day 86
# TRUTH

*Your Truth is who you are when you are around those who unconditionally love you...it's so beautiful, so authentic, so easy. To the contrary, when surrounded by those that aren't a good match for our energy, we close, become inauthentic and completely abandon our Truth. Over time this erodes our relationship to the self and causes great suffering, as we send a message that we don't matter as much as others.*

*~ Cynthia Citron \*\**

Truth is a powerful word and it carries many varied meanings and uses in our world. To live in your integrity, truth must be part of your foundation along with compassion and kindness.

Living in your Truth allows for your expansion and transformation. Being authentic and connected to your inner vision allows your personal Truth to lead the way. When you are distracted from your Truth, your relations can erode, and pain ensues. Become increasingly authentic each day and care for yourself deeply. This is the way of the Truth seeker.

As you heal and transform, you will begin to shed old beliefs, thoughts, words and actions that you outgrow. Your authenticity become brighter and your relationship with yourself become solid. Seek the higher Truth of the Universe. Allow your own reconnection from within.

**Daily Application:** Spend time in quiet, going within and connecting to your inner truth. Notice if there are ways that you are deceiving yourself and therefore not in alignment with your truth. Now, how are you aligned in truth with others. Journal your ideas and remain focused on your truth today.

**Personal Reflections:** _____
_____
_____
_____
_____
_____

## Day 87
# FUTURE

*Choose your friends with caution; plan your future with purpose, and frame your life with faith.*
~ Thomas S. Monson

I like this quote from Thomas Monson. I believe that you are here on purpose with a purpose. By living with this belief, faith is the perfect frame for your existence. In what do you have faith? Do you have faith in tomorrow, the sun rising, your life's vision or something else? Faith is the substance of our desires. As you are aware of who you call friend, connect to your personal, unique purpose and live in faith, your life creates an amazing legacy.

Your future is so bright that you may not fully believe the power of your calling or life purpose. We are not guaranteed the future yet we live in hope for that future. Do you choose your friends wisely and make plans with a purpose? How does your faith play a role in your life? These are vital questions to ponder and reconcile as you plan your future.

Having your unique plan is effective. Too many people simply get up and do the day without thought of their legacy or future. This random way of living often brings random results. With caution, purpose and faith, your future is quite bright indeed.

**Daily Application:** Take some time and ponder your future. Your personal future, independent of outer circumstances. Now, focus on your purpose and your belief in your purpose. Take at least one action today that confirms your personal future focus.

**Personal Reflections:** _____
_____
_____
_____
_____
_____

## Day 88
# APPRECIATION

*Appreciation is a wonderful thing: It makes what is excellent in others belong to us as well.*

*~ Voltaire*

Who do you appreciate? Do you tell them? Are you open about who you appreciate in your life? I believe this quote also applies to all human relationships. When you appreciate the family pet, you pay attention to that being. How do you show appreciation to others? Do you assume they know how you feel or do you express it?

    I appreciate many people and things in my life. I take pleasure in honoring my dog by showing her love in a way that she can understand. It is important, I believe, to honor others in appreciation in a way they understand. Some people respond better to words and others may respond better to actions while still others respond best to emotions. Everyone appreciates various aspects of life and relationships a bit differently.

    It is best, I have found, to show appreciation in the best way for the receiver. Appreciation is valuable in all your relations. Sometimes it is in your words and sometimes in your actions. Truly appreciating another with authenticity builds rapport and trust in your relationships.

**Daily Application:** Notice how you show appreciation today. How do you receive appreciation from others? Can you give better than you receive? Are you balanced in your ability to give and receive appreciation? Pay attention and then make any changes you may desire. Journal some of your ideas.

**Personal Reflections:** _____
_____
_____
_____
_____

## Day 89
# MEMORIES

*We all have our time machines. Some take us back, they're called memories. Some take us forward, they're called dreams.*

*~ Jeremy Irons*

Memories come in all shapes and sizes. We humans have many memories and some of us block some memories. I think the time machine idea is interesting. Are you a memory or dream type? I know some people who live in the past, memories are what they are consumed by day to day. Still others have great memories and they are fun but not consuming. I have some high school friends who are still living their high school life many years later.

     I know some people who are so into their dreams that they are missing out on today. When they wake up years from now, their memories may not be as rich as they could be due to constant future focus. How are your memories? Do you have painful memories that pose current day challenges? Are your memories fond? Depending upon your memories that you connect with, you can see where your time machine is going. You are in charge and can set the machine to any day and time. Use your time machine to serve your greater good.

**Daily Application:** In your quiet time today, be sure to reflect on memories. Any memories that bring grief or pain can be released and your inner bondage to the energy of the pain broken. The ones that bring joy, smile and allow your joy to flow. Use your memories to help propel you into the future you desire for yourself.

**Personal Reflections:** _____
_____
_____
_____
_____
_____

## Day 90
# NEIGHBORS

*Day after day, ordinary people become heroes through extraordinary and selfless actions to help their neighbors.*
~ Sylvia Mathews Burwell.

Do you know your neighbors? Would you help them in the form of a selfless action? Who are your neighbors? I have a friend who considers all humanity his neighbors. I also have another friend who considers her neighbors those living next door. One more literal than the other and the implications are many.

    We are all ordinary people walking each other home. Are you neighborly? Do you serve those around you and help when you are led to do so? I had a neighbor in my youth who would spend time with me and my friends. He was an older man and he would teach us about his vegetable and herb garden. He was so nice and he even let us eat some of the parsley. This memory is alive, even now, years later. His selfless actions made him extraordinary.

    What impression are you leaving on your neighbors? Does it take a major incident to get you to even talk to them? There is not a better day than today to start acting.

**Daily Application:** Be still. Offer gratitude for your neighbors. Reflect on your beliefs and experiences around being a good neighbor. Now, honor being a neighbor in a real way. Smile.

**Personal Reflections:** _____
_____
_____
_____
_____
_____

## After 90 Days...

How long did it take you to complete all 90 days?

*Thoughts and Feelings? Write or Sketch any impressions so far.*

*The first 90 days are the most challenging often. Send me any comments if you wish: dianne@visionsapplied.com*

## Day 91
# MUSIC

*Music gives a soul to the Universe, wings to the mind, flight to the imagination, charm to sadness, gaiety and life to everything.*

*~ Plato*

Music is universal and speaks to all of us. Music is an elixir that can heal pain, bring joy and move emotions. My mother was a pianist and she always told me that the beauty of music is not just the notes but also the space between the notes. I listen to music differently today because of her wise teaching. I also work with musicians often and we connect on this deeper level through the appreciation of the spaces.

So too with love. Like music, love is meant to flow with space and calm mixed with intensity and crescendos. Different music sets my mood differently. Right now, as I write for you, I am listening to some beautiful acoustic guitar and piano. It is making my heart sing!

Music can create peace and love and it can also be used to express more toxic emotions. Music speaks to the deepest parts of our soul and brain. I love Shakespeare's idea, music as the food for love. Let's all focus on using music to feed love and joy. Keep playing your peace and love song.

**Daily Application:** Listen to music today that sings to your soul. Allow yourself to feel loved by the notes and the spaces. Decide to feed your soul regularly. Offer gratitude for the beauty of the music.

**Personal Reflections:** _____
_____
_____
_____
_____
_____

## Day 92
# BUSY

*No matter how busy you are, you must find time for reading, or surrender yourself to self-chosen ignorance.*

~ Confucius

Confucius has a point. In today's world, we can read with our eyes, ears and finger tips. Never the less the message is important. To not, continue to grow and learn is a life of self-chosen ignorance. It is vital for a healthy and happy life to be ever expanding and learning diverse things.

When I was a teenager, I made the decision to learn as much as I could about anything that interested me. At the time, it was mostly psychology and career related material. Over the years this thirst for knowledge has expanded across many different topics, many not career related. Now, when I am in an interaction, work or leisure, I have a solid knowledge base. This has happened because of my dedication over many years.

There are many people my age who did not choose a path of lifelong learning by reading and they continue to struggle with ignorance. Some of my long-time friends have been trying to catch up and read more which is helping wake them up.

Ignorance is a slippery slope. It is time to get busy reading. Let's continue to wake up.

**Daily Application:** Take time today to read for at least 30 minutes. Try choosing something that is new yet interesting to you. Explore varied topics. Journal your experience. Make the commitment to read daily and check in with yourself in 30 days.

**Personal Reflections:** _____
_____
_____
_____
_____
_____

## Day 93
# PERSEVERANCE

*Perseverance, secret of all triumphs.*

~ Victor Hugo

Chances are that if you are reading this book that you have some level of perseverance. When you want to attain something or accomplish a goal, perseverance is often required. To persevere, you can maintain a strong focus and action plan when the journey gets tough.

Think of the times when you were successful at something because you had to persevere, whether you wanted to or not. Now, honor that ability and know that you can use this at any time. When you see a successful person, remember that beneath their success is a perseverance, desire and a drive that may not be immediately obvious. For everyone who is victorious, there is a great deal of hard work and perseverance. Even for the gifted and talented people. Your success lies in not giving up.

If you are reading this book, it means that I persevered and got it done! Triumphs come in many sizes yet perseverance is the secret ingredient.

**Daily Application:** Today, take some time to honor your perseverance. Also take time to assess where perseverance is serving you in a current project. Journal how perseverance serves you.

**Personal Reflections:** _____
_____
_____
_____
_____
_____

## Day 94
# PICTURES

*The pictures we create in our minds become the experiences of our lives.*
*~ Carole R. Gill \*\**

What you are seeing in your mind will eventually show up in your life. What are your pictures? Are your inner pictures full of life, opportunity and vibrancy? Or are you pictures dull or maybe even black and white? Regardless, your pictures create your reality.

     I once went to an event with a good friend. I was so excited to attend even though I am an introvert and was a bit nervous. My friend (the extrovert) did not really want to go when it was time to leave for the event. She wanted to attend the event when we decided to go to the event weeks earlier. She reluctantly came anyway. We were at the event for a couple of hours, meeting people and enjoying the atmosphere and the entertainment. As we drove away, we began to discuss the event, I remembered all the amazing people and experiences. She recounted the boredom and flat feeling she had. We both had very different experiences of the same event because of our pictures and expectations.

     Pictures and experiences are the glasses through which you live. Create amazing pictures and then create amazing experiences! If I can do it, you can too!

**Daily Application:** Take a few minutes and begin to pay attention to the pictures in your mind. Do you want them to show up in your reality? During your quiet time, imagine your day and the flow of events and your feelings. How do your pictures support your desire for today? Make any changes needed.

**Personal Reflections:** _____
_____
_____
_____
_____
_____

## Day 95
## MOTIVES

*Whenever a man does a thoroughly stupid thing, it is always from the noblest motives.*

~ Oscar Wilde

Oscar has a point here. Oscar had a rich life and he took many actions that were counter cultural in his day. It does seem that he was trying to do his best, even when it fell short. I think that is true of everyone. Even when things go terribly awry, that person is doing their best.

The motives may come into question because of an errant action. The seeming logic or reasoning of the person may be flawed yet most often the motives are noble. I am not speaking of intentional wrong doing here. Myself and others have made mistakes while having noble motives. Often this comes from a level of innocence or simply not knowing possible outcomes and thus experiencing unintended consequences.

Always check your motives. Practice aligning the action to the motive and assess possible outcomes. Undisclosed motives come through so being clear works in your favor. This will decrease the thoroughly stupid things as Oscar says.

**Daily Application:** Reflect today on motives and your inner motives for doing things. How is your behavior aligning with your motives? Are your motives noble or self-seeking? Journal your ideas.

**Personal Reflections:** _____
_____
_____
_____
_____
_____

## Day 96
# PLATEAU

*Everyone plateaus. What you do next is what counts.*
~ Noah Kegan

For many successful people, resting on their laurels is a foreign concept. While others are resting on yesterday's accomplishments, the success focused person is continuing to grow, create, develop and orchestrate ideas and actions for the journey. I share with my clients that life is like running up a down escalator. Stopping takes you to the bottom once again.

Because we live in a fast-paced world, we must pace ourselves. Consistency and focus are paramount for success. While you are sitting on the sidelines resting from your sprint, the more methodical, focused person will continue their progress. If you are often frustrated about your success and transformation progress, ask yourself if you are consistent or are you building in plateaus that require additional energy to reestablish momentum. Every day I hear about the power of consistent, focused action. Your consistency creates the flow that allows for your success. Your vision must be generational, not merely situational.

**Daily Application:** Meditate on any area you wish to see increased success. Assess your focus and actions over time. How can you establish and maintain consistent momentum and avoid the plateaus that rob your success? Now, share your commitments with another for accountability.

**Personal Reflections:** _____
_____
_____
_____
_____
_____

## Day 97
# FAIR

*It is not fair to ask of others what you are unwilling to do yourself.*
*~ Eleanor Roosevelt*

Fair is an interesting word and is often charged with emotion. Fairness could also be a form of justice. If life is not fair, then what? How are you to deal with life on life's terms? I experience a sense of fairness when the overall motive or intent is the highest good of all. For me, fair is not the same as equal. When we are children as in the quote, fair tends to mean equal. As adults this orientation appears to shift, thus redefining the experience of the word.

As you grow in wisdom and knowledge, fair no longer is synonymous with equal. Fair treatment would include what is right and just and appropriate for the situation. Equal means to do the same thing no matter what. For example: What is fair for an expert to do is vastly different than a beginner. Expecting them to perform equally would be insane. Thus, they are treated differently yet fairly and which may not be equitable.

**Daily Application:** Ponder the ideas of fair and equal in your life today. Take some time to explore any inner bitterness or resentment. Now, offer compassion to yourself and others. Be the example of the difference.

**Personal Reflections:** _____
_____
_____
_____
_____
_____

## Day 98
# PRINCIPLES

*Obey the principles without being bound to them.*
*~ Bruce Lee*

We all have principles that we live by and follow, even when we are not fully aware. Your hierarchy of principles and their application in your life is uniquely yours. Choosing to obey your principles without being rigid and tied to them offers your flexibility and choice in your daily actions. One of my higher principles is authenticity. There are others. By obeying without being bound, choices and options are ever-present. What principles are guiding you? There are no right or wrong answer, there is simply your answer.

Being clear about the principles you live by helps you not be so bound and rigid that your obedience comes from a toxic, fear based orientation. Bruce Lee has a valuable point. Having flexibility and freedom to grow and expand allows you to live by your principles with a loosely held grip.

Being flexible yet obedient is the cornerstone to happiness and success while living your vision. Choosing to be bound creates additional challenges. Let's be flexible and obedient to our principles.

**Daily Application:** Journal about your top 5 guiding principles. How can you be sure you are obeying them without being bound? Note your emotions and thoughts. Make any changes to release the rigid, tight grips.

**Personal Reflections:** _____
_____
_____
_____
_____
_____

## Day 99
# METHOD

*Being realistic is the most common path to mediocrity.*
*~ Will Smith*

How do you get things accomplished? Are you a realist? Are you and thinker? Or maybe you are an innovator? The method that you use to approach life and your development tell the story of your life trajectory. Will Smith is noting that using a realistic method can create a path of mediocrity. Certainly, many extraordinary people were not necessarily realistic. Their methods for achievement often broke the molds and they use a strategy that was not realistic. That method works when you are open to a diverse and interesting path that has many ups and downs.

I am a person who does not think inside a box. In fact, many people comment to me that I remember and think about the most unusual things. I think it has to do with my method of approaching life. I tend to walk off the path. The funny thing is that years ago I would have said that I was a follower. This is simply not true. As I woke up my real nature and true self, I allowed my creativity, uniqueness, talents and personal power to emerge. What about you? Are you realistic or are you a risk taker, striving for excellence?

**Daily Application:** Take a few minutes and ponder then write about your personal method for approaching life, both business and personal. Focus on what you are striving for, now check your method. Adjust accordingly. Go for it!

**Personal Reflections:** _____
_____
_____
_____
_____

## Day 100
# MILESTONES

*Remember to celebrate milestones as you prepare for the road ahead.*
~ Nelson Mandela

Yes. I always say to pay attention to mile markers because there is no finish line. It is when you get caught up in the finish line that you can become limited and short sighted. I like that Nelson Mandela is saying to celebrate the milestones. This adds flair and acknowledgement on a deeper level than just noticing them.

Milestones and rites of passage are vital to your development as a person. We all celebrated when we walked for the first time without falling after the first step, right? As adults, we celebrate the milestones of our children. What about your personal milestones. Milestones are more than birthdays ending in a zero. Do you still celebrate when you master a new skill or learn something new? Do you celebrate as you grow in your awareness or inner connection? These are all milestones that are worth celebrating.

Taking your journey for granted and missing your celebration milestones makes for a tedious and often heavy existence. As you bring more celebration, your road ahead becomes more hopeful and alive.

**Daily Application:** After your quiet time today, find ways to celebrate your personal milestones that feed your motivation. Now, notice those important to you. How can you celebrate their milestones, especially the adults who have lost sight of this important practice?

**Personal Reflections:** _____
_____
_____
_____
_____

## Day 101
# VIRTUE

*Kindness is the sunshine in which virtue grows.*
*~ Robert Ingersoll*

Virtue is something that I think eludes many people's understanding in today's world. I had a client tell me that it is outdated. Really? People with virtue have high moral standards. I believe that this is in fact still current. Having virtue means to think, speak and act from kindness, compassion and other high moral standards. This is vital in today's world. It may seem revolutionary and I assure you it is really a return to what is noble.

Kindness, as Robert Ingersoll shares, is the sunshine. The sunshine offers warmth and the light for growth. By living in the light of kindness, your virtue grows. It can't help but keep growing. I imagine each of us being these great trees in seed form when we are born. Sunshine is a vital part of our growth. The light chases the dark and grows our virtue. So, let's be more kind to ourselves and others.

**Daily Application:** Notice all your opportunities today to be kind to yourself and those around. Also notice the kindness offered you. Become aware of your experience both giving and receiving kindness. Journal and share with another your findings.

**Personal Reflections:** _____
_____
_____
_____
_____

## Day 102
# RISK

*What you risk reveals what you value.*
~ Jeanette Winterson

I'll bet you are a risk taker. Each person has a different tolerance for risk. There is financial risk, reputation risk, athletic risk, emotional risk and social risk to name a few. When you risk sharing something sensitive with another person, you are showing the value of the relationship. When you risk for your sport, you are showing its value in your life. We all have different risk tolerances. None are any better or worse than the other. It is vital to understand your risk tolerance in your major life areas.

I have a very conservative friend. She takes very few risks. She is kind and compassionate. She does not step outside of her box very often. I believe she values security. One of my colleagues, takes many professional risks and takes few personal risks. He is dedicated to his profession so this balance makes sense to me. What you value is obvious when you examine your behavior.

**Daily Application:** In your quiet time, examine the risks you take. Breathe slowly for some time. Journal how your risks are impacting your life now. Need to make changes? Journal your ideas and action plan.

**Personal Reflections:** _____
_____
_____
_____
_____
_____

## Day 103
# ZEAL

*Zeal without knowledge is fire without light.*
~ Thomas Fuller

Zeal is one of my favorite qualities. It is balanced perfectly with order. Too much zeal equals little order and too much order means little zeal. There is an amazing balance and dance that these two qualities create.

Zeal without knowledge or order has no real substance. It is simply a bunch of random energy without the light emanating. I have zeal and I resist order sometimes. Many of my clients have either more zeal than is useful with difficulty with order or the other way. I believe that being out of balance and harmony with these principles is what gives many people challenges in realizing their vision.

Just like fire without light, zeal without knowledge is not complete. Let's get excited and gain the knowledge to have a full expression of our zeal. How are you going to grow your knowledge and fuel your zeal?

**Daily Application:** Ponder today your expression of both order and zeal. How do they dance together in your life? Notice where your zeal comes alive. Honor your vision and passion and spend time learning new things in that area. Journal your ideas and thoughts.

**Personal Reflections:** _____
_____
_____
_____
_____

## Day 104
# HABIT

*Once we're thrown off our habitual paths, we think all is lost, but its only here that the new and the good begins.*

~ Leo Tolstoy

Habits will often keep us going and sometimes they can get in our way. Some habits are rooted in familiar pain and being thrown off the quiet desperation path can serve your growth. It may not feel great but then again remaining in silent misery trying to pretend all is OK doesn't work either, right? There is often much good that comes from the shakeup. Most often, you will see the good after the dust has settled from the shakeup. Keep looking for the good that comes from your habit shakeup.

Sometimes shaking up your habits can give you awareness of other opportunities where even more good can come your way. Sometimes getting thrown off your path is liberating and you may look back and wonder why you stayed so long. Habits can serve us yet when they blind us from our growth, they are no longer serving. Open your doors to the new and the good by liberating yourself from limiting habits.

**Daily Application:** Change a couple of your habits today. Check out your emotions and responses. Notice the new that is opened for you. Now, take some quiet time and reflect on your path, any habits that need to be shaken?

**Personal Reflections:** _____
_____
_____
_____
_____
_____

## Day 105
# TIME

*Don't spend time beating a wall, hoping to transform in into a door.*
*~ Coco Chanel*

How many times have you tried to force something or someone into being something that was not meant to be? What walls have you beat, hoping for a hidden door? Wasting your valuable time wanting things to be different, better, worse than they are does not serve your highest good.

Instead, use your time in your favor by remaining open to new adventures in growth and new opportunities to grow and transform. Time can work in your favor when you are open and receptive to new opportunities and awareness's.

Trying to force yourself into a mold or trying t beat a wall into a door is futile and exhausting. Relax and allow the flow to gently move you along the journey. Use your time wisely. Hold the intention for inner peace and personal development and transformation. Remain open and receptive to how you are using your time.

**Daily Application:** Create space for some extra quiet time today. Pay attention to your inner voice and impressions. Listen to your own inner wisdom. Journal and then act, using your time effectively with focused intention and action.

**Personal Reflections:** _____
_____
_____
_____
_____
_____

## Day 106
# WELL-BEING

*Chains of habit are too light to be felt until they are too heavy to be broken.*
*~ Warren Buffett*

Your sense of well-being resides within. If you are resting your sense of who you are and your value or well-being outside of yourself, you are looking in the wrong place. Your sense of well-being is directly related to how connected you are to your inner value and your inner world. I have noticed that when you are focusing your attention on others, you fall into the trap of suffering if things don't go the way you imagine.

When you are satisfied and fulfilled within, you will not be overly concerned about external appearances or situations. You have a knowingness that is beyond the mundane. How do you measure your personal sense of well-being? My friend says he must have everything in order and then he knows things are ok. Another friend, told me she only cares about the basics; shelter, food and water for her well-being. "The rest is extras," she said. Then other friends had more detailed descriptions of how their well-being shows up. Only a few mentioned their inner world is where it started for them. When I mentioned this idea, I got several ah ha's. Hint: start within, it works better that way. What chains of habit are impacting your well-being?

**Daily Application:** Spend some extra time in quiet today. Breathe lovingly. Smile. Go into the day in touch with your personal well-being. What chains of habit can you release? Draw or journal your commitment to your inner well-being.

**Personal Reflections:** _____
_____
_____
_____
_____
_____

## Day 107
# DEPTH

*So often we compare what life brings with the virtual idealization of our expectations. And we reject the real, living experience in favor of this idealized concept.*
~ Ruth Toledo Altschuler **

Many folks want to spread the good news of new things with everyone around them. Often this impulse and excitement can leave the person feeling a bit empty if they do not learn to go within and allow the new lesson or information to take root within before sharing and giving it to others. In the excitement and innocence of change, it is tempting to want to bring others with us on the journey. You may be tempted to follow your idealized concepts rather than your live adventure. This thwarts your ability to go deep within your life and thrive.

Excitement to share with others is best tempered with this understanding that we must go deep by looking within and aligning before spreading the information. As you spiritually mature, you will begin to go within, integrate and then share from your overflow which is continuously replenished. By gong wide too quickly, the distracting ego can clutter the experience and you could come away tired and drained from focusing on the idealized concepts rather then what is part of your living experience. Choose to allow new understandings to meld within. Your excitement for sharing will be better received when you are deeply rooted within.

**Daily Application:** During your meditation time today, allow your focus to go deep within and honor your journey without judgment. Make the conscious choice to connect to your own living experience. Remind yourself that the concepts are just that, concepts. This is your time to live. Breathe and Smile. Receive your personal inspiration from within.

**Personal Reflections:** _____
_____
_____
_____
_____

## Day 108
# YIELDING

*By yielding you may obtain Victory.*
~ Ovid

To yield is to pause or give way under pressure. This is evident in sports, dance and art. Great running backs excel at yielding which allows holes to open for them to exploit. The difference between the good and the great is their ability to be focused, take intense action while yielding and allowing the play to develop. Victory on the play and overall victory is the expected outcome.

Yielding in life is a learned essential. Bull dozing through life like a bull in a china shop does not serve you at all. You end up overly tired with a trail of destruction to rectify and your result still has eluded you. It seems much more appropriate to learn to yield at moments and then look for the next opportunity opening and then move through the opening while focused on your victory.

Moving too fast in a straight line can put you at a disadvantage. It is much more effective to focus on the goal and be willing to change your strategy as things develop.

**Daily Application:** Spend some quiet time apart from the busy day. Focus your mind's eye on your goals and overall vision. Take the time to be open and willing to be flexible in your approach, yielding so you can change course to get your goal met. Journal your insights and ideas.

**Personal Reflections:** _____
_____
_____
_____
_____
_____

## Day 109
# YESTERDAY

*Never let yesterday use up today.*
*~ Richard Nelson*

It is unwise to waste today on some useless guilt or regret about a yesterday. By letting old regrets sneak into today, you can easily waste today on useless spent emotions. Yesterday is a great memory for the lessons, experiences and the wisdom you have at your disposal for today. Tomorrow, today will be that yesterday. So, live so that your regrets are few and your memories last a lifetime!

Continuing to be saddened by a yesterday is a good indication that you have some work to do to heal and transform that old feeling. Restoring your peace and calm for today depend upon your letting yesterday be yesterday. Some people use the guidance of a trusted mentor or counselor to work to release the bonds to the yesterdays. Some yesterdays want to hang around and it is up to you to choose to live in today.

**Daily Application:** Breathe deeply. Drop your shoulders and relax. Now, focus your intention on this moment and visualize your amazing day. Pay attention today to your thinking. Are your thoughts more today or is yesterday creeping in? Take some time to journal.

**Personal Reflections:** _____
_____
_____
_____
_____
_____

## Day 110
# JUDGMENT

*Good Judgment comes from experience, and experience comes from bad judgment.*

~ Rita Mae Brown

Judgment means that you are assigning value to something or someone. When you are judging yourself, you are dimming your light. The way to shine more brightly is to release judgment and allow your inner light to be expressed. Being accepting and loving keeps you bright. As you are freed from the heaviness of judgment, you will feel lighter.

The better way is to use discernment as a skill for your decision making. When you are discerning, you evaluate a situation or relationship and determine if it serves you and all others involved. Then you decide from there without assigning value to the relationship or situation. Whether something is meant for you or not is not its value. It simply speaks to what is right for you in that moment. Thus, using discernment rather than judgment will brighten your light as you love yourself more fully.

**Daily Application:** Ponder the many ways you love yourself. Are there any ways that you would like to change or be more loving and kind to yourself? Take some quiet time to love yourself. Smile.

**Personal Reflections:** _____
_____
_____
_____
_____
_____

## Day 111
# STYLE

*Elegance is not about being noticed, it's about being remembered.*
*~ Giorgio Armani*

There are people that I notice. They have style. Their style is not only about what they are wearing. It is often about how they carry themselves. I remember those people. We all have a style. It incorporates how we are remembered. Because all people want to be appreciated and remembered, style points to how others will remember you.

Someone who is elegant and has that powerful presence is remembered differently than someone who has a style that is off putting somehow. Your personal style is vital to your success and feelings of being enough. It includes how you speak, how you walk and carry yourself, how you listen, how you serve others and lastly how you dress. Your authenticity and presence/beauty radiate and either downgrade the outfit or elevate your outfit. How do you want to be remembered?

**Daily Application:** As you move through your day, notice your style. Notice the aspects that are appealing. Notice things you may want to adjust. Without judgement, choose how and in what area you want to evolve your personal style or brand.

**Personal Reflections:** _____
_____
_____
_____
_____
_____

## Day 112
# NORMAL

*If you are always trying to be normal, you will never know how amazing you can be.*

*~ Maya Angelou*

Normal is a setting on a dryer. When you continue to attempt to fit into a stock mold, you will never quite fit because your uniqueness knows no mold of normal. This is good news! Your amazing inner light and talents can only shine when they are allowed to be freely expressed. Sometimes this includes leaving normal behind.

Thinking that you should fit into the *average* mold is a limited view of yourself. Your greatness is in your amazing talents and gifts that simply need permission to burst forth. Normal is part of what our society accepts as the norm. For me, most of this is not part of my desire for our society. It is our responsibility to step up and represent a way of living that his more noble than the popular view. I do not have to know you personally to be certain that you are fascinating and amazing, beyond your own perception. Normal is so out dated.

**Daily Application:** Identify where you are not normal and where you can allow your brilliance to shine forth. Journal your thoughts about choosing a non-normal path for your future. Be free of any self-imposed belief prisons.

**Personal Reflections:** _____
_____
_____
_____
_____
_____

## Day 113
# VARIETY

*As you grow older, you'll find that the only things you regret are the things you didn't do.*
~ Zachary Scott

There are things I regret that I did not do. There are things I did that I am thrilled that I took the chance and did them. Variety truly is the spice of life. So often, I hear people judging people and ways of living that are not the same as their personal way. This is so boring and single minded. Not for me.

I believe strongly in the variety of life and the wealth that comes when we authentically embrace variety. I am glad I have done so many things. I am happy that I have stepped out and taken healthy risks. This variety is serving me today. Still some of the "didn't dos" are a bit haunting. So, I am choosing to live life out loud today. Being joyous in my sharing of inspiration and education wherever I am able. I encourage you to live so you won't regret what you did not do. Variety deepens your life and makes it more rich and vibrant.

**Daily Application:** Imagine you fulfilling some of your "somedays" and creating opportunities to do those things that you haven't yet done. Sometimes it is a simple phone call or personal contact. Take some action toward your dreams and vision.

**Personal Reflections:** _____

_____
_____
_____
_____
_____

## Day 114
# COLLABORATION

*Stand next to dreamers - they tickle your imagination and support your belief in creating reality from your dreams!*
~ Sheryl Nicholson, CSP **

Collaboration is vital for success and leadership on many levels. To collaborate means that we acknowledge other ideas as well as our own, knowing that the synergy flows within the interactions and from it emerges ideas and concepts and action plans that were not available to each individual involved had they not collaborated. I have witnessed the power of collaboration repeatedly personally and professionally over many years. Many successful and influential people note the power of collaborating with others. When you can hold your vision and ideas while being open-minded to others, you become a catalyst as does the other open-minded person. In this coming together, while retaining individual differences, lies the beauty of synergy, inspiration and ultimate support for your vision and your dreams.

Be open and willing to collaborate. Release any egoic fears of losing. The only losers are the ones who shut down and hide behind pride and fear. Be open. Come together. Imagine. Create. Dream. Build.

**Daily Application:** Write your best ideas and plans regarding a life project of yours. Seek collaboration opportunities today with an open mind. Following a time of collaboration, see how your ideas and plans have been enhanced. Honor your multiplied choices and improved clarity. Now, move in the direction of your highest good.

**Personal Reflections:** _____
_____
_____
_____
_____

## Day 115
# PURPOSE

*Life without intention or purpose is an endless walk in the dark.*
*~ Carole R. Gill* \*\*

Are your lights on? Are you clear about your purpose? These are important things that make all the difference in your life. I prefer to walk in the light, at least most of the time! When you are living your purpose, your heart sings and there is a nice flow to your life. Things aren't always easy, yet you have a focus that is rooted in your purpose. As I work with people seeking a clearer understanding of their purpose, I love the radiant smile when they authentically connect to their inner vision.

To live in your purpose means that you know who you are and why you are here and what gifts and talents you are here to deliver with honor and humility. Your purpose is your inner calling or heart's desire. It is always calling you, even when you are trying to ignore the small whispers when you are quiet. Listen to that inner nudging, it leads you to life happiness and satisfaction beyond measure.

**Daily Application:** Take a few extra moments of inner reflection today. Connect to your purpose. Write about the feelings, ideas and other great things that you sense. After some pondering, begin to write your plan. Make a commitment to continue to follow your purpose so you can stay out of the dark.

**Personal Reflections:** _____
_____
_____
_____
_____
_____

## Day 116
# NOBILITY

*It's easy to make a buck. It's a lot harder to make a difference.*
*~ Tom Brokaw*

What is your motivation? Are you seeking to make a buck? Are you motivated by doing good, being altruistic? Your primary focus comes out in your decisions and interactions with others. When your motive is financial profit, your motive becomes clear when you interact with others. When your motive is service, you participate in noble profit. Noble profit is the experience of making a nice living as a result of doing what is right by others.

Making a difference takes a motive of care and compassion while focusing on the greater good for all concerned. To be noble means to serve your higher vision while remaining in alignment with your true calling. The noble profit you acquire becomes a reflection of the good you are doing rather than a reflection of greed. The greed profit will eventually fall away whereas the noble profit continues to flow. I choose nobility.

**Daily Application:** Slow down and pay close attention to your motives today. Are you acting out some financial or survival fear? Are you acting with trust in the natural order of things and attempting to offer kindness and compassion, knowing that you are taken care of by the universal good? Today, choose to make a difference.

**Personal Reflections:** _____
_____
_____
_____
_____
_____

## Day 117
# SMILE

*Never regret anything that made you smile.*
*~ Mark Twain*

Your smile is your universal calling card. All humans smile and this is a warm greeting. Even when your verbal language is dissimilar, your smile makes the connection. When you put a smile on your face, it sends the message to the energy in your body and mind to lighten up. This lighter place opens opportunities and possibilities that the heavier moods of sad or upset cannot see or experience. By focusing on your blessings, you draw to you a more warm and pleasing experience.

Smile on purpose and see how the world greets you. I imagine that the more smiles yield more returned smiles. I also imagine that your mood and outlook will be elevated by your own smile. One simple choice and action can make a significant difference in your life and the lives or others. After all, being serious and frowning all the time gives you wrinkles and separates you from others.

**Daily Application:** Smile on purpose throughout the day. Smile when encountering strangers. Smile at yourself in the mirror. Get good eye contact and feel the power of you own smile. Now, spread the smile around. Journal your experience.

**Personal Reflections:** _____
_____
_____
_____
_____
_____

## Day 118
# OLD AGE

*A man is not old until his regrets take the place of dreams.*
*~ Yiddish Proverb*

This proverb speaks volumes. Dreaming is so important to your outlook and youthfulness. What you focus on dictates what you experience and see. Old age is not a number like many might think. Old age is a mindset or an outlook toward life. I have met people in their thirties who sounded and acted like they were decades older. You become old when you stop dreaming and you start looking back with a regretful focus. What do you regret? What do you dream about for your future self?

You are not old until the regrets overtake the dreams. I still have many dreams and I am always creating. Like this book, it is a labor of love and has morphed several times. I know that I want to keep my dream alive rather than stopping and the book becoming part of any regrets in the future. Keep following your dreams, you will cheat old age.

**Daily Application:** Today is a great day to move forward with some of your dreams. Take some time today to focus and create the avenue for your success. Your chronological age is just a number, the number that reflects many amazing lessons and journeys. Let your light shine, it stops the brittle way of old age.

**Personal Reflections:** _____
_____
_____
_____
_____
_____

## Day 119
## LIMITATIONS

*Argue for your limitations, and sure enough they're yours.*
*~ Richard Bach*

Self-imposed limits are powerful and often debilitating. I hear people say that they can only change one thing at a time. This is simply not true. I hear parents warn their children that they should focus on one thing. To build a life that is rich and rewarding, it is required that you expand your territory. You may continue to choose a small number of things and it will not be because of limitations, it will be choice.

My life is full of many activities, interests and people. We explore new things and share memories and experiences. Your power is in lifting your self-imposed limits. Your talents are more than you realize and your opportunities are endless. Release the idea of having to remain within a certain number. If you argue to defend your limitations with many reasons as to why they are true, then you are correct. This is because you have created the limits.

**Daily Application:** Write down 5 things you want to explore within the next month. Plan today to be open to the new opportunities. After do the 5 things, note if any are ones you want to explore deeper and carry forward.

**Personal Reflections:** _____
_____
_____
_____
_____
_____

## Day 120
# CULTURE

*The artist has to be the guardian of the culture.*
~ Robert Longo

Culture is made up of the manifestations of human achievement, intellectually and through the arts. The artist is the one who blows out old ways and challenges the culture to expand beyond current limitations. Artists also revel the culture to itself. Musicians create music and write lyrics that reflect the sentiments of the day. Each era has its own vibe and feel. As you listen, you are immersed in the culture of the time period. The music lives on and brings out the power of the time that has passed. Just like other forms of art, the culture is both revealed and expanded by the artists.

The creative ones are the ones who seem to be the caretakers of the culture and are documenting the changes. Follow any artist and you are following some aspect of the culture. The guardians are the protectors and they are usually artists in some fashion. Our culture needs artists who are truly expressing and therefore guardians. It seems that all parts of the culture ought to be protected, even the ugly and messy, for it reveals the journey and the progress of the civilization.

**Daily Application:** In what ways are you a guardian of the culture? How are you using your visionary skills to serve the greater good? Spend some time in quiet reflecting on your role within the culture and how you want your art to emerge. Journal some of your ideas.

**Personal Reflections:** _____
_____
_____
_____
_____

## Day 121
# PROGRESS

*Make measurable progress in reasonable time.*
~ Jim Rohn

Progress in anything can be measured. It may not be measured in a yard stick or a spreadsheet. Progress can be overestimated like the time optimists that I know. A time optimist believes that the to do list can be done in much less time than is reasonable. This includes arriving at a destination on time. I have a friend who always says it takes 10 minutes to get to work. If he hits all the green lights and the bridge is not up, he can get there in about 10 minutes. What he has failed to account for is the time to leave his house, get out of his neighborhood, red lights, the draw bridge being up, other cars, etc. He tells me that he is always between 5 and 15 minutes late because of the other events. While he is getting caught up in his excuses, his progress toward his vision is suffering.

The added stress and cascading problems caused by his not being reasonable with this time is mounting. Many people over or underestimate possible progress in reasonable time. Both are essential, I think. Makes sense to me.

**Daily Application:** Today, notice how reasonable you are being with your time. Are you properly allotting the reasonable time so you make measurable progress? Wherever you notice time optimism, adjust accordingly. Check in with yourself often.

**Personal Reflections:** _____
_____
_____
_____
_____

Day 122
# SELF-DISCIPLINE

*Self-discipline is when your conscience tells you to do something and you don't talk back.*

~ W. K. Hope

Does your conscience have to yell to get your attention? Do you consider yourself to be self-disciplined? Will power and self-discipline are relatives in my life. They both remind me to pay inner attention to my conscience rather than pushing through without paying attention to my level of self-discipline.

It takes self-discipline to accomplish many tasks. It is taking self-discipline to complete this book. My conscience tells me to get to work, today I am not talking back. I have talked back and my self-discipline waivered. Some so the delay is from not listening to my conscience or talking back and some was allowing distractions. It is a good thing I can start over at any time and begin to listen more acutely. Look at your self-discipline regarding your goals, have you been talking back to your conscience?

**Daily Application:** Spend time in quiet today. Notice your self-discipline as your day unfolds. Have things been running smoothly or have there been any challenges because of your back talk to your conscience? Honor your ability to have self-discipline and allow it to serve you.

**Personal Reflections:** _____
_____
_____
_____
_____
_____

## Day 123
# SERVICE

*I slept and dreamt that life was joy. I awoke and saw that life was service. I acted and behold, service was joy.*

~ Rabindranath Tagore

Joy and service go hand in hand. Every time I hear of someone going to a lesser fortunate area, they come back changed. They think they are going to bestow some sort of benevolence on the people and yet they come away changed. I believe the extreme dire situations that they went into broke open their heart and joy came gushing forth. Thus, they experienced that service is joy.

Joy is our inherent state. When you go into your head and live from your mind only, you stifle your joy expression. So, your joy keeps knocking on your heart until it gets the opening. Often, the opening comes through service. Every time I come away from serving others, whether it be speaking or consulting, I feel a joy within that is indescribable. Service is a way of life for me.

**Daily Application:** Imagine your joy levels as you seek opportunities to serve those in your daily life. How can you serve them and let your joy come forth? Notice your freedom and write or draw your experience to remember the power of joy that comes through service.

**Personal Reflections:** _____
_____
_____
_____
_____
_____

Day 124
# SELF-RELIANCE

*Self-reliance conquers any difficulty.*

~ Yogi Bhajan

I rely on myself. Do you? Many folks in today's world do not rely on themselves. I hear people talking about everything that others should be doing for them and no conversation about self-reliance. It seems the complaining and waiting for others to come to the rescue is causing much strife and ultimately harm. Most of the people I run into are more self-reliant than they sometimes believe. Some of the leaders I work with continue to look outside of themselves for the inspiration that their own elf-reliance offers.

Some of the homeless people I have served are more self-reliant as well. They have experienced difficulty and challenges and their sense of self-reliance has been undermined. Part of the healing work we do it to restore their ability to access and use their self-reliance.

Self-reliance is valuable as a skill and mindset. As adults, we are meant to be interdependent. Some say that they should do everything on their own, an adolescent form of independence. Self- reliance is the ability to count on yourself in a reasonable way. You can cease being your own betrayer. It is OK to be interdependent and self-reliant at the same time.

**Daily Application:** In your quiet time today. Assess your personal level of self-reliance. Do you rely on yourself? Are you reliable? Journal some of your thoughts and be open to insights and directions.

**Personal Reflections:** _____
_____
_____
_____
_____
_____

## Day 125
# CHOICE

*It is not what you have, it is how you use it.*
*~ fiZ Anthony* \*\*

Every moment is a choice point. Even those things that you do not see as choices are, in fact, choices. One choice is to keep moving and to use your momentum to help you break through the blocks and challenges that appear. Some of the blocks come from within in the form of outdated beliefs and habits. Yet others seem to be from outside. In any event, you get to choose how you dance with the obstacles that arise.

One constant is your power to choose. Each moment is an opportunity for you to use your power of choice. You get to choose the power and role of emotions and events in your life. Are you going to choose to take forward focused action or are you going to use your power of choice to derail your momentum? If your choice is to keep going, you will benefit from the power of momentum. Otherwise, you will be using more energy to stop and start repeatedly. The choice is yours.

**Daily Application:** Today, notice what is motivating your most frequent choices. Do you identify nervousness or fear? Are you noticing how choices made from love or compassion impact your life? Take notice today and align your choices with your vision. Journal your insights and results.

**Personal Reflections:** _____
_____
_____
_____
_____
_____

## Day 126
# THOUGHT

*Every thought we think is creating our future.*
~ Louise Hay

Wherever your thoughts are, is where your future lies. Think about lack and fear and loneliness, you are right. Think about love, abundance and compassion, you are right. When I begin to work with a new client, I quickly learn where their thoughts have been by listening and looking at their life circumstances. Thoughts are things according to Quantum Physicists and according to others throughout the world.

When your thoughts begin to go down a road that you do not want to create for yourself, change the path. Your future depends upon your choice. So much of the messes to be cleaned up are coming from not thinking from a higher, more aligned and authentic perspective.

As time unfolds, every thought has an impact on your future. When you notice thoughts that are not serving your highest good, change them. It is that simple. No beating yourself up or getting upset. Simply make the change and refocus.

**Daily Application:** After your quiet time today, notice your thinking. Include your habitual thoughts and random thoughts. Notice ones that are creating something other than your desired result. Maybe it is time to change some thinking.

**Personal Reflections:** _____
_____
_____
_____
_____
_____

## Day 127
# PRODUCTIVE

*Focus on being productive instead of busy.*
*~ Tim Ferris*

Busyness can make you weary. Productivity has the power to enliven you. You have heard the phrase to work smarter not harder. I have a client who interpreted this phrase as an excuse for overthinking and busy work and thus worked herself to the point of exhaustion. She did not want to be seen as lazy so she kept busy. Her challenge was that she lacked clear focus in her busyness so she just wore herself down. This stops all productivity. She woke up one day, completely exhausted and realized she had not fulfilled her goals or dreams and was distracted from them with her busyness.

Productive people live through this lesson and get smarter over time. Focus is the main difference. She could not share a clear focus with me initially. After some work, she could verbalize a clear focus that she generated from within. Her productivity expanded and she was less tired. In fact, she was often on fire with inspiration now that she was aligned.

What do you want to get done? Are you using busyness to distract you knowingly or unknowingly? What results are you really looking for in your work and life?

**Daily Application:** Recall your short and longer-term goals. Become still and write down your focused action steps. Assess your focus and productivity progress. Seek to eliminate or decrease any busyness that is in your way. Share your goals and results with a trusted other.

**Personal Reflections:** _____
_____
_____
_____
_____
_____

## Day 128
# EDUCATION

*We can learn nothing except by going from the known to the unknown.*
*~ Claude Bernard*

Education takes on many forms, both formal and informal. In every case, you are moving from what you do not know into what you do know. The most effective way to do this is to stay within your zone of proximal development. Going too far, too fast can cause a crisis and therefore added challenges. Education takes being curious and being willing to stretch into the zone where you do not yet know and it is plausible that you will learn and then know.

This zone is vital. We all have one. Curiosity and the desire to grow, learn and achieve takes us into the zone and we then experience education. This is so fun. Part of my vocation is to help educate. For me to teach others, I must educate myself. Every time I stretch my limits, it exhilarates me and challenges me to go further. If I go too far too fast, I get slowed down. Now, I keep a nice rhythm and I enjoy learning and growing. Do you stretch yourself?

**Daily Application:** Ponder your movement from unknown to known in your daily life. Some things are easy, like tying your shoes. Some things more intricate. How do you like to learn, writing, listening, watching, doing or a combination? Educate yourself today and celebrate moving into the known!

**Personal Reflections:** _____
_____
_____
_____
_____
_____

## Day 129
# DECISIONS

*Strength is a matter of a made-up mind.*
~ John Beecher

To decide means to cut out all other possibilities. Your strength is in making up your mind. This is different than flirting with a good idea or thinking about doing something. A made-up mind has no wiggle room for excuses or distractions. This is where your strength is evident.

My friend kept saying she wanted to make changes yet she never really made up her mind. I told her it was as if she was enthralled by the good idea. Her strength will be in making up her mind and then following through. She continues to flirt with the ideas, not truly deciding or committing. She will experience her strength when she finally makes up her mind.

It seems easier to decide if it is something you want and you are willing to act. If you are undecided or have any hesitation, then the decisions seem murkier and therefore the action may be hesitant or distracted. Are you worthy to receive the good that comes to you as a result of your good decisions?

**Daily Application:** Notice your decision making today. Are you sure and clear or are you somewhat indecisive? What is your mind made up to do today? Does having a decisive mind help you follow through with your vision? Journal your results.

**Personal Reflections:** _____
_____
_____
_____
_____
_____

## Day 130
# EFFORT

*Continuous effort – not strength or intelligence is the key to unlocking our potential.*

*~ Winston Churchill*

I work with gifted people and many think they can outsmart the need to use any effort. They are often so smart that they can do things and figure out problems rapidly, thus feeding them the illusion of not needing effort. When having to face something that is challenging, many of my clients balk at having to use any effort. Some even say: "If I have to work hard, maybe I'll do something else." It seems some are allergic to effort.

Many of the visionary talented people I work with are eager to act and demonstrate continuous effort. They can surpass some of the smarter people because they are acting continuously. It is possible to sabotage your successes by taking an easier, softer way rather than using effort. Your potential can only show up with your action.

**Daily Application:** Take some quiet time alone. Are you avoiding effort in some area of your life while allowing the visionary part to distract from your inner avoidance? Choose an area and take continuous effort today and notice how things develop. Journal your awareness and action steps.

**Personal Reflections:** _____
_____
_____
_____
_____
_____

## Day 131
# FOOD

*Thou should eat to live, not live to eat.*

*~ Socrates*

This book is about being a leader and expanding your reach. It includes creativity, inspiration and support in caring for yourself. Eating to live rather than medicating with food is taking care of your body. Food can be abused. It is your responsibility to pay close attention to what you put in your body.

As the saying goes, if you can't pronounce the ingredient, it is not food and shouldn't be eaten. Visionary leaders are often on the cutting edge of understanding and knowledge. It is now that you use your knowledge and understanding in your human fuel arena.

Just like you would not put the wrong fuel in your vehicle, it is advisable to not put artificial fuel in your body. Let's eat to support our vision. Your body runs better with higher quality nutrition. Support you by eating to live and bring your vision to life more fully.

**Daily Application:** Spend some quiet time and reflect on the food you use to fuel your body. Journal what you eat and how much water you drink today and notice if the fuel source is of high quality.

**Personal Reflections:** _____
_____
_____
_____
_____
_____

## Day 132
# BOREDOM

*If you are bored, it means you have no inner resource.*
*~ Elizabeth J. Allen (my mother)*

My brother and I heard this phrase from our mother often. She was inquisitive and certainly a woman before her time. Boredom is a sign of not being connected within. This phrase resounds in my mind and it helps me redefine my experience: for example, not mistaking peace for boredom. It also helps to give permission to go within and connect to my inner resource. Of course, as a child we did not know the meaning of the words, not really.

The truth is that we all have abundant inner resources. Being bored is an external, temporary condition and has no real power except what you give it in the moment. I am rarely bored because, I have learned over the years to go within and either create or get moving. You have inner resources, get connected.

Sometimes these days, when I am bored, I get excited to look within and see what great creation I can bring forth! Boredom can be the birthplace of amazing inspiration.

**Daily Application:** Reflect on how you respond to the idea and experience of boredom. Are there times where you may be mislabeling another experience? Go within and enjoy your abundant inner resource and smile. Journal your inspired ideas.

**Personal Reflections:** _____
_____
_____
_____
_____

## Day 133
# HEALTH

*Health is not the absence of sickness.*
*~ Dianne A. Allen, MA*

I heard someone say that If you don't have a diagnosis then you are not sick. Wow. This idea stems from a lack of understanding. When someone outside of you can tell you if you are healthy or not, you may want to evaluate your understanding.

Health, for me, is the vibrancy felt when my mind, body, emotions and spirit are in harmony and able to do what I desire for the highest good. It is diagnosis independent. I have had times when my vibrancy was not in full force. Rather than a diagnosis, I check in with my alignment and worked there. This seems to make sense to me. This is not to preclude healing and medicine and other medical procedures.

It just seems to me that any healer or doctor has more to work with if I am responsible with my choices and in alignment the best I am able. We can all work together, and it makes authentic health much more achievable.

**Daily Application:** Are you as healthy are you desire? In your quiet time, ponder simple changes that can make a big difference. Love yourself toward a healthier you from the inside out. Journal your ideas about this and create a personal plan.

**Personal Reflections:** _____
_____
_____
_____
_____
_____

## Day 134
## ATTENTIVENESS

*Are you being a person of vision and doing what matters, or are you just reacting to the noise?*
~Brendon Burchard

Are you attentive to your inner guidance system? This inner knowingness emanates from an internal locus of control. be attentive to what matters in the greater sense and you can remain focused, acting from the inside out. When you have an external locus of control, you can easily be pulled from your vision and later regret the distraction. Even other good ideas can impair your attentiveness toward your personal heart's desire and inner vision.

To be attentive to your vision requires separating from the noise. The noise of doubt and worry in your head and the noise all around you can draw your attention away from what matters, your vision. Being attentive puts you in position to do what matters without meaningless distraction.

Attentiveness helps you get through the clutter of overstimulation, overthinking and distractions of all kinds. Focus on your vision and act from that place.

**Daily Application:** Pay attention to your inner dialogue. Are you attending to your personal vision or are you distracted? Spend some time in quiet a few times today and focus on what matters most. Write your ideas and act.

**Personal Reflections:** _____
_____
_____
_____
_____
_____

## Day 135
# GREATNESS

*Our greatness lies not so much in being able to remake the world as being able to remake ourselves.*

~ Gandhi

We are all evolving and remaking ourselves as each day passes. When I was younger, I wanted to help the world and I was unaware of the notion of remaking myself as time unfolds. Years have passed and now this statement from Gandhi seems like common sense to me. Every day, I run into someone who is still focused outside of themselves expecting that that will remake the world. It will not. Peace begins within. Harmony begins within as does Joy and Love.

Your greatness is in turning your attention inward and healing and releasing bitterness, resentment and entitlement so that you are free to help the world outside of yourself. Your greatness lies in allowing your transformed inner self to emerge and help remake our world. Now more than ever, it seems that we are best served by going within first. Then, authentic transformation of the ignorance that keeps us focused outward can happen.

As you remake yourself, you are remaking the world. Start where you have authority, within. Your inner changes touch the outer world and transform it simply with your presence. Think about the impact Gandhi has had from the inside out.

**Daily Application:** Journal for some time today about your vision for the world as well as your vision for yourself. Focus today on remaking yourself in thought, word and action. Watch how it automatically positively impacts your surroundings.

**Personal Reflections:** _____
_____
_____
_____
_____
_____

## Day 136
## FIRE

*There is no phoenix without a fire.*
*~ Dianne A. Allen, MA*

How many times have you risen from the ashes in your life? I'll bet more than two or three. Often, bright and visionary people disintegrate the old and then rise out and create the new. This is not conscious most often so it seems like you are starting over often and just when things were moving along, you fall apart and now starts a new beginning.

The fire is the cleansing agent that purifies so that the new beginning can be fresh and clean. You have walked through the fire and are on the other side, with fresh, new opportunities and possibilities for your vision. The phoenix can only rise from the fire. The phoenix does not hatch or swim up, it rises; mighty and strong from the cleansing heat of the fire.

When the fire is all around, walk through it and rise like the phoenix, using the fire to propel you into the new. Rise like the mighty bird, gaze focused upward with power and strength.

**Daily Application:** Take some time in quiet today to honor your journey through the fires. Visualize your rise out of the cleansing fires. Journal what you see. Affirm your inner strength.

**Personal Reflections:** _____

## Day 137
# PARADIGM

*Change your paradigms and you will change the way you create results.*
~ Bob Proctor

Your paradigm is the framework you use to negotiate the world. Most people do not pay much attention to their paradigm until they run into someone with a different paradigm and they want to communicate. Some people have the good/bad paradigm, some the school paradigm (we are here learning lessons) and some have the paradigm that science is the only answer to the larger life questions. There are many others.

When you are stuck or feeling like you are going in circles, your paradigm could be the culprit. Make some changes in your framework and see how things change. I understand that wherever my attention goes, I create more of that thing. So, I have changed my paradigm from fighting disease and sickness to focusing on healthy functioning and healing opportunities rather then fighting. I am getting much better results now. I just needed a paradigm change.

**Daily Application:** Ponder your personal framework for creating results in your life. Is it working? What changes could create even more effective results? Journal your ideas and thoughts.

**Personal Reflections:** _____
_____
_____
_____
_____
_____

## Day 138
# POWER

*Power does not corrupt. Fear corrupts, perhaps the fear of the loss of power.*
*~ John Steinbeck*

It seems that John Steinbeck has a point. Fear is much more of a problem than you might think. Power can be used for benefit of others when used with compassion and understanding. Whenever I see an abuse of power, fear plays a major role in that misuse of power. I have also witnessed the positive and inspiring use of power where fear did not move in and corrupt.

Many folks in power have known and unknown fears of the loss of that power, unless of course they are able to live by higher principles of non-attachment. The self-centered fears of losing what you have or not getting what you want can bring corruption to your leadership or management behaviors. As a visionary leader, you are responsible for your healthy use of personal power. How do you use your power? Is your fear of losing your power impacting your use of that power?

**Daily Application:** Write the areas in which you have power. Note any fears that impact your perceived loss or change in power and how it changes your use of your power. Any part that is not aligned for you, make changes accordingly.

**Personal Reflections:** _____
_____
_____
_____
_____

## Day 139
# IMPROVEMENT

*Your legacy should be that you made it better than it was when you got it.*
*~ Lee Iacocca*

I first learned the idea of leaving things better than I received it in girl scouts when I was young. I remember we were attentive to our camp sites and nature to be sure we left it better. I remember feeling so happy and proud of all of us for doing the right thing. Leaving things better than when I found them became part of my everyday behavior into my adulthood.

This translates into our adult business and personal environments well. Making the decision to leave things better than when we arrive on the scene is a practice that is honorable. It becomes part of your legacy. Do you notice how you can improve things around you? Is your impact one of improvement? I believe as you focus on building up and improving rather than diminishing, you will find great joy and satisfaction. This idea of improvement comes from an intention of service. Are you a service oriented leader?

**Daily Application:** Setout today to make things better. Focus your thoughts, words and actions toward improving with humility. Allow yourself to feel your satisfaction in making things better.

**Personal Reflections:** _____
_____
_____
_____
_____
_____

## Day 140
# CHILDREN

*If you want your children to turn out well, spend twice as much time with them, and half as much money.*

~ Abigail van Buren

Children are one of our greatest resources. There is so much potential is each child as they are born. So often, children are taught limiting beliefs that stem from fears of the adults that surround them. The limitations that the adults project on the children only holds back the child. It is not noble to spew your fear onto another in the name of love or care. You must realize that each child is born fully equipped to grow into the world with a purpose and a mission. It is the responsibility of the adults to support, nurture and encourage each child to grow along the lines that are aligned for their highest good without selfish motive or agenda.

With all the children I have interacted, it is the ones who are encouraged to be their individual personalities and respect others and themselves that seem to excel. Let's do our children a favor and shed our limiting beliefs then encourage them to follow their heart's desires.

Spend time with the children. Encourage them. Love them. Support them. Enjoy them.

**Daily Application:** Be the supporter and encourager of a child today. Remind the children in your life that they are worthy and valuable. Smile with them. Spend time and leave the money at home. Write your experience and encourage other adults to invest face to face time with children.

**Personal Reflections:** _____
_____
_____
_____
_____
_____

Day 141
# STEWARDSHIP

*Your own self-realization is the greatest service you can render the world.*
*~ Ramana Maharshi*

Stewardship means to take the best care of something left in your care. To be a good steward means that you take excellent care of what you are charged with protecting. Leo understands the idea that being a good steward of time means that wasted hours do not flitter by. He has learned over time, like many of us, that having discipline and taking good care of the time allotted, yields prosperous results.

Squandering time yields lacking results and maybe even perceived failures. A good steward takes good care of their time by using it wisely. This does not mean acting like a machine, rather it means to honor all aspects of your life in good use of your time. Take care of your emotional, mental, physical, spiritual and social areas by investing your time with fore thought and care.

**Daily Application:** Plan your day in advance. At the end of the day, see how you took care of your time. Were you a good steward? Do you want to make any changes? Note your successes and desired changes in your journal or below.

**Personal Reflections:** _____
_____
_____
_____
_____
_____

## Day 142
# DIRECTION

*Stay close to your growing edges. If you notice that you are experiencing an unhealthy amount of depression then look to where you have moved away from your personal direction for growth. You only need to move 1/4 of an inch in the right direction to start feeling better.*

~ Don Ollsin **


Be aware of your edges and your direction. The smallest adjustment can yield massive results. This is true for your emotions and your sense of well-being. Many people are random about their direction and then they find themselves in a mess. Your directional focus and actions lead you into each event of your life.

I have a friend who tends to become melancholy and somewhat depressed when he does not play tennis to burn off his physical over excitable energy. When his direction is more sedentary or only work related, he becomes snippy and irritable. Just a small change like playing tennis a couple of days in a row, gets his healthy direction going again. His melancholy lifts.

When you are feeling too far "off", look around and see where you changed direction and may not have known. Assess your options, seek guidance and then act toward your higher good.

**Daily Application:** Spend some time alone and ponder your current direction. Are you fulfilled and satisfied or are there some directional changes that will serve you? Journal some of your thoughts and self-feedback.


**Personal Reflections:** _____
_____
_____
_____
_____
_____

## Day 143
# PURITY

*Iron rusts from disuse; water loses its purity from stagnation... even so does inaction sap the vigor of the mind.*

~ Leonardo da Vinci

I have noticed that when I am stagnating for too long, I feel blah. My mind then becomes less disciplined and focused. In those times, my excitement and thrill for life seems to elude me. I know that if I do not keep learning and feeding my mind with information and ideas, I become lackluster. For me, purity is about having clarity and a clean way. Like clear water that remains clear because there is an inflow and an outflow.

Taking in and releasing are the natural ways of life. So, I practice releasing and allowing anything that is old or stagnate to leave, gently. Keeping your mind active keeps you young and alive. Doing crossword puzzles helps your mind remain flexible and youthful. Sharing with others face to face builds a connection that is not colored by electronics, thus is purer. Purity is desirable for those who wish to be moving along the road of life without pollution. Want to join me?

**Daily Application:** How much vigor do you experience in your thinking? Meditate on how increasing action and flow in your thinking can make your mind active and clear. Journal your ideas and awareness.

**Personal Reflections:** _____
_____
_____
_____
_____
_____

## Day 144
# RECOVERY

*Hardships often prepare ordinary people for an extraordinary destiny.*
~ C. S. Lewis

My operating definition of recovery is "to feel better". So many times, when we go through a setback, we have a time of recovery. If you fall, you recover by getting up and taking care of any injury. If you have a career setback, you recover by making changes. Recovery is an active part of life.

Last night, I was working on a quilt. I made a mistake on a seam. My recovery was to get the seam ripper, take out the thread and then re-do the seam properly. That is a form of recovery. All hardships in life require a recalculation much like your GPS. Every time you transcend a hardship, you are positioning yourself for an extraordinary destiny. The harder the challenge, the more extraordinary the destiny.

In my work over decades with people suffering addiction and mental illness, I have had the privilege of helping people come out of the darkness and into an extraordinary life they never thought possible. The road is not for the weak or unwilling. To have an extraordinary destiny, you must be willing to let your hardships prepare you for that greatness.

**Daily Application:** Reflect on your past hardships and see how you have grown and transformed. Know that your extraordinary destiny comes from walking through each hardship asking the question: "How can this hardship help me grow?" Allow yourself to grow through the struggles.

**Personal Reflections:** _____
_____
_____
_____
_____
_____

## Day 145
# OPPORTUNITY

*I see my life as an unfolding set of opportunities to awaken.*
~ Ram Dass

Opportunity follows service and giving. This is an age-old understanding yet so many people continue to have a poverty consciousness which keeps real opportunity away. Do you remain mindful so to see clearly the opportunities for your life as they arise? I notice that the more open and aware I am throughout the day, the more I experience a sense of hope. I am then free to give more and serve others more which seems to continue the cycle of opportunity.

It seems that people with an internal locus of control who are looking for ways to give to others are afforded more opportunities than those who are focused on what they can get from others. I think the opportunities abound and it is our motive, intention and perception that makes some more available than others. Are you mindful of opportunities because you are serving others? Are you wanting more opportunities? Start first by giving and the doors will be opened.

**Daily Application:** Seek opportunities to serve others today by giving freely of your time, talent or treasure. Note what opportunities are available to you. Write them down and then act with good conscience.

**Personal Reflections:** _____
_____
_____
_____
_____
_____

## Day 146
# SACRIFICE

*Nothing comes without a price. Sacrifice has a benefit for the long-term goal.*

~ Dave Moore **

Sacrifice is familiar to all of us. What have you sacrificed to attain your goals? I have sacrificed time with friends and family, social events and outings as well as time alone for reflection. All of these at different times and in different amounts, of course. Dave and I talked about some of the sacrifices he has made to achieve his goals. The sacrifices paid off because he was able to achieve his heart's desire and live his vision. You can be clear about your long-term goals and then know that the price and sacrifice is worth the attainment of the goal. Understanding this energy exchange makes sacrifice and goal attainment make sense.

We all pay a price for what we seek. Taking the easier softer way will not yield outstanding results. The benefit for your long-term goal is profound when you are willing to make appropriate sacrifices with the goal in mind. Clear focus on your long-term goal allows for strategic sacrifice which then benefits your goal. There is a great chasm between excellence and mediocre, you choose your outcome.

**Daily Application:** Are you willing to pay the price for your goals? Reflect in your quiet time today about your willingness to make sacrifices on the road toward your long-term goal. Be willing to pay the price, remain focused, take a few breaths and take action.

**Personal Reflections:** _____
_____
_____
_____
_____

## Day 147
# DESTINY

*There is a destiny that makes us brothers, none goes his way alone. All that we send into the lives of others comes back into our own.*

*~ Edwin Markham*

This quote was on a wall hanging in my bedroom when I was in high school. I used it for a school project in a history class. I was told by my teacher that this idea is not accurate and she told me to change my project. That did not sit well with me. I knew that there was a truth here that she could not see. I redid the project for the grade and I kept the wall hanging in my room. I had a deep inner sense of a connection greater than I was able to understand or verbalize at that time. Years later, I have more awareness and understanding. There is a destiny that connects each of us.

Are you aware that no matter what, you are not alone and you do not travel alone? Are you aware that whatever you send into another's life returns to you? I think I am singing to the choir and I still hear people say that there is no connection. Really? We are all connected and everything effects everything. You always receive what you have put out, even if from another place.

**Daily Application:** Imagine all your positive thoughts and actions are white balls that multiply when you are kind and compassionate. All your doubt, worry, fear and selfishness are black balls that multiply. Do you have more white or black balls at the end of the day? Where is your destiny headed?

**Personal Reflections:** _____
_____
_____
_____
_____
_____

## Day 148
# STRENGTH

*Don't expect to build up the weak by pulling down the strong.*
~ Calvin Coolidge

Have you ever tried to help another and later felt tired and weak? When you are the strong one in a situation and you spend your strength on others, it depletes your reserves. Allowing others to pull you down does not work.

Pulling down bright visionaries can happen because of the cultural idea that the weak need to be brought up no matter the cost. I believe strongly that the strong can serve from their overflow and thus maintain their strength. To pull down the strong does not work because then all people end up weak.

If you wish to help those who are weak, build them up and teach them from your overflow. When our society attempts to become focused on pulling down the strong to help the weak, they have it backwards. This has proven not to work over millennia. This ineffective way creates resentment and entitlement. This steals inherent strength from all those involved and no one is built up. Use your strength to serve and lift others from your overflow. Now, both are built up.

**Daily Application:** In quiet time, honor your strength and your gifts that you can share to build up another. Take the opportunity to build others up without depleting your resources. Journal and teach a better way to help.

**Personal Reflections:** _____
_____
_____
_____
_____
_____

## Day 149
# INTIMACY

*The opposite of loneliness, it's not togetherness. It is intimacy.*
~ Richard Bach

Intimacy for me is defined as "In To Me See". There are several levels of intimacy and most of them are not sexual as most of our culture would imagine. I wrote a book on loneliness. In it I discuss that loneliness is more about disconnection from self and cannot be fixed simply by being around people.

The intimacy that is most beneficial is self-intimacy first. Then, intimacy with the Divine and Nature. Then intimacy with others. These 3 areas of intimacy are the trifecta to being connected and fulfilled. Simply having a warm body near you does not intimacy make. There are many people who can attest to that! So, intimacy is valuable when you focus on connecting with yourself and your calling then with others. When struggling with loneliness, try connecting to nature or your heart's desire before searching outside of yourself. Your cure for loneliness comes from within.

**Daily Application:** Be Still. Connect to your inner self. Are you comfortable there? Now, expand out to the Universe and connect with nature. Then check your availability for being intimate with other people. Journal your awareness.

**Personal Reflections:** _____
_____
_____
_____
_____
_____

## Day 150
# TRIUMPH

*The triumph can't be had without the struggle.*
*~ Wilma Rudolph*

I have many triumphs in my life. I'll bet you have had many as well. With each triumph came great celebration. Somehow the struggle, pain, sweat and tears were worth the victory. Even when I felt like giving up, I kept going and I triumphed. I'll bet you can relate to this.

When I was in high school, I remember excelling at academics. I triumphed in difficult classes that pushed me at times. I rose to the occasion along with my classmates. The ultimate result of our blood, sweat and tears was being able to get college credit for much of our hard work. Boy it was worth it to enter college with credits already in hand. In that era, this was not common and we had to work to take additional tests. That triumph set the stage for many other endeavors in my life. I learned that the struggle was worth it when the victory was at hand. What are some of your triumphs?

**Daily Application:** Ponder any struggles you may be having now. Are they a part of your triumphant journey or are they part of a self-imposed distraction? Relax your mind and breathe. Focus on your goal. Journal your willingness to work for your triumph.

**Personal Reflections:** _____

## Day 151
# HERO

> *I think of a hero as someone who understands his degree of responsibility that comes with his freedom.*
>
> ~ Bob Dylan

Who are your heroes? Do you have everyday heroes in your world right now? Are you an everyday hero? A hero is a person who is responsible and respectful of their freedoms. Freedoms include psychological safety, freedom of choice, freedom of speech and expression without harm to others and freedom to pursue noble goals. As you waken to your freedom, you become more responsible for the care of that freedom.

When someone is demanding some sort of freedom while attempting to imprison others with ignorance, that person is missing the mark. Freedom demands being personally accountable for your thoughts and actions and how you verbalize these things. You are a hero when you honor and respect the responsibility of freedom and you act accordingly.

**Daily Application:** Spend some quiet time reflecting on the times you have been a hero and may not have honored your role. Name your heroes and then take time today to thank them in person, writing or in a blessings or prayer. By honoring the hero within and without, you awaken your responsibility and personal power.

**Personal Reflections:** _____
_____
_____
_____
_____

## Day 152
# AFFIRMATION

*Affirmation without discipline is the beginning of delusion.*
*~ Jim Rohn*

I love this quote. In my professional circles, I hear many business owners and others making affirmations for wealth, prosperity, love and the like. When they do not see immediate results, they waiver then return to their previous defeatist stance. It takes focused action with discipline to achieve your goals. Doing varied tasks each day with on and off motivation does not yield powerful results.

A delusion is a fantasy of sorts. Making affirmation without discipline is basically a nice idea. Do not expect to make great strides without the discipline needed to succeed. If you are whining to yourself now, know that all successful people have had to be disciplined to move forward toward their goals. If the goal is truly your goal from the inside out, be focused and disciplined in your approach. Affirm your success and move your feet. Your action makes all te difference between delusion and success.

**Daily Application:** Note a few goals in your life right now. Now, write the disciplined actions, words, thoughts and beliefs that are required to meet your goals. Now, do it on all 4 levels. Don't look back.

**Personal Reflections:** _____
_____
_____
_____
_____
_____

## Day 153
# INNER PEACE

*Inner Peace can only be reached when we practice forgiveness.*
~ Gerald Jampolsky

Inner peace is something many people say they want and I am not sure how many people think it is even possible. Do you think it is possible to attain inner peace? I do. In fact, I have inner peace often. For me, compassion for self and others seems to be the first step on the road to peace. Forgiveness means *to have compassion for*. Compassion for the grand adventure of being human.

I used to be very hard on myself, demanding more than was reasonable. Over time, suffering heartache and experiencing great joy, I have learned to hold a compassionate or forgiving heart for all of us. Yes, we all make mistakes and there are messy times. There are also great and triumphant times, right?

So, yes, I think Gerald Jampolsky said it well. As you practice forgiveness you will experience more inner peace. Forgive yourself first then offer forgiveness to others. Respect your boundaries.

**Daily Application:** Spend time in quiet several times today and open your heart to the feeling of compassion. No matter what you are experiencing or you have heard about, hold all involved with you most loving compassionate heart, free of judgment or condemnation. Smile then journal you experience.

**Personal Reflections:** _____
_____
_____
_____
_____
_____

## Day 154
# CONSCIENCE

*Labor to keep alive in your breast that little spark of celestial fire, called conscience.*

~ George Washington

Conscience is a vital part of your leadership and your success in life. That still small voice that speaks to you is a guiding light. When you dismiss the voice, the results are often problematic. I love how George Washington calls our conscience that *little spark of celestial fire*. The imagery is beautiful You have that spark within you and it is heavenly and magnificent. This is your conscience.

I have worked for years with people seeking help for addiction. Many committed crimes while under the influence. The drugs silenced their celestial spark and they could not hear their own conscience. Their choices were poor and they paid the price. Once they cleared up and were abstinent, their conscience returned. Then came the healing for the guilt for not following their conscience. The moral of the story here is to never let anything get between you and your conscience. Keep your inner fire burning.

**Daily Application:** Be still and quiet. Rest in your connection with your inner voice and conscience. Be aware. Move into your day and pay attention to the inner spark.

**Personal Reflections:** _____
_____
_____
_____
_____
_____

## Day 155
# INTEREST

*An investment in knowledge pays the best interest.*
*~ Benjamin Franklin*

My mother used to tell me to get my education because it is the one thing no one can steal. She was a big proponent of being well educated, both formally and through experience. She was right, it has been the best investment that has paid the most interest. She was well learned and I wonder if she knew of this quote from Benjamin Franklin.

How do you invest in your knowledge? Early in my career I decided to learn as much as I could because one day I will need this information. I did not understand the gravity of that decision at the time. Now, 3 decades later, I use much of my knowledge and skill to work with my clients and to teach seminars and workshops. I can also relate to many different people and varied world views. This would not have been possible if I did not make the investment in knowledge. It has paid and continues to pay the best interest.

How about you? Do you see the interest being paid on your knowledge? All influential people invest in their knowledge.

**Daily Application:** Take some time to review your portfolio of knowledge. Assess the interest. Is there some information that you want to invest in to expand your knowledge base? Focus on your vision, learn something new today. Enjoy your dividends.

**Personal Reflections:** _____
_____
_____
_____
_____

# Day 156
# MIND

*If you correct your mind, the rest of your life will fall into place.*
~ Lao-tzu

Your mind is powerful and in control. Your body is neutral. Your body reflects your primary thinking in the form of health, struggles and vibrancy. This way of seeing things is common in many world views. It even dates back thousands of years. It seems that traditional Western culture has squashed this truth and now it is emerging once again.

Your life follows your mind. As you think, your world is created. I had a client once who took this to heart and he changed his thinking. He changed his relationships, his career and his health using the power of his mind. He is a living testimony to the idea that your thinking creates your experience.

Think about it for a minute. What you think about you attract. Your life right now is an exact reflection of your primary thinking over the past year or so. Use your mind to create your best life now.

**Daily Application:** Be still. Breathe a few deep breaths. Listen to your mind. Is it thinking about what you want to see in your world? If not, make the change now.

**Personal Reflections:** _____
_____
_____
_____
_____
_____

## Day 157
# CHAOS

*If life feels chaotic, threatening, confusing, or stressful, it doesn't really reflect the true strength and power that you possess inside.*
*~ Sandy Freschi* **

Life can be full of chaos at various times. Being able to acknowledge the chaos and then transcend the impact is one of the hallmarks of a peace-filled person. Many people talk about peace and wanting to see peace in the world yet they are angry and often causing discord in their lives. If you are not peaceful within then it is impossible to transcend conflict and suffering within or without.

Conflict, chaos and suffering are everywhere it seems. Thus, peace within helps you transcend the outer influence. By having inner peace, you are free of the toxic energy of the chaos everywhere.

Peace is the experience within that births great ideas and compassionate action toward yourself and others. When you buy into the discord and anger of others or of your inner conflict, you deny yourself the ability to think, speak and act in your best interest. Peace can free you from the chaos around you.

**Daily Application:** Spend 10 minutes twice today, breathing and focusing on inner peace. Allow your own inner peace to guide you through the chaos of the day. When you find yourself off your center, stop, breathe in peace then resume. Notice the results.

**Personal Reflections:** _____
_____
_____
_____
_____

## Day 158
# EXPECTATION

*I strive to foster an expectation that becomes a reality.*
*~ Gabriel Aluisy *\**

What are your expectations? I have found that the more you focus on your expectations, the more present they become in your life. By focusing on expectations of good stewardship, kindness, respect and honor, you will begin to see them more frequently in your world. Whatever you are focusing on and expecting, comes to pass.

I hold expectations of myself and others based on the situation. Expectations of good service, delivering more than expected to the customer, being of service and of course doing the right thing. By holding this expectation for myself, it becomes the reality for me and my business. If you are expecting great service then you will automatically seek businesses that provide great service. If you expect your work to be of a high standard, then by focusing on your expectation, you can make this goal a reality.

Living up to your personally set expectations is the most effective way they become the reality for you and others. Are your actions in alignment with the reality you seek?

**Daily Application:** In your quiet time today, ponder what you expect of yourself and others. What expectations do you want to see more of in your daily life? Write your thoughts.

**Personal Reflections:** _____
_____
_____
_____
_____

## Day 159
# DIGNITY

*We must reach out our hand in friendship and dignity both to those who would befriend us and those who would be our enemy.*

~ Arthur Ashe

Dignity is a quiet yet powerful action. Many times, I hear about people fighting for human dignity in not so dignified ways. This has me perplexed. I think Arthur Ashe has made a powerful point. To act with dignity and extend dignity, you must first be clear about who you are and be able to stand in your knowingness of self. After you have done the inner work to come to yourself, you can then freely extend the hand of friendship to all others.

This does not preclude boundaries and maintaining integrity in your words and actions. Today's quote reminds us that dignity is extended from the inside out. It starts with you. Dignity cannot be demanded from others when you do not hold dignity within.

Dignified strength is powerful and changes relationships and paves the way for a meeting of the minds. Arthur Ashe was an example of dignity.

**Daily Application:** In your quiet time, make the choice to reach out your hand today. Remain aligned within yourself while extending yourself. Note your experience and share with others

**Personal Reflections:** _____

_____
_____
_____
_____
_____

## Day 160
# WORK

*To work with calm confidence and joy, ground your efforts is "faith". I define this faith as an unwavering trust in a positive future for you, that you cannot yet see, and a deep belief in a profoundly loving & intelligent higher reality that guides your life. Your destiny is utterly beautiful and completely secure.*

~ George Kao **

Work for many is a necessary evil to "make it". What if you practiced what George Kao is suggesting in this quote regarding work? Work can emerge from your inner unwavering faith in a positive future for you. Isn't it easier to invest in your work when your vision of your future is desirable and secure? I think so. Having calm confidence in your positive future allows you to connect to your higher guidance. Can you see the beauty that is your destiny?

     I believe that making an inner transformation toward work being part of your greater good has the power to uplift your work life immeasurably. When you can stand in quiet confidence as you focus on your future and your work You are now in charge of creating the life you imagined, and better. Work becomes an extension of your joy and magnificence and you become authentically joyful and productive.

**Daily Application:** Journal about your inner experience of trust as part of your work journey. Write the positive future you envision. Allow yourself to feel the immense beauty of your heart's desire. Now, in faith, take proper action.

**Personal Reflections:** _____
_____
_____
_____
_____

## Day 161
# ATTITUDE

*Weakness of attitude becomes weakness of character.*
*~ Albert Einstein*

Some say that attitude is the single determining factor in success. I have had this discussion with others. I believe that the attitude you hold creates much of any outcome. I once worked with someone who always said that attitude was all he cared about in our employees. He said if people weren't happy in their jobs then he was doing something wrong as the business owner.

What about the attitude people arrive with as they enter your life? Everyone lives from their own autobiography. We see things through those lenses. Maybe attitude can be influenced by events yet I believe that attitude reveals real character. What are you thinking now? Does your attitude determine how your character develops? I believe they are interconnected and one reflects the other.

**Daily Application:** Ponder attitude and character. How do they work in your life? What do you look for in others regarding attitude and character? Journal some of your ideas. Enjoy your day with an uplifted attitude!

**Personal Reflections:** _____
_____
_____
_____
_____

## Day 162
# ETERNITY

*Nothing is worth more than this day.*
*~ Johann Wolfgang von Goethe*

Live in the moment. The past is a memory and the future is yet to be. By living in the moment, you are living in a perpetual eternity. How are you spending your moments during your days? Is your unfolding eternity as you anticipated? After all, living fully in the present gives your life a sense of timelessness in the grand schema.

Are you waiting for what eternity brings after you die? Do you even believe in eternity? Eternity is about being timeless and transcending time. There are several ways to look at eternity. Are you excited for the flow of timeless beauty and love? Or do you experience eternity quite the opposite as in taking an eternity to get something done which then yields a level of frustration or annoyance.

I choose to see eternity as a beautiful flow. A flow of experience, love and time lived in the moment. By focusing on what is at hand, you can live in a state of perpetual ease and flow.

**Daily Application:** Spend some time in quiet reflection a few different times today. How are you spending your day? Make any changes as you become aware. Journal your thoughts. There is nothing more than this day.

**Personal Reflections:** _____
_____
_____
_____
_____
_____

## Day 163
# SENSUALITY

*Sensual is everything that refers to the delight of the senses. And that's what artists do, is stimulate the senses in any possible way.*
~ Shakira

Are your senses alive and awake? Do you acknowledge your senses as a vital part of you? When your senses are delighted, you experience uplifting emotions like joy, peace, harmony and happiness. Your senses tell you the safety level and the pleasure level of everything you encounter on a regular basis. This is how artists touch you so deeply and in meaningful ways.

Stop and smell the roses. Smell the goodness of baking bread or cookies or of a beautiful spring day. Notice your sense of touch as you pay attention to all that touches you from the air temperature, fabric, another's skin or your own skin. Notice that your sensuality is directly tied to your connection and appreciation of your senses. The delight of your senses is how you feel alive and vibrant. What artists stimulate your senses?

**Daily Application:** Today, notice how sensitive your senses are and how you take in information through your senses. Honor your own sensitivities and share your sensual nature.

**Personal Reflections:** _____
_____
_____
_____
_____
_____

## Day 164
# PROSPERITY

*If there's a will, prosperity can't be far behind.*
~ W. C. Fields

You are a prosperous being, I know it. You have prosperity all around. If you are ever experiencing any lack, you may want to look at what your will is doing. Will is an amazing power that we all possess. Where your will goes usually tells much of the story.

Will is the ability to choose, decide, lead or command. It is a great power to possess. If you try to live life by will alone, which is called will power, prosperity will elude you. True prosperity is much more than currency. It encompasses authentic love, kindness, compassion. Will is a needed element but is not the only element. If you have the will and use that power, you are on the right path to unlocking the prosperity waiting for you.

**Daily Application:** Spend time alone in quiet. Focus on your ability to receive prosperity in your life. How can you use your will to support your goal? What other qualities are needed? Journal your ideas.

**Personal Reflections:** _____
_____
_____
_____
_____
_____

## Day 165
# IMPERFECTION

*Imperfection is beauty, madness is genius and it's better to be absolutely ridiculous than absolutely boring.*

~ Marilyn Monroe

We are all perfectly imperfect. This is the beauty of humans. Each of us possessing our own unique beauty. I love this quote from an icon who was heralded for her beauty. She was more focused on not being boring. To be absolutely ridiculous is much better than being boring.

Any imperfections that you are secretly holding against you are causing more internal damage than embracing your imperfections. Face it, we all have imperfections. Humans are a bit goofy. Either you focus on things that are unreality or you focus on your genius and beauty.

I say we all focus more on our inner beauty radiating out into the world, allowing our genius to show up and to embrace our ridiculousness with a smile! Your imperfection reveals your beauty.

**Daily Application:** Rest today in your authentic you-ness. Notice all your perfectly imperfect parts and quirks. Notice their beauty and brilliance. Notice the imperfection all around and see the beauty. This will stop boredom in its tracks.

**Personal Reflections:** _____
_____
_____
_____
_____
_____

## Day 166
# OBLIGATION

*We become happier, much happier, when we realize that life is an opportunity rather than an obligation.*

~ Mary Augustine

When you act out of obligation, you are acting from a place of fear. To have the consciousness of being obligated holds you back. To be obligated means you don't really want to but you feel like you should for fear of some future retribution. Examples include going to an in-law's house for the holidays when you don't want to go or a child being obligated to hug a distant relative they do not know because of fear of the parents' scorn.

By changing your inner dialogue to opportunity which is more open and comes from a love place. Your experience is much different. Both the scenarios above, if approached from an opportunity stance would turn out very different. See life as an opportunity, really.

When you do something because you are obligated, everyone can feel your underlying unwillingness. Instead, work with yourself to act from a place of love and kindness. By shifting your focus and vibe, you are more attractive and others will resonate better with you.

**Daily Application:** Be still often today. Ponder your underlying motive for your actions. Is there any underlying fear lingering? Journal ways to can make shifts to more love and less fear in making your decisions.

**Personal Reflections:** _____
_____
_____
_____
_____
_____

## Day 167
# SHARING

*We share with people who have earned the right to hear our story.*
*~ Brene Brown*

When you choose someone to share something important with, you go about it with great care. It is the highest honor to be chosen to hear someone's story. To be present and listen as they share is a sacred time and space. Sharing what is authentic takes risk. Therefore, to earn the right to be that trusted other you must be able to hold the space and focus without bartering the others information.

When you want to share something. It is essential to choose someone who has earned the right to be the listener. Not just anyone. A big mistake I hear about is just blurting out a sensitive personal story to anyone who is around. This does not work. You must use your discernment to choose wisely. Some content is not meant for just any ears. Sharing is a powerful and healing action.

**Daily Application:** With whom do you share your life? Who chooses you to be the listener? Journal your ideas and insights. Take some quiet time today to honor your relationships that are trusted.

**Personal Reflections:** _____
_____
_____
_____
_____
_____

## Day 168
# FLEXIBILITY

*For a flexible person, it is incomprehensible not to reach his destination, because by using his ability to be flexible, he can easily define a nearer new destination.*

*~ Mehmet Murat ildan*

Flexibility is not just for yoga. Flexibility is evident in the body and is also present in the mind. How flexible is your thinking? Are you easily upset when things do not go as you plan or anticipate? Do you attempt to control outcomes? Are you adaptable and able to change courses if indicated for your best result? Your flexibility is an asset for living your vision and reaching your goals.

Flexibility is most prominent when you are in the flow of life. Flexibility does not mean that you have no input, rather it means that your input is greater because of your ability to improvise and bend as needed to complete projects and tasks. Are you flexible enough not to break? You can even be flexible and change your destination as it suits you.

**Daily Application:** Take time throughout the day to check on the tension and rigidity of your muscles. Tight muscles and rigid thinking are signs of inflexibility. To be flexible, breathe into your work and activities and consciously open your mind. Allow things to go differently than you imagined and see what happens.

**Personal Reflections:** _____
_____
_____
_____
_____
_____

## Day 169
# INFLUENCE

*A teacher affects eternity; you can never tell where the influence stops.*
~ Henry Adams

Who do you influence? Family, friends, employees, others in your circles? Leadership is independent of position. If you are influencing others then you are leading them. This type of leadership is proving much more effective than the older method of being authoritative or somehow controlling. Visionary leadership influences others from a visionary orientation. This transcends position and titles.

What kind of influence are you exerting? Are you conscious of the impact you have on others that stems from your influence? Your sphere of influence and how you influence is the cornerstone of your legacy. We are all influenced by others? Are the people influencing you demonstrating great leadership and offering successful strategies? Influence is powerful and can be found in most scenarios. If you want to be a successful leader, then it will be your influence, not your controlling way that will make the difference.

**Daily Application:** Spend your quiet time in contemplation about your influence and who is influencing you. Journal ways you can use your influence for the betterment of others. Focus on your vision and your leadership.

**Personal Reflections:** _____
_____
_____
_____
_____

Day 170
# SPRING

*Autumn is a second spring where every leaf is a flower.*
~ Albert Camus

Spring is a time of awakening after the quiet and stillness of winter. Autumn is a time of slowing down in preparation for the quiet of winter. There is no accident that the beauty that the colors of both spring and autumn bookend winter. Many great things emerge out of stillness and quiet. When your season is nearing a completion, you want it to be a graduation into winter, a time of rest. By trying to fight the seasons of life, you end up miserable and creating more divorces than graduations.

Spring is a great season. It represents new life and new growth. As you journey through life, there is more than one season happening in your world than the one that is predicated in nature. So, enjoy the seasons of your life. Enjoy the beginnings, the growth, the slowing down and the ending. Thus, is the cycle of life.

**Daily Application:** What seasons are your experiencing in your life? Be still and ponder these amazing cycles at work all the time. Tune into your inner wisdom and celebrate.

**Personal Reflections:** _____
_____
_____
_____
_____

## Day 171
# PERSISTENCE

*We are made to persist... that's how we find out who we are.*
*~ Tobias Wolf*

Some of you are more persistent than others. Persistence can be taken in many ways. Persistent questions can seem a bit off putting. Persistence through difficult challenges can be seen as heroic. Athletes that persist toward excelling are often heralded for their efforts. I am sure you persist in areas and situations in your life. You may not even notice how persistent you can be at times.

I have a friend who is very persistent in learning and being engaged in many activities. It seems exhausting at times for the onlookers. Yet her persistence toward her vision and dreams inspires her and yields her success and happiness. In her persistence, she is clear who she really is underneath the superficial descriptors.

I'll bet you have persistence. I'll bet you can step back and see how your persistence has helped you see more of your *real* value and depth. You were made for this journey of persistence.

**Daily Application:** How does your persistence show up? In what areas? Reflect in quiet on what you are learning about yourself by what you are most persistent about now. Journal any insights or changes you want to remember.

**Personal Reflections:** _____
_____
_____
_____
_____
_____

## Day 172
# INTEGRITY

*Integrity is doing the right thing, even when no one is watching.*
~ C. S. Lewis

Integrity is looked for in our relationships. Integrity is a behavior, not a moral judgment. When you have come out of integrity, it means that you did not do the right thing. It does not mean you are a bad person. In my business, integrity comes up often. I contracted with an amazing videographer for some work. He was paid in advance. After months of waiting for the work, I requested a refund. Much of the work was time dependent. He said he would refund the money. It took many actions including an attorney over many months to get the refund. He was out of integrity when he over promised and underdelivered, when he promised return of money and when he did not do the right thing.

He is not a bad person at his core. For some reason, he lacks the integrity to do the right thing even when no one is watching. He is causing himself great emotional pain. He is causing others pain and frustration. The cure here is a behavior change. By doing the right thing, integrity is restored and continued pain stops.

**Daily Application:** Spend time in quiet. Rest in your inner stillness. Look at your words and actions. Are they in alignment? Is there any improvement needed for your integrity? Journal your ideas and any changes you wish to make. Take action today.

**Personal Reflections:** _____
_____
_____
_____
_____
_____

## Day 173
## MOVEMENT

*Movement isn't progress.*

*~ Thomas Leonard*

Just because you are moving does not mean that progress is being made. Take the rocking chair, lots of movement with no progress. Movement is good for your body and your health depends upon it. Not all movement equates to progress.

One of my clients some time ago was busy doing things all the time. She was moving all the time. She came to me because she could not understand her lack of progress toward her business goals. Upon further discussion, the movement was for good reasons and causes, it just wasn't toward her stated goal. Her movement was not yielding progress.

I like to say that acting and moving with a focus on the goal with your vision in your heart yields great progress. Moving without these can be very random and even counterproductive.

**Daily Application:** Spend your quiet time being still. Set your intention to notice your movement throughout the day. Has your movement furthered your progress? Share your progress related actions with a trusted other.

**Personal Reflections:** _____
_____
_____
_____
_____
_____

## Day 174
# UNIVERSE

*You can't send negative out into the universe and expect positive back.*
*~ Raymond Hinst* \*\*

Our Universe responds to our intention and vibration. When you send low vibration negativity into the Universe, it answers in kind. Grief, guilt, shame, pain, doubt, fear and anger are all low vibration and you will see it coming back to you. On the other hand, positive vibrations like love, joy, gratitude, kindness, compassion, honesty and gentleness yield more of the same. Ever wonder how angry people experience an angry world and a kind person experiences a kind world? Well, it is directly related to what they start with by sending it out into the Universe.

When turning the tide, you may get a bit frustrated because initially the old negative continues to return until the positive has been put out and has had a chance to return. There is some time between your shift and your being able to experience the results. You must learn to trust the universe to be as it should, trust the process.

**Daily Application:** Take a few deep breaths and relax. Monitor your thinking for a moment. Positive or Negative? What do you want back from the Universe? Are your thoughts aligned with your desires? If not, make the appropriate shifts. Remember you get back what you put in.

**Personal Reflections:** _____
_____
_____
_____
_____
_____

## Day 175
# HEART

*Few are those who see with their own eyes and feel with their own hearts.*
~ Albert Einstein

Do you feel with your heart? I notice that many people think their way through life and never allow an authentic emotion. I notice a lot of people joining emotionally charged bandwagons yet when I inquire about their inner emotion, they are at a loss. This is a very difficult way to live; never being fully aware of your own experience, rather living through others.

When you look around your life, through what are your viewing? Are you using your eyes or are you using the eyes of your family, friends or ancestors? Have you cleaned your inner windows so you can see the scenery of your life more clearly? Allow your heart to feel. Remove the barriers so you can see and feel your life and not live through another's.

**Daily Application:** Put your hand over your heart. Feel it beating? Now, breathe and honor your personal feelings. Notice today what you see and feel. Be one of the few that Einstein references.

**Personal Reflections:** _____
_____
_____
_____
_____

## Day 176
# FOCUS

*Focus on where you want to go, not on what you fear.*
~ Anthony Robbins


Where your attention goes your energy flows. Focus on fear and you will get more fear. Focus on where you intend to go and you will be drawn in that direction. Fear's function is telling you to *get ready*, not to focus on the fear thereby making it larger and more powerful.

Driving a race car, the driver looks ahead at where they are driving, not the wall. By focusing on the wall, the driver will inevitably crash into the wall. When you are focused on what you fear, you get more of the same. When you are focused on your vision and goals, you will be moving along toward your goals.

Sounds so simple, yet it can be challenging at times. Focusing on where you wish to go can be undermined by old fearful beliefs or fearful emotions. Begin today to learn to focus on your goals consistently.


**Daily Application:** Journal some of your thoughts. Write them all, no matter the content. After some time, re-read your thoughts. Are they based in fear or on your action plan? Create a visual reminder of your goals and focus your intentions there.


**Personal Reflections:** _____
_____
_____
_____
_____
_____

## Day 177
# ENTHUSIASM

*Creativity is a natural extension of our enthusiasm.*
*~ Earl Nightingale*

I am alive, alert, awake, enthusiastic. This the line of one of my favorite songs. I was singing it as I typed it in fact. Enthusiasm is an amazing and powerful energy that can move you to great heights. Most of the enthusiastic people I know are also naturally creative. When you let your enthusiasm and creativity come out and play, expect great things!

Remember when you were young, your enthusiasm for life and your natural creativity was evident in so many ways? I think this natural way of being is somehow lost in the world if you, as an adult do not nurture your creativity and your enthusiasm. I had a long day today and I had planned to work on some writing projects this evening. My enthusiasm level was a bit low because of the long work day. I took the time to charge my batteries and not my creativity is flowing as is my enthusiasm for what I am creating. I believe we are all inherently enthusiastic and it is the perceived weight of life that can squash creativity unless you focus on allowing it to emerge and be recognized.

**Daily Application:** Create something today. Notice your enthusiasm level before and after the project. Notice how these go hand in hand. As you are enthusiastic you are creative. Your creativity shows your enthusiasm. Now, take time today to honor your enthusiasm!

**Personal Reflections:** _____
_____
_____
_____
_____

## Day 178
# COMFORT

*If we're growing, we're always going to be outside of our comfort zone.*
*~ John Maxwell*

This quote really hits home for me because I am most often outside of my comfort zone. Years ago, I thought it was because something was wrong with me. Then I learned that it simply meant I was growing. Part of my growth was to outgrow the old beliefs and identities that I adopted that were no longer true.

There have been nights of growth and being uncomfortable when I yearned to have some comfort. Today, I am excited by my growth and the growth of others. The comfort zone is not always the best place to be hanging out.

You are often growing and evolving whether you are focused on your growth or not. Making friends with being outside of the comfort zone helps your path become more manageable. I have learned that trying to remain in the status quo yields increased pain and discord. Now, my comfort is in being outside of my comfort zone. I guess you could say I am comfortably uncomfortable. This is my sign of growth.

**Daily Application:** Are you outside of your comfort zone? Are you growing or simply attempting to keep the status quo? Take some time to reflect. Are you willing to be comfortably uncomfortable as part of your growth? Write your thoughts. Happy growing.

**Personal Reflections:** _____

_____

_____

_____

_____

_____

## Day 179
# PATH

*Obstacles do not block the path. They are the path.*
*~ Zen Proverb*

Your path is uniquely your destiny. There is much discussion about genes and what the future holds. I believe that the expression along our path is more about what we think, do and believe and less about our genetics. As you are empowered, your path opens and greets you.

I was told when I was young that I would need eye glasses before I was 40 years old because everyone related to me had glasses. They said that it was in our genes. I did not want glasses. I remember being about 7 years old and saying: "No, I will see well and my eyes are healthy." I have affirmed this and taken great care of my eyes. I am over 40 years old and still do not need glasses. Everyone else has glasses in my family. I believe it is my mental attitude and focus that has changed things for me. My genes do not decide my destiny.

As I learned the power in empowerment. I am happy that my path is divergent from others in my family. You have the power to create your own path.

**Daily Application:** Be still and ponder your sense of personal power. How do you relate to your path? Are you paying attention or simply saying that it runs in the family? Journal and remain open to new ideas and paradigms.

**Personal Reflections:** _____
_____
_____
_____
_____

## Day 180
# DEPENDABILITY

*Ability is important in our quest for success, but dependability is critical.*
~ Zig Ziglar

Dependability is vital. People tell me that I am dependable. This is important to me. My personal code has dependability included. I am not perfect. Are you dependable? Are there dependable people in your life?

In all relationships, business and personal, dependability is important. I have a great artist friend who is dependably 10 minutes late for any engagement. I also have a great client who is dependable in arriving for our meetings early. I am dependable in that is I put something on my calendar, I show up. No matter how far out I commit. How are you most dependable? How does your dependability show up in your daily life?

When you are focused on life success and happiness, focus on being dependable and being around other dependable folks. Ability is a variable that we you can work with and being reliable and dependable sets you apart from the masses.

**Daily Application:** Become still for some time and breathe into your inner wisdom. Ponder your dependability in your personal and professional worlds. How do you want to move from here? Journal your ideas. Go forward and align your actions with your desired result.

**Personal Reflections:** _____
_____
_____
_____
_____
_____

## Day 181
# CONSISTENCY

*Trust is built with consistency.*
*~ Lincoln Chafee*

My operating definition of trust is consistency over time. Many of my clients come to me stating that they cannot trust a certain person or organization. As we explore, what I hear them say most frequently is that the person does not do what they say over and over. For me, not doing what you say is an integrity issue.

I have this great client and he is so smart and creative. He is a free thinker. His wife is more consistent and less spontaneous. They were having relationship challenges. After some discussion and defining things more accurately. It was not a trust issue they were having because she could trust he would be late, he does it every day, he could trust she would spend lots of money when she was mad because she did it every time. Both can trust the other's response that they taught each other over time.

The real question for them is what consistent behaviors and emotions do you want in the marriage and what are you willing to do to achieve this goal. The next question is what are you no longer willing to do.

**Daily Application:** Be still for some time and ponder how you use the word trust. What operational definition are you using? Is it serving you? Journal any awareness you have.

**Personal Reflections:** _____
_____
_____
_____
_____

## Day 182
# EXCELLENCE

*Excellence is not a skill. It is an attitude.*

~ Ralph Marston


Have you ever noticed that perfectionistic people can be rigid and difficult? Do you stress yourself out trying to be perfect or do something perfectly? Excellence is a much better way to go. You will live longer and be happier. The good news is that shifting your paradigm can be done with some information, redefining key words and practice. All good skills come with focused practice.

Have and attitude of excellence. This means you are open to growth and expansion of your current understandings and behaviors, no matter the origin. An attitude of excellence is one of being open, always doing your best, having frequent feedback and being flexible about the road to the result. Notice how being rigid and controlling are absent. When you live from a place of excellence you have more ease and flow in your life. Change your attitude and change your life.

**Daily Application:** Ponder excellence and perfectionism in your ideas and thoughts. How open are you to your ever-unfolding life? Focus on excellence. Note the response life gives you.


**Personal Reflections:** _____
_____
_____
_____
_____
_____

HOPE REALIZED

# Half Way There...

How long has it taken to go this far?

*Take a moment and reflect on your progress, transformations and lessons. Write a few notes to honor your path.*

## Day 183
# ARTISTS

*Every artist dips his brush in his own soul and paints his own nature into his pictures.*

~ Henry Ward Beecher

There is so much to life. So much that goes beyond words. Artists offer us personal opportunity to experience depth of being without words. When any art speaks to you, you are connected to the very nature of the artist through whom the art emanated. As you experience the unspoken depth, you transcend the ordinary. Artists are a vital part of your culture as they express the human condition in ways that are powerful and real.

When you engage in your art, regardless of form, you dip into your deeper nature and touch others in ways that make words pedestrian. As you share your art form, you change yourself and others. This connection can never be repeated exactly. Honor this and experience deep authentic richness.

**Daily Application:** Connect with some art today. When it resonates deeply, allow your inner nature to come alive and shine through your life. How is your life richer because of the connection to the art and the artist?

**Personal Reflections:** _____
_____
_____
_____
_____
_____

## Day 184
# INGENUITY

*Success is the maximum utilization of the ability that you have.*
*~ Zig Ziglar*

Ingenuity is a word that is rarely used in many circles. It is a valuable resource for you as you create your life experience. When you are maximizing your gifts and talents, you are able to follow multiple paths to reach your vision and goals. There is more than one way to accomplish your mission.

Using your creative ability, construct a great plan and path to unfold your vision. Use your natural talents. You know you are successful when you are able to maximize your resources. We all have different resources and this makes us able to achieve, work and play with variety and diversity. For me, this benefits the collective whole.

Do you use your ingenuity? I am sure you do. You are creative, clever and innovative even in ways you do not yet see. This is great news!

**Daily Application:** Put your your creativity to work today. Maximize your talents on a project and see how things shift as you focus. Spend time in quiet gratitude and relax.

**Personal Reflections:** _____
_____
_____
_____
_____
_____

## Day 185
# RELEASE

*When you release endorphins, you just feel good.*
~ Jesse Metcalfe

Releasing can feel so good. Endorphins are the feel-good chemical. When we release them into our system, we feel good. Some things just feel good. For me, it is being on the water, sailing and feeling the wind and the water. I just feel good. I have a friend who loves to run long distances, he just feels good. Endorphins being released changes how we feel.

We all are releasing endorphins and we feel good. For some, the thought of releasing is scary and they want to hold on. Holding on causes more problems than releasing. Holding on to ideas, people and situations that are restricting will hold you back.

Releasing old ideas, beliefs and the stuff that accumulates feels good as well. At first you may not want to let them go but afterward, when you are free, you feel good! Amazing how releasing can be a source of pleasure. Releasing the tight shoe, feels so good.

**Daily Application:** Notice where releasing is freeing you up to have a richer experience. Notice where releasing feels good. Today, give yourself permission to release what is holding you back. Journal how good it feels.

**Personal Reflections:** _____

## Day 186
# LANGUAGE

*Language is wine for the lips.*
*~ Virginia Wolf*

Gourmet conversation is like a nectar. Soulful poetry is the language of ultimate beauty emerging. Great language is wine and can be intoxicating. Having a good command of language affords you more opportunities and options for self-expression. Restricted language leads to restricted views and an inability to express yourself.

Do you pay attention to your language? Do you use language like a wine to your lips? Certain words just roll off my tongue. I love to use them because it feels so amazing. Soft smooth words have such a different feel that the hard consonants that convey yet another vibe.

We all use language and it seems that when we appreciate and taste our words, we experience them on a different level. How do you use our language? My mother always taught me to have a good command of the language. I am grateful for her teaching.

**Daily Application:** Pay attention to your language today. Pay attention to the language of others. Is your language like wine to your lips?

**Personal Reflections:** _____
_____
_____
_____
_____
_____

## Day 187
# SECURITY

*Anyone who trades liberty for security deserves neither liberty nor security.*
*~ Benjamin Franklin*

Benjamin Franklin has a point, I believe. Security can be achieved by understanding that security is relative. Liberty and freedom are important for many people yet they compromise their freedom for security. We see this so prevalently in our society today. People are willing to give up their freedom for security when in fact the security is an illusion.

The only secure thing I know of is the ever-changing world around us. Security that is meant to keep the status quo is unrealistic. For me, security is in my faith and connection to the ever-present flow of life. Nature and the Universe offer an elegant sense of security that is all encompassing.

In what do you find your security? How does this impact your life daily? How does your sense of security impact your relationships?

**Daily Application:** After your quiet time, look at your inner freedom and liberty as well as your sense of security. How are they related. Any changes needed? Plan. Now, take the first step.

**Personal Reflections:** _____
_____
_____
_____
_____
_____

## Day 188
# VERSATILITY

*Nobody ever made a difference by being like everyone else.*
~ PT Barnum

How versatile are you? Are you trying to fit in and not doing so well? Those of you who are making a difference, and I'll bet it is all of you, are making the difference by being versatile and flexible. Change makers and catalysts are those who make the difference and are most often not following the crowd. The important factor is to use your versatility for the highest good of all.

PT Barnum was on the cutting edge in his time. Whether we agree with him or not, those who make the difference are versatile and are not like the masses. Fitting in and being one of the many never brings about change. Make a difference in the life of someone, anyone. It is OK to be different because it is in the difference that the real transformation and change occurs.

**Daily Application:** Enjoy some inner quiet time. How are you going to make a difference today? Now, journal your intention. Check back later to see how you are doing. Remember, your versatility is a gift, use it.

**Personal Reflections:** _____
_____
_____
_____
_____

## Day 189
# FLOW

*Water will not flow from a faucet that is not connected to its source.*
~ Mary Morrissey

Flow is that balance between angst and apathy. When you are in flow, you are connected to your source, no matter what it is called. In the flow, time takes on a different meaning and dimension. Being a sailor, the flow of the air and water are important to how fast the boat goes. The flow of the air and the flow of the water work together to propel the boat forward. Flow is important.

Your lungs have a flow of air that sustains your life. Your blood system has a flow that rushes vital nutrients to your organs. Flow makes life possible. Being connected to your source is vital for any flow to happen. See it in nature. Block the flow of a creek and it stops flowing because it is disconnected from its source.

Are you connected to your source? How do you know?

**Daily Application:** Breathing in your quiet time, pay attention to the flow. The flow of air, the flow of your thoughts, and the flow of your life are interconnected. Notice any blocks and disconnections. Now, journal some ways you can begin the flow again.

**Personal Reflections:** _____
_____
_____
_____
_____
_____

## Day 190
# DARING

*To dare is to lose one's footing momentarily. To not dare is to lose oneself.*
*~ Soren Kierkegaard*

To dare is a powerful action. Even if you stumble, you can remain focused on your goals and desires so any stumble is temporary. When you dare to succeed and you take right action, your success is assured; even when the outcome looks differently than your first vision. You may lose your footing or have challenges. You may even fall once or twice. Who you become on the journey toward your vision is a result of your being willing to take risks.

As you journey toward your goals, being daring in your focus, you achieve even more than you anticipated. Always remember that you are here to journey toward yourself rather than away from yourself. So, to not dare to be great means that you become lost.

When you are daring and you take calculated risks, you set yourself up for ultimate success and freedom.

**Daily Application:** Today, be daring. Be the one who is in the game of life with full participation. Let your light shine and your good will be evident. Journal your feelings before and after stepping out. Keep your eyes focused on your vision.

**Personal Reflections:** _____
_____
_____
_____
_____
_____

## Day 191
# ACKNOWLEDGMENT

*Celebrate what you've accomplished, but raise the bar a little higher each time you succeed.*

~ Mia Hamm

Being acknowledged is something many people want. Some need acknowledgement so much that they appear clingy and needy. I like Mia Hamm's point. Acknowledge your accomplishments and also raise the bar to keep progressing and moving forward. Once you have succeeded at something, it is time to stretch and grow further. Acknowledgment of your progress is an important factor in your foundation of growth.

How do you acknowledge your personal and professional accomplishments? Do you celebrate your milestones? Paying attention to your milestones and your vision helps you achieve your desires.

By raising the bar, you support growth and you can be rid of complacency. Complacency can undo accomplishments and this is typically not the vision or goal for most leaders.

**Daily Application:** Journal some of your recent accomplishments and acknowledge your effort and focus that contributed to the accomplishments Now, acknowledge your goals and your vision. Set the bar and write your action plan.

**Personal Reflections:** _____
_____
_____
_____
_____
_____

## Day 192
# ALIGNMENT

*It is through the alignment of the body that I discovered the alignment of my mind, self, and intelligence.*

~ B.K.S. Iyengar

I love yoga. I loved hot yoga the first time I took a class. I remember thinking that is was one of the hardest things I have ever done and wanting to do more because of the benefit and the feeling. I wasn't thinking about alignment at that time. After months of daily practice, I began to experience alignment that I never knew was possible. Aligning my mind and emotions as well as my body was a profound realization for me.

Alignment today has many orientations for my life. I now also assess my inner alignment and my alignment with my peers. What is your awareness of being aligned? Do you notice? Does alignment have any effect on your life? For me, aligning my self makes for profound shifts and opportunities that being out of alignment could never have created.

**Daily Application:** Paying attention to the alignment of your body; are your mind and emotions aligned as well? How does alignment serve you? Journal about an area that could use an alignment check and then decide on your actions to create and maintain alignment.

**Personal Reflections:** _____
_____
_____
_____
_____
_____

## Day 193
## DETERMINATION

*For the resolute and determined there is time and opportunity.*
~ Ralph Waldo Emerson

Too many people make excuses. I think this quote reminds us that determination and resolve open doors to opportunity. When you are focused, and have a driving force from within, then you can create opportunities that the excuse makers never see. In my work, I spend time with those who make excuses and therefore lack determination in the areas they say they want growth. Then there are the determined ones who take any morsel of guidance or instruction and take off running with the information or focus.

      Determination is vital in all aspects of life, especially those areas where you want to excel. A determined person outshines and out preforms others who struggle with being determined. Use your determination to open doors of opportunity. Allow time to work in your favor as you focus your attention.

**Daily Application:** Reflect on your goals. Choose one or two and raise your determination level today. Take focused, determined action. Allow increased determination to lead the day and seize opening opportunities.

**Personal Reflections:** _____
_____
_____
_____
_____
_____

## Day 194
# BEAUTY

*Everything has its beauty, but not everyone sees it.*
*~ Confucius*

Beauty emanates from within. Many people struggle to see beauty in the world. This is often because they struggle to see any beauty within themselves. The lens through which you view things colors your perception. You will experience beauty differently than another because of your perceptions. Each life experience combined with your unique make-up adds depth and color and texture to your life.

Your autobiography colors your lenses and offers you a multitude of beautiful choices. As you move through life, you see what you want to see on some level. Your brain is intricately connected to what you see as beautiful and how you see. You can change your mind and change how you experience beauty all around.

If you desire to have more choices and become more joyful, clean your lenses and allow the light to enter. You are choosing your perception of beauty, knowingly or not. Begin to see beauty in all things and people.

**Daily Application:** Throughout the day, notice beauty all around you. Pay attention to the place where you see beauty where you did not expect. In some way, honor the beauty and see how your experience of beauty in your world expands.

**Personal Reflections:** _____
_____
_____
_____
_____

## Day 195
# ALERTNESS

*Alertness is the hidden discipline of familiarity.*
~ David Whyte

Heads up! Pay attention! Being alert is a significant advantage over those who are sleep walking through life. Many people are hyper-alert from previous life experiences. Then there are those who have an amazing ability to focus intellectually and emotionally. They may have an overexcitability as part of their gifted brain development. Being alert is also a discipline. You may have a natural gift of being alert or you may want to develop the skill.

My alertness comes from my autobiography and is rooted in the overexcitabilities. Thus, some things become familiar to me faster than others. It all comes down to my alertness. The discipline of being alert and paying attention serves me well in my work and my athletic endeavors. Sometimes others do not understand. It is all good. I have the freedom to use being alert naturally for the service of others and in my sport. How do you use your alertness?

Being alert comes from a calm, intensely focused inner landscape. It is not frenetic and chaotic. This is the discipline. When you are moving too fast, your ability to be alert wanes. Your inner world greatly impacts your ability to remain alert.

**Daily Application:** Take a few deep breaths and relax your body and mind. Breathe and relax. Let your mind slow for a time. When you open your eyes, notice how alert you are right now. If you determine changes are needed, journal your plan.

**Personal Reflections:** _____
_____
_____
_____
_____

## Day 196
# UNION

*In union there is strength.*

*~ Aesop*

Yes, when you are in union with your inner most being and your body and mind and breath, you are strong beyond measure. Yoga means union and it is amazing. There are so many different types and styles yet they are all heading to the same place, union. Have you tried yoga? You are either saying yes or wishing I would move on now, right?

Authentic union has many levels and there are many ways to journey toward and achieve a sense of union. Union within is most important. If you are not a unified whole within, then what you show the world is fragmented. Yoga, breath and mediation are a few of the avenues that can support your journey. Union with the greater Universe, nature or the Divine is another union. Prayer, meditation, spending time in nature, digging in the dirt, growing food and herbs and exploring various terrains can open this journey for you. Union with other beings is the third union. Connecting with animals, connecting authentically with other humans and connecting to the global community are a few of these examples. All of these develop strength.

**Daily Application:** How do you express your union and connections? Spend some quiet time pondering your ideas and actions. Try a new practice today and notice how it serves your strength.

**Personal Reflections:** _____

_____

_____

_____

_____

_____

## Day 197
# BALANCE

*Life is a balance of rest and movement.*
*~ Osho*

Balance is an interesting word and carries many concepts in daily life. I was taught at an early age that the beauty of music laid in the space between the notes, not the notes themselves. I believe that the beauty of life is found in the rest that punctuates the movement. After all, driving fast on a highway has completely different experience than taking a beautiful winding road with places to rest and take in the beauty.

Balance is essential to health, wealth and welfare on many levels. Too much of anything can create a mess. I balance my days with work, spiritual practice (meditation and mindfulness), physical exercise and connection with others. My balance scale is not the typical visual of 2 sides, mine is more of a circle mobile that all move together in harmony. What does your balance scale look like?

**Daily Application:** Journal your operating definition of balance. In your quiet time, take a look at your life. Without judgment, decide if any changes are needed then create action steps. Realize that balance is fluid and you are not seeking perfection; rather a flow that is satisfactory for you.

**Personal Reflections:** _____
_____
_____
_____
_____
_____

## Day 198
# AUTHORITY

*Nothing strengthens authority so much as silence.*
~ Leonardo da Vinci

There is power in silence. To have real power, you must have authority within. Are you standing in your authority from a personal vision place? In other words, do you know who you are and what you are doing here on Earth? Do you walk through life with confidence in your steps? That walk demonstrates your personal authority.

Silence is golden. Trash talk and incessant chatter reduce your authority. Have you ever been oversold and then did not buy because the sales person would not stop talking? They were not standing in their authority. When you are in your authority, words are not needed to convey a message. Words are used effectively with silence as well.

When you are faced with a challenge, are you loud or silent? In your silence, you retain your authority and then you can take more effective action.

**Daily Application:** How do you see your personal and professional authority? Do you cover up insecurity with chatter and noise, thus eroding your authority? In your meditation time today, check in and see where your ability to remain silence is serving you. Journal in silence.

**Personal Reflections:** _____
_____
_____
_____
_____
_____

## Day 199
## DOMINION

*Begin to act from your dominion. Declare the truth by telling yourself that there is nothing to be afraid of, that you no longer entertain images of fear.*

~ Ernest Holmes

Dominion means to have province over or control over your world. When you act from this knowing, you can declare that Truth. Fear, then, must leave. When you are clear on all levels of your co-creating ability and dominion, you quickly realize that there is nothing to fear, really.

I love this idea as it set me free when I first grabbed hold of the idea years ago. If it is true that we have dominion, then we can directly have authority over our life and the world around us. This is a far stretch from the paradigms that would have you in a tight box without any influence on your world.

Declare the truth and experience an absence of the power of fear in your world. Check out some of Ernest Holmes' ideas and writings. Be open and see how they resonate with you.

**Daily Application:** Having dominion is our human birthright. This gives you power to remove fears tendrils of control and influence in your life. Declare your truth out loud and in writing. Rest in peaceful assurance. Enjoy today.

**Personal Reflections:** _____
_____
_____
_____
_____
_____

## Day 200
# DESIRE

*What we think we desire is what the world tells us we should, but what our heart wants is for us to just go within and desire to know and accept ourselves.*

*~ Cynthia Citron* \*\*

What desire did you awaken with today? I'll bet it included doing that would help or serve someone in some way. That someone includes you too. When fear enters, it is tempting to act in unevolved ways. Your actions then do not match your motives or intentions.

The two most powerful fears that can usurp your desire are the fear of losing what you have and the fear of not getting what you want. When these bandits ride into your consciousness, there is trouble. You will most likely act in ways you regret later. The moral of the story is to allow your true desires to emerge from within. Put fear in its place. The fear is telling you to get ready, not to be a jerk. Follow your heart's desire and act from a place of calm assurance. When fear shows up: stop, breathe and regroup.

**Daily Application:** Be still and allow your real desires to become forefront in your thoughts, words and actions. Breathe calmly and feel your emotions. Sit with this calm assurance for some time. Move into your day. Use fear as your messenger to get ready. Don't let fear pull you out of integrity so you act like a jerk.

**Personal Reflections:** _____
_____
_____
_____
_____
_____

# Day 201
# STRUCTURE

*Unless structure follows strategy, inefficiency results.*
*~ Alfred D. Chandler*

I love structure. In fact, I find it freeing. I wasn't always this way though. Years ago, I wanted freedom to be spontaneous and do what felt right at any given time, without the constraints of structure. I am grateful for the time and the lessons while I am happy to be where I am today, using structure to implement my strategy. I now see how inefficient and wasteful my previous way of operating was. Being random can seem fun but the results are underwhelming.

Today, having a structure in my life and my business is essential. It enables me to implement my strategies efficiently. Times of frustration and nearing the giving up stage have gone by the wayside. Even now, when I find myself irritated, I look to use a structure to bring my strategy into reality. Structure is my ally in my life now. How about you?

**Daily Application:** Notice any areas of your life that you would label inefficient. Are you missing a strategy or the structure or both? Take some time to create a working strategy to help with those inefficient places. Document your plan and when you will evaluate the plan.

**Personal Reflections:** _____
_____
_____
_____
_____
_____

## Day 202
# PARADOX

*The curious paradox is that when I accept myself just the way I am, then I can change.*

~Carl Rogers

This is so true. The paradox is that acceptance brings about change, or at least the potential for change. Acceptance does not mean being static yet many believe that to accept means to stop changing and growing. At the moment of your authentic self-acceptance, you then are free to make any personal or professional changes you deem desirable.

This is a great paradox. For me, the more self-acceptance I experience, the more my creative mind thinks of possibilities that require some sort of change. The change then is attractive rather than feeling like change must happen due to being unworthy or somehow not enough.

Being comfortable in the paradox is important to your success and happiness. It seems Carl Rogers understood this process. Get excited when you experience a paradox. It means change is a foot and you are growing.

**Daily Application:** Practice self-acceptance today. Even with your blunders and with your accomplishments. Allow the paradox of acceptance to show itself to you and enjoy your awareness. Journal after your quiet time.

**Personal Reflections:** _____
_____
_____
_____
_____
_____

## Day 203
# EXCITEMENT

*I always had this thirst for excitement.*
*~Nicole Miller*

Excitement excites me! What excites you? Good food? Gourmet Conversation? A sporting event? Solving a challenging problem? Adrenaline producing activities? Reading a good book on a rainy day? All these and more are exciting.

Excitement is part of what gets new projects and activities started. You launch a business or a new division with excitement. You create amazing memories with excitement. You participate in activities with excitement. And with all these there are the other parts of the experience. The work that doesn't thrill you but must be done, the parking or crowd issues, an unanticipated delay or challenge are all ways that the real world can dull your excitement if you let them.

Or you can be excited about the challenge and the journey on the detour. It is your choice. Excitement gives you energy for great things. Use it.

**Daily Application:** Allow you excitement to show today. Share some of your ideas with trusted others and allow them to feel your real excitement. Use your great energy and the synergy for the good.

**Personal Reflections:** _____
_____
_____
_____
_____
_____

## Day 204
# HUMILITY

*Pride makes us artificial; humility makes us real.*
~ Thomas Merton

Humility means to be courteous and respect self and others. Humility has boundaries. To be humble does not make you a door mat. In fact, it means quite to opposite. If I think you are trying to harm, I now have choices and options. It does not mean to allow the harm. Respect for what I and you are capable of doing is part of humility.

To be meek and humble is to be unresisting yet respecting the situation and the people involved. If I respect myself, I have the power to move away from a disrespectful person or situation. It is this deep knowing that keeps us real.

Pride comes from shame and the fear. It creates an illusion and a fakeness that can incite more challenges. Be courteous to yourself first. Respect yourself. Then move forward without the fear and unworthiness that is the root of pride.

**Daily Application:** Spend your quiet time in nature if that is available to you. Allow yourself to be respectful of you and your surroundings. Be courteous as you plan your day. Journal any awareness or insights. Enjoy your day today.

**Personal Reflections:** _____
_____
_____
_____
_____
_____

## Day 205
## PATIENCE

*Nature does not hurry, yet everything is accomplished.*

*~ Lao-tzu*

They say that if to pray for patience that you will experience the life lessons that make you learn patience. I think of this in a different way. My view of developing and honoring patience is more about getting into the flow of the Universal energy. I focus on nature and the natural order of things to remind me that my impatience is outside of the natural flow. Nature does, in fact, get everything accomplished with beauty and magnificence. Even fires, floods and wind events are part of the natural cleansing of the earth.

We humans may not like it and at the same time, we need to be more aware of the natural order of things. After all, nature and natural laws are more powerful than humans. I believe that if we would simply follow the example set in nature that we would be happier and less stressed.

**Daily Application:** Notice the rhythms in your life. What areas are in Spring, Summer, Autumn and Winter. Notice that with patience and natural rhythm, your life becomes less chaotic. Enjoy the natural flow of life.

**Personal Reflections:** _____
_____
_____
_____
_____
_____

## Day 206
# STILLNESS

*To the mind that is still, the whole universe surrenders.*

*~ Lao-tzu*

Be still. Quieting your mind may be challenging. Some overthinkers must learn the art of stillness. When I began to quiet my inner self and mind, it took some time and patience before I could celebrate a still mind. Today, it is easier to become still. I have learned that if I am over tired or over stressed, that being still is trickier than when I am properly rested.

When your mind is still, all the possibilities for your life begin to emerge and appear. This is a powerful way to make important choices and decisions. When you are still, everything becomes more open and available. This is the optimum place to be when making life decisions.

Your best decisions and actions come from a still mind. Practice stillness regularly and allow your quiet mind to be open as a beginner is open to learning. In stillness, rest and have your being.

**Daily Application:** Journal to free your overthinking. Then take some time today to enjoy your inner stillness. Rest in a calm assurance as you expand your awareness. Be still.

**Personal Reflections:** _____
_____
_____
_____
_____
_____

## Day 207
# CALLING

*It is not about what you can do; it is about what you are called to do.*
*~ Dianne A. Allen, MA*

You have many talents and things you can do. You are excellent at many activities and chances are your work has taken different roads. When you focus your attention and intention within and you choose actions based on what you are called to do, any dissatisfaction dissipates. Most people who have a sense of something missing or being stuck are often using their talents yet not fully paying attention to what they are called to do from the inside out.

Being focused on the external world and denying your heart's desire can cause you great dissatisfaction and sadness. Being stuck without bringing your personal vision forward is where many disillusioned people remain. From this comes bitterness and resentment. By listening to your heart's desire and calling, you have the ultimate power to make the change and then the unhappiness leaves. Follow your inner calling. It always takes you on an awesome journey.

**Daily Application:** Take some quiet time today without distraction. Then write your free flow thoughts regarding your calling and heart's desire. Does it align with your current focus? Act to ensure proper alignment for your happiness and fulfillment.

**Personal Reflections:** _____
_____
_____
_____
_____
_____

## Day 208
# ACCOMPLISHMENT

*There can be no great accomplishment without risk.*

~ Neil Armstrong

How do you experience accomplishment? What is your mantra or saying that keeps you motivated to use all your gifts and skills? You are an innovator by nature. This positions you for great accomplishment and achievement should you want these things. They say that the greatest compliment is someone copying you.

I am not speaking about plagiarism or stealing music or content. I am speaking about risk while focused on your vision. Your own vision then comes through uniquely you and at the same time complementary with others.

Be the innovator that you know you are deep within. Allow your creations to spring forth. This is what innovators do every day. Accomplishment is the perfect happening as you bring your vision forward. Keep innovating and risking in healthy ways while you leave the imitators on the sidelines!

**Daily Application:** What innovation are you wanting to bring out in the near future? Ponder other innovators and notice where you can emulate their strategy for your innovation. Now journal and ponder your next steps. Take action as warranted.

**Personal Reflections:** _____
_____
_____
_____
_____
_____

# Day 209
# QUIT

*The way to get started is to quit talking and begin doing.*
*~ Walt Disney*

Action is my favorite word. It helps me focus on what I am doing to get me where I say I want to go. There have been many times in my life when I wanted to quit. I was afraid or unsure. I kept moving though and the doing is what set me apart from others. I know many people who are great talkers and planners yet they do not take proper action. Then there are those who take action and do little talking. I think there is a balance. When it is all said and done, it is the action takers who make the progress and attain their goals.

Let's quit talking. Let's quit doing what gets in our way and then make excuses. Let's quit idle chatter. Are you a quitter? Be a quitter of mere words. It is time to back up your words with action for your greater good.

**Daily Application:** Use few words today. Quit the long explanations and distracting conversation. Start your doing and see what happens. Remind yourself that it is OK to quit distracting yourself from your goals. Journal how quitting helped you today.

**Personal Reflections:** _____
_____
_____
_____
_____
_____

## Day 210
# SOLUTIONS

*Identify your problems but give your power and energy to solutions.*
~ Tony Robbins

When your attention is on solution, then your energy goes that direction. You have seen people stuck thinking about problems, talking about problems and then having to deal with problems. The most effective way to begin to change the tide is to think and talk about solutions to whatever the identified problem may be. Identify the challenge, then begin with as many "how" questions as you can ask to look for solutions. How can it be done? How can we succeed? These more effective questions foster more effective solutions.

Yes, you must know what the problem is in order to solve it yet you do not want to remain stuck there. I think of changing a channel on the radio or television. The problems are the commercials and the solutions are the other programming. I know the problems are there yet the solutions have my attention. To keep yourself from being stuck in the problem, focus on the solutions and only speak to the solution. It works.

**Daily Application:** What solutions are you seeking now? What "how" questions can you ask to lead toward solutions? Spend quiet time, ask the questions and proceed with your day, trusting that the answer will come to you. Journal the answers that arrive.

**Personal Reflections:** _____
_____
_____
_____
_____

## Day 211
# VALUES

*If you don't stick to your values when they are being tested, they're not values, they're hobbies.*

*~ Jon Stewart*

What are your values? Companies post their values. People have values, even if they don't talk too much about them. Think about this for a minute. Do you value integrity, authenticity, inclusion, diversity, service and the many others? Are you clear about your top three values? These would be the values that you stand on, no matter what.

Some "values" are great ideas and are comfortable when life is going smoothly yet they falter when the challenges and obstacles appear. Maybe they are values in the making or even good ideas yet when tested they don't cut the mustard. Having this awareness of what is nonnegotiable for you helps in your decision making, hiring of employees and choosing business or personal alliances. As you evolve and transform, you may adjust and this is perfectly normal. This is the chance to go within and check on your progress.

**Daily Application:** What values are nonnegotiable for you? How do you live them and communicate them to others? Ponder your alignment and authenticity in this area. Are you compromising any aspect of your values in your professional or personal life? Journal any changes you wish to make. Act in alignment with your awareness and ideas.

**Personal Reflections:** _____
_____
_____
_____
_____
_____

## Day 212
# WILLINGNESS

*Willingness to learn is important, but willingness to act on what you learn is critical.*

*~ Kevin Kelly*

Being willing to step out in action is what sets leaders apart from the dreamers. If you have heard me speak, you have heard some derivative of action. It is great to know stuff and great to be well informed. The next and most important question is: "What are you going to do now?"

To take the right action, willingness and discernment are required. To be willing means that you are eager and prepared. Does it mean that you act without discernment? NO. You then take your eagerness and you explore what the right action is for you in that moment. Your best action may be a hesitation or a differently timed action.

Be willing to learn and discern. We willing to act on the learning. This is where success resides. Your eager availability to move toward your vision and goals is where you as a leader excel. Be willing and pay attention to timing.

**Daily Application:** Be open. Be willing. Spend time in quiet today. Open your mind to new ideas and be willing to examine them. Be willing to use what you learn today. Pay attention to your timing.

**Personal Reflections:** _____
_____
_____
_____
_____
_____

## Day 213
# CONSENT

*No one can make you feel inferior without your consent.*

~ Eleanor Roosevelt

Eleanor Roosevelt has a point. We live in a society that attempts to focus blame and responsibility on others rather than one self. What anyone says about you is truly none of your business. They are really telling on themselves with their fear based words and actions.

Start by paying close attention to whom you give power in your life. Are you consenting to feeling inferior because of another? This is the moment to wake up and begin to take responsibility for how you feel about yourself. If there is something you wish to change, get about that change.

Remember that no one outside of yourself has the power to make your feel anything, including being inferior. You are completely in charge of your life and it is time to pay close attention to whom you give consent in your life.

**Daily Application:** Notice today the consent you give others to influence your life experience. Take time to focus inward and act from the inside out rather than reacting. Any feelings of inferiority can be eliminated with proper focus.

**Personal Reflections:** _____
_____
_____
_____
_____
_____

## Day 214
# VULNERABLE

*We are never so vulnerable as when we love.*
*~ Sigmund Freud*

You know what it is like to be powerless and susceptible. Sometimes it can be unnerving, right? This can happen when you are open to love. When you want to share a personal truth, you choose the listener carefully so you can be vulnerable and not be hurt after sharing. Being vulnerable takes courage and willingness to be exposed in a safe manner. Love is a powerful force that can expose inner doubt, fear and worry.

Think about the love in your life. Being vulnerable helped make your love stronger when you were safe. Being willing to be open and powerless in many ways shows grit and fortitude. Just like shutting down and refusing the risk of vulnerability can close you off from love and therefore create isolation and loneliness. It takes good discernment and thoughtful choices along with an inner strength that can stand tall as you choose vulnerability in your life.

There is authority in vulnerability. You come out the other side stronger and wiser. Love and share. Listen with your heart and be safe for others to share. Trust yourself.

**Daily Application:** Being vulnerable takes courage and strength. In your meditation time, review some of your vulnerable times. Breathe and allow your strength to be felt. Journal any emotions as you reflect and sit quietly.

**Personal Reflections:** _____
_____
_____
_____
_____

## Day 215
# SOLITUDE

*You will find that deep place of silence right in your room, your garden or even your bathtub.*

~ Elizabeth Kubler-Ross

Solitude is vital for your creative genius to emerge. Solitude serves everyone, even you extroverts. As an introvert, I love solitude. Solitude is an inner quiet and stillness, much like the stillness of winter after a gentle snow fall. It is the place from where your heart's desire and calling emerge. It is where you determine what is most important in your life.

Solitude does not necessarily mean perfect silence. It means having time alone to go within and reflect. Reading this book offers you daily time for solitude and a word and idea to ponder. Solitude is a necessary part of your seasons of life. When there is great change and transition, solitude may be the best choice.

In death, birth and rebirth, solitude is part of our process. There is nothing wrong and you do not need to keep talking to numb your experience. It is all working perfectly as you allow.

**Daily Application:** Give yourself some solitude today. What comes up? Grief, regret, sadness, joy, love, what? Maybe a bit of all of these and more. Use your solitude to acknowledge and shed light on what you are carrying around. If something is not serving you, release it with gratitude and love.

**Personal Reflections:** _____
_____
_____
_____
_____

## Day 216
## MINDSET

*There are better starters than me, but I am a strong finisher.*
~ Usain Bolt

I have new client who told me: "I want to be successful". She is a young woman in college and she is looking toward her future. She is working with me because her mindset is to relax and hang out without taking much responsibility for the outcome. She has awareness of this challenge which is why she called. She is working to transform her mindset.

Your mindset sets the stage and creates your reality. If your mindset is success, then you will design your life around your personal definition of success. For some, success is being employed with a large corporation while for others success is in being an entrepreneur. There is no right and wrong. The bigger question is" "Is your mindset serving you authentic inner vision or not?

Mindset helps you reach your goal, it is not the goal. When your mind is set on something that you really want, you can go get it, even if it is hard. What are you willing to do? What are you willing to no longer do?

**Daily Application:** Give yourself some time to reflect on what your real inner mindset is toward success. How do you define it? Where are your doubts and fears? How can you use your mindset to transcend the challenges? Journal your ideas and insights.


**Personal Reflections:** _____
_____
_____
_____
_____

## Day 217
# REALITY

*Reality leaves a lot to the imagination.*
*~ John Lennon*

The word reality can conjure up different feelings and thoughts for different people. What is your reality? Your reality is created by your belief systems, self-talk, world view, autobiography, existential beliefs and your experience of life. There certainly is much room for your imagination.

Some say that reality is an illusion, others say that reality is all there is. What a vast variance. I think we are all correct based on our world view and beliefs. How does your reality serve you? How does your view of reality get in your way? Arguing over reality is futile in my view. Because of the infinite possibilities encompassed in this single word, it seems we are all correct.

Imagine a world that is operating for the highest good for all beings. Is it possible? Use your imagination for your highest good. See what happens!

**Daily Application:** Take a few long, slow deep breaths. Notice your reality right now. Meditate on the idea of reality. Use your imagination to create your reality today. Open the doors of possibility. Journal and share your ideas.

**Personal Reflections:** _____
_____
_____
_____
_____
_____

## Day 218
# STUMBLE

*Men stumble over pebbles, never over mountains.*
~ H. Emilie Cady

Have you ever stumbled? Have you ever fallen flat on your face? I have a friend with small children. I stumbled over a Lego. Wow, it hurt. At that same friend's house, I had to watch out for furniture and I could navigate without stumbling. Maybe it is because I was paying less attention to the small things and that is what tripped me. The larger things were more obvious.

In life, you may stumble over the pebbles due to not seeing them or minimizing their impact until you stumble. The larger mountains take more thought and strategy so your stumbling may be less. And mountains are big so stumbling is not the option.

When you stumble, put the event in its proper place. Your stumble is along your path that has many pebbles as you climb the mountain. After all, it is the climbing of the mountain that matters. Don't let a stumble along the way stop you.

**Daily Application:** Take some time alone today and in your mind's eye, gaze at your mountain, your goals. Know that there are pebbles and you may stumble and that with focus and continued action you will climb the mountain. Sketch or draw your path. See your success.

**Personal Reflections:** _____
_____
_____
_____
_____
_____

# Day 219
# BELONGING

*I knew that if I cut a tree, my arm would bleed.*
~ Alice Walker

When you have a deep sense of belonging, you have a similar experience as Alice Walker. Belonging at the core is when we experience our connection and oneness with all that is. There seems to be no real separation and everything and everyone belong together as a great whole.

There is also belonging in our profession and our family or peer group. There is a human experience and the spiritual experience of belonging. You may not feel that you belong in your family or among another set of people. How do you create a sense of belonging in a world that appears so segregated and divided? For many, it comes down to choosing to honor their inherent belonging in the Universe and act from that place. If others do not understand yet, love them anyway.

**Daily Application:** Go within and ask yourself if you belong, really. What do you think about? How do you feel? How can you use these responses for your personal transformation? Journal your ideas.

**Personal Reflections:** _____
_____
_____
_____
_____
_____

## Day 220
# LAW

*Always bear in mind that your own resolution to succeed is more important than any other.*

~ Abraham Lincoln

You want to succeed, right? Each one of us has a different functional definition of success. Our resolution to succeed must also follow spiritual law and be aligned as the most important piece. Your personal resolve to follow the higher laws of compassion, gratitude, love, generosity and the like are paramount in your personal and professional success and happiness.

The word "law" can sometimes get a bad rap. Some people always think of getting in trouble with the law. The law for visionary leaders is about following the higher spiritual laws of the Universe. It is these natural laws that are vital for happiness.

Your resolve is most important. It means that you are unwavering and are focused with acuity. Your focus and actions create the opportunities for your successful attainment of your goals. Follow the higher laws and the human created laws and you will have the success you deserve and more.

**Daily Application:** Having resolve is critical for your success. In your quiet time, consider your resolve and the laws operating within your world. Visualizing your success, journal your thoughts and ideas. Breathe deeply and honor the law.

**Personal Reflections:** _____
_____
_____
_____
_____

## Day 221
# PREJUDICE

*Prejudice is never the answer.*

*~ Gandhi*

To pre-judge never serves anyone, ever. Preconceived, biased opinions only harm and hold others and yourself back. To be prejudiced means you are holding yourself in a self-made prison of limitation and bondage. No one else is doing it to you. You are creating the bondage. When someone holds preconceived biases toward you, how do you respond? I am sure you do not enjoy being the subject of the bias.

We are all different, unique people. Even on common topics, our underlying views and understanding can vary greatly. I hear a lot of prejudice against people with addiction or mental illness. I have worked with people who have these illnesses. They are all as different as could be and no two fits into the biased comments I hear from others. This form of ignorance does not serve us as leaders. It is time to raise ourselves higher. Hear Gandhi.

**Daily Application:** Be still and relax for some time. Do you hold any prejudices? Is there any opportunity for you to make some shifts to take yourself out of your bondage? Ponder, journal your ideas and plan your actions. You will be glad you did.

**Personal Reflections:** _____
_____
_____
_____
_____
_____

## Day 222
# BREVITY

*Brevity is a great charm of eloquence.*
*~ Marcus Tullius Cicero*

To be eloquent means that you have a way with words that is smooth yet powerful. Over speaking causes the power to be diminished in your words. I teach the leaders I work with to speak in 5-word sentences and no more than 5 sentences at a time. This is to practice brevity. When you master delivering your message in a concise manner, you open doors that others cannot see. You give yourself increased flexibility as well.

Think about listening to a speaker who keeps talking and does not get to the point. It is an entirely different experience when the speaker is brief and eloquent. This is the charm that exudes from the person that has your attention.

My friend said once that she can make a short story long. Due to the length often, any power in the story is lost. Also goes any charm and connection. It is a word overload with too much fluff. More is not always better.

**Daily Application:** Breathe and relax. Monitor your inner dialogue for some time. Are you eloquent? Are you able to be brief when is serves everyone? Ponder some of the reactions you receive when you speak, do you want to make any adjustments? Document your thoughts.

**Personal Reflections:** _____
_____
_____
_____
_____
_____

## Day 223
# DISCERNMENT

*He who knows others is clever; He who knows himself has discernment.*
*~ Lao-tzu*

To discern is to decide what is right for you or not right for you. You enter judgement zone when you then place value or lack of value. To make something good or bad is judgement, to discern means you know what is right for you without labeling it good or bad.

Knowing yourself without judgment yet being honest and clear is discernment. From this place you are then equipped to decide what you wish to include in your life. Simply because something does not resonate with you does not necessarily make it right or wrong. So, discernment and judgment operationally are different.

Knowing others is nice but knowing yourself really is where your discernment emanates. How well do you know the real you? You know, those parts of you just below the surface. There is always more to be revealed, more to emerge.

**Daily Application:** Today, notice how often you assign value to something. Pay attention to your inner discernment relating to who you are amid the experience. Be still and enjoy discerning for yourself.

**Personal Reflections:** _____
_____
_____
_____
_____
_____

## Day 224
# PRIORITIES

*Make room in life to focus deeply on the top one or two most enjoyable priorities in your life. Put everything else on hold until you have thoroughly enjoyed those things.*

*~ Sandy Freschi \*\**

Who are you? Really, who are you in there? Your self is created over time based upon your choices and beliefs. Many of your beliefs started when you were very young. You make choices every day based on your beliefs and life experiences. All this comes together to create your "self".

Your "self" is fluid and is evolving or devolving based upon choices and actions. Both choices and actions come from your thinking and mental attitude. Sometimes the smallest of choice can yield a major shift in your "self". Sometimes what seems to be important may end up a smaller part of you.

Understanding your fluid nature offers you opportunity to discover more of your inherent depth. Your "self" is ever changing. You might respond one way today that is very different had the event happened years ago. Your "self" changes with every choice. With choice comes wisdom.

**Daily Application:** Spend extra time today in quiet with your "self". Notice many of the choices that have impacted your "self" today. As you plan your day, pay attention to your choices and how you would like them to impact your life. Document your feelings and thoughts as you wish.

**Personal Reflections:** _____

_____
_____
_____
_____
_____

## Day 225
# POTENTIAL

*There is no heavier burden than unfulfilled potential.*
~ Charles Schulz

You have potential. I remember hearing as a young woman from my mother that different young men I would date had potential. We all have potential. The question is for what? In the dating scenario, it could be concluded that the potential referred to being a desirable mate.

I'll bet you have some potential that is yet to be fulfilled. I'll bet you even feel it from time to time. What is your potential that is yet to be fulfilled? You can find it where you feel heavy or sad somehow. My vocation is to inspire people to live their vision and fulfill their potential. The biggest barrier and obstacle that I see in my clients is fear and doubt.

If it is in your heart and you can feel it, see it and taste it, then it is yours to do. You may not know exactly how you will live your potential but you don't have to yet. It is more about who you are becoming along the journey that lifts the burdens.

**Daily Application:** In your quiet time today locate any heavy spots that may seem burdensome. Look within the darkness to see the potential that is buried within and give yourself permission to see it and let the light shine on the potential. Now, journal what you see, without judgment about how you will fulfill the potential. Just sit with it and breathe.

**Personal Reflections:** _____
_____
_____
_____
_____

## Day 226
# PLAY

*We don't stop playing because we grow old; we grow old because we stop playing!*
~ George Bernard Shaw

How much fun do you have every day? Do you need a child as a decoy to have fun? When you are playing, and laughing, no matter how silly, you are revitalizing your youth. By lightening up and playing, you awaken your creativity and you see life from a fresh perspective.

When I was younger, I was very intense and serious. I did not play much and as I look back, I can feel the heaviness I must have been experiencing. Today, I have fun and play nearly every day. Some play is more grown up than fun activities. From swinging to skipping to laughing with friends, play is an active part of my world these days.

It is true that even when someone is older by age and they are having fun with play that their vibe is much younger. I think this is why Betty White is so loved and revered. She is not only talented and amazing on many levels, but she reminds us to play. To stay young, let yourself play.

**Daily Application:** Take yourself on a play date. Swing, dig, jump or create and let your inner child come out and laugh. Now look in the mirror and see your youth. Enjoy.

**Personal Reflections:** _____
_____
_____
_____
_____
_____

## Day 227
# DIGEST

*Only consume as much as you can digest, physically, mentally, emotionally and spiritually. Move toward solutions.*

~ Don Ollsin **

Digestion is the key to health. In our culture, taking in too much is reinforced. This is a bad idea. With every amount taken in, there must be a digestion time. I also call it integration. Taking in too much too fast without proper assimilation into your system is hazardous to your health. Moving forward toward solutions to your challenges requires honoring your personal systems' tolerance for taking in food, information or the like.

One of my amazing musician clients and I are always in this conversation about integration and digestion. He has many food sensitivities and he has overexcitabilities and has an incredibly sensitive system. I think this is why he is such a gifted musician with a great spiritual connection. His gifts and intensities, though, mean that he must take in things in smaller portions at times. When I am teaching him things, there are times we must wait for his integration. He forgets this sometimes and when he is reminded he then slows down. He is eager and smart and intense, digesting "slowly" at times is a challenge.

**Daily Application:** Ponder your digestion on all levels. How well are you integrating information and "food" on all these levels? Notice your systems and journal your consumption today. How are you digesting?

**Personal Reflections:** _____
_____
_____
_____
_____
_____

## Day 228
## ISOLATION

*Isolation is the enemy of improvement.*

~ Tony Wagner

Two heads are better than one. When you have connection to others, your improvement can happen. Your own brilliant and creative mind works better when bouncing ideas and concepts off other minds. Isolation can stop your progress. Visionaries work well when in tandem with others who are like-minded.

I have been alone for much of today, working on this book. The aloneness began to feel like isolation. I took a break to speak with a friend. Just speaking about the project and sharing my thoughts has recharged my dedication and resolve. Coming out of isolation served to enhance my creative flow and helped me move forward. This is true for all of us.

Our brains are designed to be in relation to others. We are pack animals so the connection with others sparks our neurology. Come out of isolation with your ideas and creative energies. By connecting with another, the enemy of isolation is defeated.

**Daily Application:** Reflect on your connection to others. Are you isolated often? How can you increased connection to support your improvement? Journal your thoughts.


**Personal Reflections:** _____
_____
_____
_____
_____
_____

## Day 229
# STRETCH

*You must do the thing which you think you cannot do.*
*~ Franklin Delano Roosevelt*

Stretching is reaching beyond your perception of what you think you can do and go just a bit further. You stretch when you try something new and expand your talents and abilities. This can be physical, emotional, mental, spiritual or social in nature. Stretch your mind each day and learn something that takes you beyond what you think you know.

Expand spiritually by becoming more open and receptive to guidance. Stretch socially by reaching out to others and exploring new avenues to connect with people. Stretch mentally and learn something of which you are unfamiliar. Stretch your muscles, breathe and fuel your body for improved functioning. This expansion via stretching is vital to your overall success and happiness.

It is time to do what you think you cannot do. As FDR said many moons ago, the saying remains valid today. As visionary humans, it is time to stretch and expand.

**Daily Application:** Be still and imagine you are stretching today. What might you do to expand beyond what you think you can do. Journal your thoughts. Release your fear and doubt then go for it!

**Personal Reflections:** _____
_____
_____
_____
_____
_____

## Day 230
# WONDER

*Always be on the lookout for the presence of wonder.*
~ E.B. White

Wonder is described as a combination of admiration and amazement. Always be on the lookout for things that excite you and things that you admire. Wonder is everywhere if you are paying attention. I experience wonder when I am listening to someone share their knowledge and their story. I also experience wonder with the weather and the seasons of the year. Nature never hurries yet everything unfolds right on time. This simply amazes me.

I was just outside gazing at the night sky. The stars and the moon were accentuated by fast moving clouds through which I could see the light of the moon. How awesome. I stood there experiencing wonder and awe as I watched the weather and the solar system do her thing.

Sometimes others express wonder when I am sharing with an audience. This is also amazing. I also experience wonder as I share. The entire experience is full of amazement and I admire that our connections are so profound. What brings wonder alive for you?

**Daily Application:** Be still a few times today and check in with yourself. Notice all the amazement and wonder all around you. Stop for a minute and honor the wonder. Journal and awareness or thoughts.

**Personal Reflections:** _____
_____
_____
_____
_____
_____

## Day 231
# JUSTICE

*Justice is sweet and musical; but injustice is harsh and discordant.*
~ Henry David Thoreau

Being fair and honest are important. When an injustice occurs, what do you do? How do you respond? Are you using injustice to fight injustice or are you employing justice to move injustice out?

Whatever you focus on you get more of in your life. By focusing on injustice and giving it your attention and energy, you are creating more of the same. When you place your attention and intention on justice, you produce more justice in kind. Whatever you fight, you get more resistance and more of the issue you are fighting.

I am not suggesting allowing injustice or to turn a blind eye. Quite the opposite. I am suggesting that there is a powerful way to right the wrongs by using the higher laws of the Universe. We get more of what we focus on. Focus on the sweet, musical justice and create more of this. It will drown out the harshness of injustice.

**Daily Application:** How do you express your belief in justice? Meditate on being just and the best ways for you to respond to injustice by using justice. Journal your plan and share your actions with trusted others.

**Personal Reflections:** _____
_____
_____
_____
_____
_____

## Day 232
# CERTAINTY

*The quest for certainty blocks the search for meaning. Uncertainty is the very condition to impel man to unfold his powers.*

~ Erich Fromm

I love to live in the mystery. Living in certainty is great at times. Holding on to the need to be certain all the time stops your evolving connection to your vision and meaning. Within the uncertainty is the space to support your exploration and unfolding of your spiritual powers. Here is where you can connect with your powers of zeal, order, love, will and more. Without the mystery you would not have the space or opportunity to discover your inherent powers.

The drive for certainty is fueled by fear, control and perfectionism. All this causes even more issues that radiate out from the fear that must be certain and control things. Certainty has its place in some academic pursuits. It can be a hinderance in your quest for your personal unfoldment.

It is OK to be uncertain. The mysteries support your journey of unfoldment by inciting questions and curiosity. Your authentic power lies beneath uncertainty and inner mystery.

**Daily Application:** In what areas are you driven to be certain? How do you handle mystery and uncertainty? Take some time apart and ponder these ideas. If you are searching or meaning, get comfortable with uncertainty. What's your resistance? Journal and be open for change.

**Personal Reflections:** _____
_____
_____
_____
_____

## Day 233
# LINEAR

*Life is not linear.*
*~ Dianne A. Allen, MA*

Do you expect that things should go a certain way? For example, keeping track of how long you invest your time into something and expect a certain result. Many people say things like "I've been doing this for 30 days and I should see results by now." This is not always how life unfolds. Most often life unfolds with twists and turns that are often unexpected and circular.

When life does not happen to your expectations, step back and allow yourself to experience the beauty and richness of the twists and turns. Sometimes the greatest learnings and beauty are off the beaten path. Always remember that the fabric of your life is created in *all* circumstances. Give thanks for the circular and rhythmic movement of life.

One of my clients struggles with the circular nature or the seasons. She would rather have a linear problem to solve. She struggles tremendously with some of life's events because of her inner resistance to embrace a softer, more organic lifestyle. Her rigidity comes from fear and doubt. It is time to realize that the organic flow of life adds to the beauty, it does not distract. You can have both linear and circular at the same time!

**Daily Application:** Today, notice your opportunities and enhanced experiences when you are off the beaten, linear path. Allow creativity and beauty to enter your life via delays and chance meetings.

**Personal Reflections:** _____
_____
_____
_____
_____
_____

## Day 234
# BETWEEN

*Music happens between the notes.*
*~ Igor Stravinsky*

My mother played the piano and she always said that the beauty of the music is the space between the notes. She played amazing classical music. I never really understood the meaning as a child. I understand this now. The beauty is in the silence between what is being played. I think this is true about life as well.

I work with musicians often. When we are working toward their realized vision, they understand the spaces. They are often more pliable and able to flow more easily than some of my gifted clients who tend to be more linear. The space between is pregnant with possibilities and beauty.

The space between your actions and thoughts and words is where your beauty emerges in a tempo fitting for the situation. Slow tempo or fast, the music of your life is happening in between the events, words and ideas. When you are wanting to push like a machine, remember the music of your soul. You can hear it playing beneath your waking hours. Go inside and feel your personal groove and rhythm.

**Daily Application:** Be still and turn your attention inward for some time. Now, pay attention to your personal melody that is playing through your heart. Listen. Enjoy and allow it to emerge. Share your song.

**Personal Reflections:** _____
_____
_____
_____
_____

## Day 235
# DIFFERENCE

*Never feel too small or powerless to make a difference.*
*~ Anita Roddick*

Your presence changes things. Your entering a room changes how it feels to others whether you see it or not. You make a difference with every thought, word and action you take. Your difference is visible and tangible. The question is: In what direction is the difference you are making?

You are more powerful than you know. Are you using your power for the good or are you using your power to fuel fear and worry? You may think you are too small to make a difference yet this is simply not true. Try sleeping with a mosquito buzzing around. You are a human being, fully equipped and able manifest your vision. You have been given power, dominion, over your world. How are you using this power?

**Daily Application:** Do you want to make a difference? What are you doing to make the difference? In your quiet time today, reflect on your desires and ways to bring your inspiration into the world. Now, act with calm assurance.

**Personal Reflections:** _____
_____
_____
_____
_____
_____

## Day 236
# INSPIRATION

*To be inspired, that's the secret.*
~ Andre Agassi

When you are inspired, you rise to the next level and beyond. Inspiration is like a magic carpet, it swoops under you and carries you to places you never dreamed possible. I see this in college sports and athletics where people are representing their country. The inspiration that comes from who they are representing often motivates and excels the athlete farther than they might have gone alone. Andre Agassi played inspired tennis.

When your personal life is inspired and your professional life is inspired, you find yourself being drawn toward a new level of performance and experience. My clients that follow their vision are inspired and they can achieve what they previously thought impossible. What inspires you? I am most inspired by the range of emotion and achievement that humans can make.

**Daily Application:** In your quiet time today, connect with your inner spark of inspiration. How can you fan that flame today to create an even more brilliant light? Reflect on ways you can live an inspired life. Journal any ideas.

**Personal Reflections:** _____
_____
_____
_____
_____
_____

# Day 237
# ACHIEVEMENT

*The starting point of all achievement is desire.*
~ Napoleon Hill

What do you want, really? What is burning deep within you that you desire? If you do not have words, describe the feeling. That is your desire. To the extent that you marginalize or squash that desire, you hamper your achievement. If your actions are random and not connected to your desire, any achievement will be short if at all.

Think about some of your achievements. What was your desire? Many of my clients have made great achievements. Every achievement came from having a desire first. Create the desire and then act in keeping with the desire and you will achieve. For example, I have a strong desire to create a mediation book for visionary leaders. I am writing and creating this book from that desire. Without desire the hours of planning, writing and creating would make the completion elusive at best. The hard work and discipline that it takes are easier to do when my desire is alive and focused. The same is true for you and your desires.

**Daily Application:** Ponder your desires and how they have underpinned your achievements. In your stillness, allow yourself to connect to your current desires. Visualize following through and achieving your vision. Journal your vision and how you will feel while experiencing the achievement.

**Personal Reflections:** _____
_____
_____
_____
_____
_____

## Day 238
# DISHARMONY

*If you are depressed, you are living in the past. If you are anxious, you are living in the future. If you are at peace, you are living in the present.*

~ Lao Tzu

I have heard it said that all real healing begins within each person. All the violence and hatred comes from a deep inner disconnection first that then radiates out and becomes obvious in the world around us. Healing means to make whole again. If we are to begin to be make progress on all the disharmony, we must first go within and mend our own sense of separation and disharmony. Then, we are fully equipped to assist the community at large in mending their separation, pain and fears.

For me the frequency of love is one of compassion and kindness wherever possible. It does also include boundaries. Having a loving presence does not mean to be a door mat. Look at Gandhi, Nelson Mandela, Mother Theresa for example. They all held this more harmonious existence which allowed them to stand up for what was right for them. See, real power comes from within and then acts upon the world. Being reactionary, fighting for a cause, still focuses on the problem and thus perpetuates the issues.

**Daily Application:** Spend some quiet time within. Notice any beliefs or thoughts that are disharmonious. How can you create harmony in those areas? Begin to take those actions and your personal power will explode. Journal your ideas and progress.

**Personal Reflections:** _____
_____
_____
_____
_____
_____

## Day 239
# COMPANY

*The key is to keep company only with people who uplift you, whose presence calls forth your best.*

*~ Epictetus*

I have heard it said that we evolve at the same rate as the people we hang out with regularly. When someone has angry or fearful energy, it is difficult for me to lift myself out of that energy field. I do my best to uplift and support others without agenda. I believe that if your vision is coming from within you authentically, then my role is to support you. Authentic visions always are about serving or doing good for our world in some way.

The company you keep strongly impacts you and can lift you up or hold you down. This can happen without anyone being aware of the way it works. One of my clients just made some changes in her social and professional circles. In a short time, we are seeing changes in her outlook toward her business and her personal life. The company does impact you. Pay attention.

**Daily Application:** Spend some time in quiet pondering the company your keep. As you go about your day, ask if the people and situations are uplifting. Do you need to make some adjustments?

**Personal Reflections:** _____
_____
_____
_____
_____
_____

## Day 240
# FEELINGS

*I'm looking forward to the future and feeling grateful for the past.*
*~ Mike Rowe*

Feelings are the energy that tell you that you are alive. They are our friends and allies, not the enemy like we have been conditioned. Sensitive and creative people have more intense feelings and these feelings are the energy source for great things.

Today is a day to honor your feelings no matter what they may be, for you are alive. You can name your feelings whatever you wish. The most misunderstood feeling is grief. Grief is a conflicting mass of human emotion following any significant change in behavior. It happens not only in death. We are taught to be alone while our biology requires connection for the healing. No wonder there is so much despair.

Breathe deeply and allow your feelings to give you messages without you judging or trying to change. Just breathe and be with your feelings. The more you align with your inner genius, the more authentic power you possess.

**Daily Application:** Breathing now, slowly and calmly. Allow whatever emotion wants to arise. Simply allow without thinking or over analyzing. Throughout the day, stop and breathe and honor your feelings. They are here to serve you.

**Personal Reflections:** _____
_____
_____
_____
_____
_____

## Day 241
# ANIMALS

*An animal's eyes have the power to speak a great language.*
~ Martin Buber

Animals are amazing. Humans can sometimes be the least aware of animals. My dog is amazing. She is so expressive. It is as if we speak the same language through her expressions and eyes. I also notice this depth in other animals' eyes It is even obvious in photos and video. Have you ever really gazed into the eyes of a calf or cow? They are so warm and soft. How about a snake? Each animal speaks through their eyes. It is their window of communication.

I have a couple of friends who care for and protect many different animals as part of their vocation. I admire them and their ability to speak the great language of the different species. From giraffes to birds to alligators to big cats, gorillas, penguins and horses; they communicate and somehow connect to these animals. They know when the animal needs care or is sick. They know when everything is going well. The language is amazing and inspiring.

Too many people ignore the eyes and language of animals other than humans. Some even miss the eyes of other humans. This is a great tragedy. Look into the eyes. Listen to what is being said.

**Daily Application:** Connect with an animal or two today. Breathe slowly and notice their eyes and the message they are communicating. Enjoy.

**Personal Reflections:** _____
_____
_____
_____
_____
_____

## Day 242
# PHILOSOPHY

*Knowing yourself is the beginning of all wisdom.*
~ Aristotle

As you grow in knowledge and experience, you have the opportunity to become wise. This starts with knowing yourself according to Aristotle. This was his philosophy. Knowing your philosophy is an important part of growing in knowing yourself. Your personal philosophy is the theoretical basis upon which you base your life. It includes your framework. One simple example is whether the world and people in it are inherently good or bad. Each person has their view and the important part is to realize that this view shapes their thoughts, words and actions.

My philosophy shapes my life on every level as does yours. As you grow in wisdom, you can be more in tuned to your personal philosophy and can change it is you are led. I believe this is fascinating. I love to engage with someone and listen to how they see the world and what it means to them. Chances are that repeating challenges are due to a philosophy that could use some updating. Be open.

**Daily Application:** How intimately are you aware of your philosophy? Spend some contemplative time and become even more attuned to your personal basis for your decisions. Journal your awareness and any changes you wish to make.

**Personal Reflections:** _____
_____
_____
_____
_____
_____

## Day 243
# KINDNESS

*Remember there's no such thing as a small act of kindness. Every act creates a ripple with no logical end.*

~ Scott Adams

Kindness is so powerful. A kind word or a kind deed can speak volumes and move mountains. Kindness in action can unknowingly help someone decide to continue another day. Kind words ring in the listeners mind for days and even years to follow. Kindness that comes from within and emanates out into the world truly has a lasting effect.

Hugging an animal and showing kindness for their being is crucial of our own health and welfare. People who have rescued animals will say that the animal rescued them. Most likely, the human was rescued from self-centeredness and self-will by the unconditional love the animal shared in return for the kindness done.

This is the ripple effect in action. Sharing kindness yields powerful goodness for our world and the universe. Kindness to other humans helps soften a hardened heart. You may never see the softening yet the softening exists none the less. Offer kindness to yourself and others. Love the animals. Smile. Watch the world around you become transformed.

**Daily Application:** Pay special attention to extending kindness from your heart today. Be authentic and allow your natural kind nature to find the desirable avenue for expression. Go with it. The avenue that pops into your mind may surprise you. Give your inspired ideas a chance to express. Enjoy.

**Personal Reflections:** _____
_____
_____
_____
_____
_____

## Day 244
## SELF

*It is not what is done to us in this life that matters the most, it is what we do to our self that is everlasting.*

~ Jennifer Kaye**

Your brain believes your own voice above all others. As you choose to grow and transform, you will want to release the stories of the events that have happened. The deeper healing is in freeing yourself from the inner perpetual pain that you are carrying forward. Many people I have guided over the years perpetuate the inner disconnection and suffering because of the stories they consistently tell themselves.

What are you doing to yourself? How are you supporting your freedom and transformation by changing your inner dialogue? Are you ready to be free of the stories that are keeping you bound to pain and old grief? Let's continue to explore alternatives to ongoing suffering and pain.

**Daily Application:** Write your personal story. Really, what are the things you tell yourself about you and your life thus far. Now sit quietly and ponder your thoughts regarding what you have written. Shift any part of the story that doesn't serve you. Write what you could feel or think instead of the pain and discord. Focus on your personal freedom and inner desires.

**Personal Reflections:** _____
_____
_____
_____
_____
_____

## Day 245
# JOURNEY

*Life is a journey, not a destination.*
~ Ralph Waldo Emerson

Destination addiction seems to affect many people in our society. So many people are focused on "getting there" rather than enjoying the journey.

Just the other day, I was speaking with someone about this very topic and they said: "Yes, I love the journey and I don't pay much attention to the destination anymore. I can't wait to get there." Wow! I was amazed at the apparent contradiction in one sentence after another. This person didn't even realize how seduced they were by the addiction to the destination until we began to talk about it later.

I believe many people fall into this trap. They think they are enjoying the journey yet their sights remain focused on the destination.

Rather than destination, I speak to milestones or markers that denote rites of passage. There is not finish line so focusing on a destination can rob you of your enjoyment and lessons.

**Daily Application:** Take 3-5 ten-minute breaks during the day and honor your journey while releasing destination thoughts. Look around and see the grandeur that is your life. Trust the process and you will thrive.

**Personal Reflections:** _____
_____
_____
_____
_____
_____

## Day 246
# WALKING

*He who limps is still walking.*

*~ Stanislaw Jerzy Lec*

Sometimes you are making great progress, power walking and enjoying the scenery. Other times, you are walking slower, still making progress though. Then there are the times when you are limping. I think of marathon runners and iron man triathletes. Often, they are limping over the finish line and sometimes they are crawling yet they get over that line.

If you are limping, you are still walking. In other words, it counts to limp toward your goals. You are not always moving along at the same pace, in fact, there are many times you may be limping. Don't stop or give up.

Sometimes there are challenges. No great mission or goal has been accomplished without challenges and opposition of some kind. It takes perseverance to reach your goals. Your progress at any given time will vary. Remain focused and continue toward your goal, even limping. Keep walking, just keep walking.

**Daily Application:** Pay attention to your walk today. What is it saying about you and your journey? Reflect on your progress and how you can focus on walking toward your goals. Draw or write about your vision so the milestones along the way become more obvious.

**Personal Reflections:** _____
_____
_____
_____
_____
_____

## Day 247
# LIBERTY

*Life without liberty is like a body without a spirit.*
~ Kahlil Gibran

Liberty is the ability to act with autonomy and self-determination. A body without a spirit is lifeless as is life without autonomy. We are all spiritual at our core. This is where our animation and life reside. It weighs nothing but makes all the difference! Life without liberty and the sense of autonomy would resemble being lifeless on many levels. It would be dark and dreary.

Your body is animated by your spirit and this is from where your freedom, free will and self-determination emanate. They go hand in hand, one without the other doesn't work well. When you were not in touch with your spirit, you were heavy energetically. This is depression, grief and doubt in action. When your spirit is bright, you are alive with great energy!

As you continue to experience great opportunities, take a moment and reflect on your liberty.

**Daily Application:** Spend time in quiet. Enjoy your time apart. Notice your beating heart and your still small inner voice. They work together for your highest good! Journal about your sense of liberty. Take some time to share your ideas with others in an encouraging manner.

**Personal Reflections:** _____
_____
_____
_____
_____
_____

## Day 248
# FEAR

*We fear things in proportion to our ignorance of them.*
*~ Titus Livius*

I find this to be relevant today in many cases. I notice when someone doesn't know or understand something, that I hear judgment, anger, fear and other strong fear based emotions being expressed. I also notice a wall of deflection when inquiry occurs.

The function of fear is "to get ready". Above the ways we respond is the function. Fear is always telling us to get ready; whether it is to learn something or do something, *get ready*. When I embraced this understanding, I noticed my irritation and aggravation greatly diminish. Most often the *get ready* message is to learn what needs to be learned. It does not mean the fear leaves, it simply means that is comes with a message.

Ignorance and fear are cousins and they play together well. Knowledge and faith and trust are great answers to stop the destruction of fear and ignorance.

**Daily Application:** Take some quiet time today and pay attention to your breath. Notice that as you settle your breathing you become more aware and calm. Notice any fear today. Journal what you are to get ready for and then get ready.

**Personal Reflections:** _____
_____
_____
_____
_____
_____

## Day 249
# NIGHTMARES

*Vision without action is a daydream. Action without vision is a nightmare.*
*~ Japanese Proverb*

This is so true in an affirming sense to me. Yes, I am a visionary and you may be as well. Regardless, we all have dreams for our lives. Dreams are where hope comes from. Your dreams are the fuel to keep you going. So, what about the nightmares? Sometimes your dreams may turn into nightmares along the path of their realization.

Your nightmares are also great motivators. They show you where not to go and things that can become problematic. Nightmares can be instructive even when they are upsetting or disconcerting. I usually write down my nightmares and a few days later, look at it for the meaning. Then the information can be used to propel me forward.

Dream your dreams. Allow your vision to become clear in your dreams. Use the nightmares as grist for the mill. Nothing goes to waste when you are focused.

**Daily Application:** In your quiet time, reflect on the idea that nightmares are a vital part of your dream life. Journal the lessons and teachings that the nightmares offer. How does it relate to your dreams? Take a few deep breaths then use the information for your greater good. Journal your insights.

**Personal Reflections:** _____
_____
_____
_____
_____

## Day 250
# NATURE

*Look deep into nature and then you will understand everything better.*
*~ Albert Einstein*

There is an elegant simplicity to the power, diversity and awe of nature. Stopping to simply observe, you will see the flow without distraction. The sun's rays are on point, rain does not change direction as it falls, the plant and the animal cycles remain consistent over time.

All of nature has a beautiful flow and rhythm. Nature is vibrant and alive, even when the cold of winter or extreme heat of summer sends the teams of life for protection. I have never seen a tree upset and afraid because of what the wind might do tomorrow. I think humans could use the powerful and ever-present message from nature to allow the flow and trust.

**Daily Application:** Take time today and be in nature. Offer heartfelt gratitude for the power and presence of the beauty all around you. Notice the cycle of nature alive in what you witness as you become even more open to the awareness of the elegant simplicity of nature.

**Personal Reflections:** _____
_____
_____
_____
_____
_____

## Day 251
# CHILDLIKE

*The child in me wants to play.*
*~ Charlie Chaplin*

We all have an inner child who wants to come out and play. There are days you want to have a blast and be childlike. Childlike is different than childish. Childish is acting immaturely. To be childlike is to be open and curious. Asking good questions, paying attention and being open.

When your child wants to play, you call out that aspect of you that is open, lighthearted, curious and fun. This is the way to be able to receive your higher messages. When I feel my child wanting to play, I let her. Often it entails playing with my dog or creating something or playing in nature. Nevertheless, I allow that part of me to come into the light. She always has a message and is right on time.

**Daily Application:** Breathe deeply and become aware of that child in you that wants to play and be heard. Invite curiosity to emerge. Be open and teachable. Now, go have fun today. Play!

**Personal Reflections:** _____
_____
_____
_____
_____
_____

## Day 252
# TRANSFORMATION

*Transformation can't happen if you are always right and everything always works! Mistakes are valuable when you learn from them.*
~ Judi Snyder \*\*

Powerful transformation can catapult you forward toward your vision. Often your greatest talent and gift will become obvious following what you perceive as a great failure or disappointment. Being open to learning and releasing the ego need to right fight can be the most liberating experience. When you are married to being right all the time, you put yourself in a prison that is fully self-imposed.

Being teachable and open to learning from others, sets you up for transformation and authentic success. Think of any mistakes as mis-takes. You have the power and ability to re-do any aspect of your life you wish. You are the director of your life, you have the power to control how the play turns out. Use adversity and mistakes as fuel for a great outcome.

**Daily Application:** Spend a few minutes in quiet reflection. Focus on ways any mistakes can be used as fuel for your transformation. Be open to the possibilities.

**Personal Reflections:** _____
_____
_____
_____
_____
_____

## Day 253
# STRATEGY

*However beautiful the strategy, you should occasionally look at the results.*
~ Winston Churchill

Strategy is a word I hear all the time in business and in vision planning. I asked someone the other day about their results and they stumbled. He told me that his strategy was all that mattered. He knew it was a good one and he was focused on following through. I asked him what his evidence procedure is to determine the effectiveness of his strategy. He was confused. He was so focused on following a strategy that he was not paying attention to if it was working or not.

I have a client who arrived all focused-on results and she could not tell me her strategy. She seemed to be doing many things hoping something would give her the number she is seeking. She is the other extreme of my colleague. In my business and personal ventures, I like to look at both strategy and results. I remember when I had little strategy and just followed my ideas. Now, having a nice balance is working well.

Have a strategy and the evidence procedure for your results. This way both your strategy and results can be duplicated and enhanced.

**Daily Application:** Ponder your life strategy. Do you have one? Write it down to make it real and so you can really see what you are operating with to make decisions. Ponder the results you are receiving in work, relationships, health and fulfillment. Does your strategy yield the results you are seeking? Make any needed changes.

**Personal Reflections:** _____
_____
_____
_____
_____
_____

## Day 254
# DIVERSITY

*Diversity: The art of thinking independently together.*
~ Malcolm Forbes

I enjoy diversity in my friendships, business experiences and relationships. Diversity brings everyone together and enfolds the greatness of all. Malcolm Forbes calling it an art makes good sense to me. As I sit and think about the art of diversity, the creativity is evident. Coming together and retaining personal individuality offers the best of both worlds. This thrills me.

How diverse are your relationships and your connections? Does everyone seem like clones when they are together? Are they very different and therefore rich in diversity? We can think and create independently together, and the results have a synergistic vibe.

I am often surprised when some people notice the diverse nature of my clients, friends and colleagues. I enjoy the differences, life stories, similarities and brilliant ideas. I love the rich diversity in music and literature. If everything was similar, life would be boring, and I desire flair and connection.

**Daily Application:** Picture your colleagues and friends in a large room together. Is there variety? What is happening? Is there any area where some diversity could add to the environment? Journal ways you can add variety and diversity. Take at least one action.

**Personal Reflections:** _____
_____
_____
_____
_____
_____

## Day 255
# DISAPPOINTMENT

*If you will shake off the disappointment, the self-pity, the blame, then you will discover that nothing in life happened to you, it happened for you.*

~ Joel Osteen

Many folks think life is to be endured. I believe that life is a grand experience that is designed to work in my favor. Self-pity and blame are common in a society that is litigious and focused on giving one's power to others. My inner world is more in charge of my life than the outer world. Even when I get distracted, I go within and remember that the world is for me, not against me.

      I have had many disappointments in my life. When I focused on ways to transcend and use the experience to move toward my vision, that is what happened. When I held onto the problem, it continued to fester and cause pain. Now, I allow my experience and expression of disappointment. I feel it and then I focus on how it can work for me rather than against me.

**Daily Application:** Notice any areas of your life that are influenced by blame, self-pity or disappointment. Now, journal ways you can use this experience for your benefit and success. Take charge by changing your orientation.

**Personal Reflections:** _____

_____
_____
_____
_____
_____

## Day 256
# WIND

*The winds of grace are always blowing, but you have to raise the sail.*

*~ Ramakrishna*

As a sailor, I love the wind. Feeling the breeze on my face is always so refreshing. For me, wind is much like the Divine. You cannot visually see the wind yet you can see the effects of it. From the movement of leaves early morning to the fierce wind of a storm, still the wind is only visible through what it impacts. Wind has great power from a soft caress to violent chaos that comes in the storms.

Inner storms have a wind that clears away emotional debris. When you are holding on to old pain or fears, the deadened areas need to be cleared away for new growth. It may not feel great, like a storm but in the aftermath, there is a clearing and cleansing that only the wind can do.

**Daily Application:** In your quiet time today, allow the wind to loosen and release the old, outdated ideas, emotions and beliefs. As you release what is not serving you, allow only love, peace and joy to be present. Journal your insights.

**Personal Reflections:** _____
_____
_____
_____
_____
_____

## Day 257
# QUESTIONS

*The most important thing is to not stop questioning.*
*~ Albert Einstein*

I am sure you have heard it said that there are no bad questions. Asking inward questions that are designed to move your thinking forward are essential for a successful life. It is the curious that create what others cannot yet see. Using better questions leads to better results.

No matter the appearance of your progress, keep asking questions. Focus on solutions and insights that are waiting for your understanding and implementation. Questions can yield powerful results and you are meant for the powerful results. One question I use often is: "Is what I am about to do going to get me where *I say* I want to go". This question helps me remain in my personal alignment and integrity.

*How* questions tend to open doors. Use them frequently. How can you continue your visionary journey with focus and a calm assurance? Questions keep the fire burning.

**Daily Application:** Today, ponder questions you use in your life. Are they helping you move forward or are they holding you back? Now, choose a motivation or clarifying question that you can use regularly. Practice using your question (or you can use mine) and see how it helps your focus.

**Personal Reflections:** _____
_____
_____
_____
_____
_____

## Day 258
# APATHY

*Apathy is a vice.*
~ Oscar Wilde

Apathy is a form of indifference that often appears lazy. Apathy comes when you are burned out on something and you do not seem to care any longer. It can also become evident when you are subjected to things that are overwhelming and you eventually shut down. Constant news that contains violence can create apathy and a disconnect within each person.

As you become more disconnected and apathetic, the power of the vice becomes evident in your flat affect, emotionless response to things that historically you acknowledged. To be free of apathy, evaluate how things in your life are serving you. When you experience a shutting down, stop and reflect so you can remain connected within more fully. There are too many people wrought with apathy. You are meant to be fully alive and connected, decline subjecting yourself to what which disconnects you.

**Daily Application:** In your daily quiet time, assess any inner apathy spots you may have. Ask yourself what steps you can take to become more fully connected and alive. It may require releasing something that is overwhelming on an inner level. Plan your strategy to become free of the apathy within.

**Personal Reflections:** _____
_____
_____
_____
_____
_____

## Day 259
# CONTENTMENT

*Health is the greatest gift, contentment the greatest wealth, faithfulness the best relationship.*

~ Gautama Buddha

My second book is a guide to contentment. To be contented is amazing. Too many people walk around discontent and struggle feeling the lasting pleasure of contentment. Buddha says that contentment is wealth. I never thought of it this way yet as I read this quote, it makes perfect sense.

When you are living your vision, contentment is one of the many exciting pay offs. It seems your blood pressure is healthier as is your emotional state. You are then wealthy. As your vision unfolds, have a blast and enjoy the satisfaction and gratification of following your heart's desire.

One of my youngest clients is struggling with being content as she told me she thought it meant complacency and being satisfied and therefore being done. She has great goals and did not want to stop. When we discussed that the gratification is an ongoing experience as she travels the road toward her vision, she began to look visibly relieved. Being content as you focus and act on your vision is powerful and inspiring. You are then wealthy.

**Daily Application:** Go within and feel your inner contentment level. Are you happy? Be still and allow yourself to relax. Now, are you content? Ponder how you can enhance your sense of being content. Document your answers and take action toward the goal.


**Personal Reflections:** _____
_____
_____
_____
_____

## Day 260
# EVOLUTION

*There is nothing noble in being superior to your fellow man: true nobility is being true to your former self.*

~ Ernest Hemmingway

Oh Evolve! This is my favorite bumper sticker. In fact, a client gave it to me on a key chain as a memento. You are different today than you were last week or last year for that matter. You are evolving every day with all your lessons and experiences. You know when you are truly evolving as a person when you are able to reflect on who your used to be and be compassionate and authentic. What was true in your earlier development may not be true today. Can you be real and compassionate to your former self?

Looking outside of you is the wrong place to look. Comparing yourself to others is not noble and in fact it hinders all involved. Your only real comparison is with your previous self as your grow into new arenas and territories.

As you evolve, do not expect things to be the same. Be true to you and embrace your natural evolution and growth. You will not pass this way again.

**Daily Application:** Go apart for a while today and contemplate your personal evolution and growth. Have you been stifling or are your flourishing? Take several deep breaths. Enjoy your progress and visionary road. Smile and be kind to you along your road.

**Personal Reflections:** _____
_____
_____
_____
_____

# Day 261
# RESOLUTION

*Always bear in mind that your own resolution to succeed is more important than any other.*

~ Abraham Lincoln

Your inner resolution is the most important part of your ultimate success. Without an inner resolution, the path becomes murky and any distraction can take you off course easily. To have resolve is to decide on a goal/outcome and the needed actions and feedback necessary to move you forward. Your personal resolution is the only real important one as Abraham Lincoln urges.

Great ideas without a resolve behind them are just that, great ideas. These often do not come into fruition as the idea alone does not have the inner power or the discipline needed for actual success. To go from ideas to results, having resolve is the defining ingredient.

**Daily Application:** Look at your challenges or stuck spots. Look within to determine where your resolve is in the situation. Are you expecting results from a good idea? Note 3 actions you can take today that will bring forth the resolution you want to meet your goals. Tell a supportive other and ask for support and accountability.

**Personal Reflections:** _____
_____
_____
_____
_____
_____

## Day 262
# CELEBRATION

*Creativity is a celebration of one's grandeur, one's sense of making anything possible.*
~ Joseph C. Zinker

I sailed on a boat named Celebration. The owner was a great, creative man. He taught so many by his welcoming spirit that was always creating something for everyone. He was an industrious type of fellow. He worked hard and was very intelligent and creative in his thinking. One thing I celebrate that he created was laughter. His great laugh and the humor he shared made every day a celebration. We all had a great time and his grandeur was evident.

Celebrating life and your personal grandeur is essential for your leadership. Your unique vision shows in the celebrations you share with others. It is time to celebrate your life and your milestones. Working all the time without celebrating does not serve you, in fact it adds stress and dims your inner light.

There are a multitude of ways to celebrate using your natural creativity. How do you celebrate? Are there ways you want to celebrate and haven't?

**Daily Application:** In your quiet time, vision your next celebration. Smile and see the great creativity that emerges from the celebration. Go out today and smile and celebrate your life.


**Personal Reflections:** _____
_____
_____
_____
_____
_____

## Day 263
# EXPRESSION

*Simplicity is the glory of expression.*
~ Walt Whitman

How you express yourself tells more about you than just about anything else. Your expression is in your words, clothing and actions. When you overly use adjectives or adverbs, you are complicating your speech. Often this expression can be cumbersome. There is value in simplicity of speech. I often tell my clients to deliver their message in 5-word sentences and no more than 5 sentences. Be simple and be powerful.

The same goes for clothing and actions in most cases. If you are a performer, then simplicity may not be part of your show. Shows aside, over doing the outfit or jewelry can hinder how you are received by others. The expressions that are over the top can lose their power.

In writing, be simple, clear and concise.

**Daily Application:** Ponder your preferred expression style. Be still and identify any ways you may want to simplify your expression. Breathe deeply and relax. Express simply.

**Personal Reflections:** _____
_____
_____
_____
_____
_____

## Day 264
# COMMITMENT

*To believe in something not yet proved and to underwrite it with our lives: it is the only way we can leave the future open.*
~ Lillian Smith

In what are you committed? Are you able to make a commitment and follow through? I notice that many people shy away from using the word commitment. I have a colleague who is generally committed to her views and ideas. She hesitates to use the word because she told me that she is afraid of being restricted in her options. It seems to me that commitment gives me the momentum to keep moving and to expand my future options and possibilities. We see this differently. I also notice the difference in opportunities that we both enjoy.

Nothing in front of you is proven. It is all a great opening that you can choose how you enter and pass through. Are you committed to your vision and your action plan? Are you hesitant due to doubt, fear or worry? It is time to begin to open your future by acting on your beliefs in a committed manner.

**Daily Application:** Breathe deeply, relax your jaw and drop your shoulders. It is a great time to become friends with your breath and your amazing future. Picture your vision unfolding and notice your inner dialogue and feelings. Journal your ideas and relax in the feeling. Choose actions that support your commitment.

**Personal Reflections:** _____
_____
_____
_____
_____

## Day 265
# POSSIBILITIES

*We must safely place ourselves in impossibilities in order to discover what is possible.*

~ Michelle S. Royal **


What is possible was once impossible, right? Before it was possible for you to walk, it was impossible. You learned to walk and now it is possible. Since you are reading this, it would appear that the learning to walk environment was safe on some level. The same process of moving from impossible to possible can be said about all the inventions and accomplishments over time.

As adults and people who have a desire to grow and transform, this quote is particularly applicable. The idea of safely placing ourselves in situations that are currently impossible in order to discover what can be made possible takes vision, grit, courage and perseverance. We are swimming in an endless sea of possibilities that we cannot even imagine until we grow into them safely.

You can only grow to the level of safety you feel. Being open and paying attention to safety physically, emotionally, mentally and spiritually is vital for your success, I enjoy stretching as I focus on ongoing transformation and growth. How about you?


**Daily Application:** In your quiet time today, ponder how you can choose to safely place yourself in an impossibility. Be open. Be willing. Be curious. This evening, write some notes about your awareness and journey today.


**Personal Reflections:** _____
_____
_____
_____
_____
_____

## Day 266
# ADVENTURE

*One way to get the most out of life is to look upon it as an adventure.*
*~ William Feather*

Yes. Life is a grand adventure. There have been times in my life when I could not see the adventure. Life seemed to be drudgery and maybe even a problem at times. Now, however, adventure is the word I would use to describe the amazing roller coaster with the scenic views of life. All the varied terrain and happenings make for a grand adventure.

Think about a vacation you have taken that you still fondly remember. It was an adventure. It stands out from the ordinary, right? What would happen if we all treated each day as a unique adventure? I believe that being open and bright eyed like when you are on vacation in a new place changes your life for the better. What great things are you missing every day? Let's get the most out of life and seek to see the adventure, even in the mundane.

**Daily Application:** Go into your day with an adventurous spirit and mentality. Notice how things are different. Get the most out of this day then journal how this practice has served you. Enjoy.

**Personal Reflections:** _____
_____
_____
_____
_____
_____

## Day 267
# INSIGHT

*Insight – There are no problems, only solutions in hiding.*
~ Mark Victor Hansen

Your insight into your vision and the road of unfoldment can help you make great decisions. What do you believe about problems, challenges and solutions? The words merely point to the meaning of an idea. Problems and challenges are simply outer reflections on your inner doubts. Your answers and solutions are alive within you at this very minute. Sometimes they seem to elude you because you may be more focused on what is wrong than the possibilities of what is right.

You are fully equipped with all your solutions. That is the good news. The bad news is that you may have to get dirty digging and unearthing your solutions that have been buried. Just like buried treasure, you know it is there. You must find your solutions and then bring them out of hiding. It is possible. You can do the excavating.

Developing insight is vital to your success and overall happiness. Your insight helps you make better decisions. When you are blinded or have limited insight, you can be fooled or mislead, and the results may not be favorable.

**Daily Application:** Are you aware of your inner solutions? Ponder this and be still. Listen to your inner voice and pay attention to the impressions that you experience. Take some deep breaths and look deeper within. Enjoy your journey. Journal your awareness and insight.

**Personal Reflections:** _____
_____
_____
_____
_____

## Day 268
# HONESTY

*Tricks and treachery are the practice of fools who don't have the brains enough to be honest.*

~ Benjamin Franklin

Honesty is an important value and behavior. People who use tricks and deceitful actions, according to Benjamin Franklin, are fools and they don't have the brains to be honest. This is a strong statement yet it rings true. Tricks cause betrayal and other consequence that prove that the person is not smart nor wise.

How do you show and express your honesty? How do you discern it in others? I imagine that openness and vulnerability demonstrate a level of authenticity and honesty. In a world where people think there are different honesty levels, it is most important that you come from your personal authenticity with aligned integrity. Telling the truth is only part of being honest. There are deeper levels of inner honesty that also show up I your world. If you find yourself making excuses, stop for a minute and check your honesty level, or have you been seduced into trickery?

**Daily Application:** During your quiet time today, look within at your personal sense of inner and outer honesty. Remembering that self-talk that is not honest is a form of dishonesty. Make appropriate changes to your self-talk that reflect self-love and self-care which is then honest.

**Personal Reflections:** _____
_____
_____
_____
_____
_____

## Day 269
# ELIMINATION

*Art washes away from the soul, the dust of everyday life.*
~ Pablo Picasso

The art of elimination makes things clean and clear. The good artist knows what to release or strip away from their work to add impact and feel. Art that touches your inner life has a way of cleansing away the static or stagnation. The cleaner the art, the more power to help clean away your inner cobwebs.

Everyday life can also become dull and covered in the film of monotony. To bring vibrancy back, art is the answer. Art in the form of visual or sound will work. Clean your inner life with some art and feel your soul spring to life!

I appreciate art that is simple and clean appearing. The simplicity refreshes my inner self and allows my soul some breathing room. How about you? What art, sound or visual or both, awaken your soul and cleans the dust away?

**Daily Application:** In your quiet time, notice the art around you where you are sitting. Does it clean the dust from your inner world? As you eliminate the dust, you come alive. Go forth and share your beautiful vision. Share your art with another.

**Personal Reflections:** _____
_____
_____
_____
_____
_____

## Day 270
# REJOICING

*Rejoicing in the good fortune of others is a practice that can help us when we feel emotionally shut down and unable to connect with others. Rejoicing generates good will.*

~ Pema Chodron

Today is a day to rejoice! When you celebrate the good fortune of others you as richly blessed. Sometimes, life gets going and things happen. If you get caught up in the race and pace of things, it is easy to turn off emotions and just keep going. I know people who are much like the energizer bunny and then they eventually run down. This is counterproductive and causes issues you do not want.

Rejoicing in the good and having that powerful vibe moving through you makes all the difference. You awaken in your core and you begin to feel alive and vibrant again. Celebrating others adds value to them and you. There is always room for more good will and celebration.

**Daily Application:** Spend a longer time in quiet today. Become excited about going forth and sharing your good will with others. Seek opportunities to become the bearer of a positive and uplifting presence. Journal your ideas.

**Personal Reflections:** _____
_____
_____
_____
_____
_____

## Day 271
# EXPLORATION

*Exploration is curiosity put into action.*
*~Don Walsh*

Successful people are naturally curious. Checking things out and asking questions are their calling cards. If you ask a lot of questions, that's an asset. When you use your curiosity to fuel your exploration of ideas and concepts, you are following your inner questions which will always lead to an exciting answer. Explorers brave the unknown to make it the known.

You are an explorer as a leader. Using your curiosity in your relationships as well as your academia is helpful in leading others. Be curious and explore their beliefs and how they came to them as well as what brings others joy. When these things are brought into the known, authentic connections result. Being willing to explore knowledge and connection with others takes action and risk. It is well worth it to reap the results.

Take time to explore your inner landscape. Be curious about your beliefs and inner workings. Act accordingly.

**Daily Application:** Let yourself become curious about your inner beliefs and knowledge. Now, go within and explore your connection to others, self and The Universe. Journal ways you can continue to explore your inner world and your outer world. Take some action.

**Personal Reflections:** _____
_____
_____
_____
_____
_____

## Day 272
# QUALITY

*Quality is never an accident; it is always the result of intelligent effort.*
*~ John Ruskin*

Have you noticed that quality seems to be dropping over the years? There is a planned obsolescence in what is being manufactured to keep us buying and spending. Where is the quality these days? Sometimes this is irritating and I have to really search for things that have quality.

Intelligent effort brings about quality in products and also relationships. Your relationships that have meaning and connection have come about as a result of quality effort. Both people have had to invest intelligent effort for the success to occur. Intelligent effort can be seen in the people who have attentiveness to building depth and have a long range vision. They think generationally. This type of visionary is a real asset because the longer-range plans are much more effective than short sightedness.

If you are a generational thinker, you might become frustrated with the short sightedness of others. Stay the course and believe in your strategy. In the search for quality, you will stand out and attract other quality people and relationships.

**Daily Application:** Reflect on your belief in quality. Do you invest intelligent effort to have more quality in your life? Notice the situations and people that you connect with and their quality. Share intelligent effort today. Journal your results and action plan.

**Personal Reflections:** _____
_____
_____
_____
_____
_____

# Day 273
# GENEROSITY

*I am in the habit of looking not so much to the nature of the gift as to the spirit in which it is offered.*

~ G.K. Chesterton

The spirit of giving is so amazing. Some of my favorite gifts are the handwritten poems or cards given to me by some of my clients who suffer with severe mental illness. When someone creates something from their heart and then gives it to me, I am touched and honored beyond words. Their generosity is so beautiful.

Giving from your heart and spirit has a quality and substance that enhances the gift. Things bought without much thought and given without the spirit have a lesser value than the ones that have the spirit within the giving.

Just yesterday, I received a handwritten note. Some of the spelling was interesting. The message was one of thank you and gratitude because I helped this person. The paper was not special and there was no envelope. This note is cherished by me because of the spirit of the giver. It brought tears to my eyes. I am so sentimental and when I can see the generosity and love that went into the note, that is what touched me so deeply.

**Daily Application:** What can you give that has spirit and soul? Develop a consciousness of spirit giving that enhances depth and connection. Keep supporting and encouraging spirit giving. This is authentic generosity.

**Personal Reflections:** _____
_____
_____
_____
_____
_____

## ¾ COMPLETE...

*Document your thoughts and experiences. Honor you and your journey. This is important.*

## Day 274
# HEALING

*We do not heal the past by dwelling there; we heal the past by living fully in the present.*

~ Marianne Williamson

We hear the message about living in the day and being present in varied ways and over centuries. This is the clue that this is vital to your health and well-being. When you have one foot in yesterday and one foot in tomorrow, you ruin today. To heal means to be made whole again; to reconnect to the source. This is a spiritual lesson that then translates into the physical body.

As long as you focus on intervention care, authentic healing will elude you. Being stuck in the past with resentment, bitterness and grief causes ongoing medical challenges. Living fully present in today begins to free your spirit and emotions and thus allows a physical healing to occur.

**Daily Application:** In your still and quiet time today, notice how much energy you have in the past. Now, lovingly bring your attention to the present. Dwell in the current and put the past in the past.

**Personal Reflections:** _____
_____
_____
_____
_____
_____

## Day 275
# DEVOTION

*Devotion is diligence without assurance. If faith were rational, it wouldn't be by definition faith. Faith is walking face-first and full speed into the dark.*

~ Elizabeth Gilbert

I was once told that I was devoted to helping others. This definition is true for me. I am diligent about my service and work and I have no real assurance of any outcome. My inner knowing and calling are guiding me so I follow the impressions that come through. Many of my ideas are not immediately rational. I simply can see that not all of life in linear and I must step out of the dullness to shine.

Taking action without assurance is like being non-attached. Being fully involved yet not holding on to any outcome. The outcome is not predictable anyway, not fully. Much of my work is not rational and it does not follow any certain pattern. I am devoted to living a life of service, wherever it may lead. What are you devoted to? How do you know?

**Daily Application:** Ponder the idea of being devoted and how it relates to your faith. Notice the aspects that are not rational. Celebrate your ability to be focused and not need to have assurance of outcome. Honor your devotion. Share some of your ideas.

**Personal Reflections:** _____
_____
_____
_____
_____
_____

## Day 276
# HUMOR

*Humor is an affirmation of dignity, a declaration of man's superiority to all that befalls him.*

~ Romain Gary

I love good humor! I love to laugh and I enjoy my friends who bring laughter into my life. When you can laugh in the face of difficulty, you are taking a stand that will serve you later. This does not mean to laugh at something or someone. It also does not imply emotional dishonesty. Humor is your way to rise above whatever comes along that could distract you from your vision.

My brother has amazing humor. He can laugh no matter what is happening. He taught his children to also have a sense of humor about life. This has served all of them. I struggled with humor in my teens and I started to get ulcers. When the idea of surgery was mentioned, I quickly found some humor to stop the damage. I did learn good humor and my intensity was rechanneled and all worked out well. My humor was my declaration of my triumph over the potential medical issues.

We all have great stories about how humor saved the day, right? Reflect on some of these and allow yourself to laugh as you remember. Share your humor freely. Appreciate others' humor.

**Daily Application:** After your quiet time, find something funny to do that will strike your humor. Smile and notice how humor has helped you move forward in your life and overcome your obstacles. Pass this along to another.

**Personal Reflections:** _____
_____
_____
_____
_____

## Day 277
# INDIVIDUALITY

*Let no man pull you low enough to hate him.*
~ Martin Luther King, Jr.

We are all individuals made up of the same amazing essence. We all have our own unique expression which makes things very fascinating and interesting. You are a deep and creative human. Others are also deep, complex and amazing as well. I find this to be fantastic.

When we want everyone to be the same, think the same and act the same, we are looking for a group of automatons. We are all humans, with unique natures. Your individual self is perfect and right on time.

When people become ignorant and afraid, they can sometimes make a real mess of things. Fear drives separation which does not honor the amazing power of being individually different while honoring the same energy from which we are created. Never allow anyone to get you to the point of such upset that you experience hatred. You will then actually also be hating that same aspect within you. We are all connected and individual at the same time. All that you wish upon or think of another also impacts you. Pay attention and do not be pulled down.

**Daily Application:** Spend quiet time and open your heart. Allow yourself to honor your individuality. Ponder any inner upset or discontent. See your reflection and offer humble compassion for yourself and the other. Then take right action. Journal your ideas.

**Personal Reflections:** _____
_____
_____
_____
_____
_____

## Day 278
# ANSWERS

*Dreams are todays answers to tomorrow's questions.*
~ Edgar Cayce

I dream in color, even when I am sleeping! Your dreams contain answers. Sometimes they do not make sense right away. Time passes and then they may become more obvious. Your dreams contain answers to your inner questions. Sometimes it takes interpreting yet still they are answers. I am thrilled that my answers often come in dreams and flashes that come when I am dreaming while awake. This is valuable to me, my growth and my clients.

You have questions you haven't yet formed. Paying attention can yield answers that you will use at a later date. This happens to me often. I will get the answer and it is often 18 months ahead of itself in linear time. Over the years, I have learned to wait and see how things unfold. Historically, I would get frustrated because I thought that the answer was to be used at once and my timing was horribly off base. Now, I allow life to lead me and I am poised as events unfold. I am much more serene now.

**Daily Application:** Be in a quiet place. Notice the answers and inspired ideas that are coming through for you these days. Smile and know that the answers will have their perfect time and place. No hurry. Document your answers for future use. Smile.

**Personal Reflections:** _____
_____
_____
_____
_____
_____

## Day 279
# DREAMS

*You are never too old to set another goal or to dream a new dream.*
~ C.S. Lewis


Age seems to be a focal point for ability and timing in many situations. When I challenge the idea of being too old (or too young for that matter), some people tend to make excuses. They believe the excuses yet out here, they make no real sense.

If you are breathing, then you are capable of dreaming the new dream and setting another goal. This is the true nature of life. If you stop dreaming and setting goals, you are setting yourself up to be controlled by outside forces which are a form of being imprisoned in someone else's vision.

I have a friend who is active and jovial. She is older than many of the people at her work. She sets goals and dreams and she has more fun than the others. My great aunt and I traveled together often. She would look at people younger than her who were discontent and say: "I hope I never get that old". She was young until she passed on in her 90's. Age can work on your side. Let your life experience and wisdom dream amazing dreams. Enjoy.

**Daily Application:** Close your eyes and dream about your future. Dream a new dream and allow your inspired thoughts to show you the way. Write your dream and be willing to move toward its realization.


**Personal Reflections:** _____
_____
_____
_____
_____
_____

## Day 280
# HAPPINESS

*Happiness is a direction, not a place.*
~ Sydney J. Harris


Are you happy right now? The place to determine that answer is within. Far too many people rest their sense of happiness on external situations, environment and people. Once you realize that your real happiness emerges from the inside out and is entirely independent of other people or circumstances, then your direction will reflect this inner state.

Today is the day to allow your authentic happiness to emerge more fully. Remember that happiness is the journey and there is no happiness-happiness land to visit. I know people who rest their happiness on external events, they always seem to be up or down and are the puppets of outside circumstance. This way of living seems exhausting to me.

To conserve your energy, make the choice to be happy from the inside out. Because your happiness is your flash light at night, let it show you the way!

**Daily Application:** Is happiness leading your life direction today? Spend some time in quiet, checking in with yourself. Now, any place where happiness is not leading the direction, breathe Joy into the space and let your resistance to happiness go. Let it go. Create an affirmation to remind you of your personal happiness direction.

**Personal Reflections:** _____
_____
_____
_____
_____
_____

## Day 281
# DOUBT

*I show you doubt to show you that faith exists.*
~ Robert Browning

Doubt is a real foe for many people. Visionaries, leaders and sensitives often struggle with doubt. I have a friend who struggles with doubt often. She has many gifts and she is aware of them. I often wonder what happens to her faith when the doubt emerges and sabotages her goals. She is a professional, gifted person with many talents. She often shares how she is doubtful and struggles with feeling like she can do things. She is known for her connection spiritually yet doubt sneaks in like an odorless smoke and wreaks havoc. It is faith that conquers doubt.

You can use doubt as it emerges as an avenue to demonstrate to yourself the faith you have in yourself. Doubt is common in many people. Faith is stronger than doubt. Isn't it time that you use doubt and a call for faith to come forward rather than giving doubt control and sabotaging your vision? It is time to put doubtful thinking in its place.

**Daily Application:** Take a few deep breaths. Do you have any lingering doubt? Take a couple more deep breaths and bring forth your inner faith. Allow the faith to transmute any doubt. Now, choose faith. Journal your thoughts and ideas.

**Personal Reflections:** _____
_____
_____
_____
_____
_____

## Day 282
## CURIOSITY

*We keep moving forward, opening new doors and doing things because we're curious and curiosity keeps leading us down new paths.*

~ Walt Disney

Questions, questions. Are you naturally inquisitive? Do you seek answers and want to know as much as you can about things that interest you? Being inquisitive sets you apart from the person who simply knows things. It is in your questions and inquiries that your unique leadership style is found. Leaders often are good question askers. Asking questions to determine the reasoning of things is the sign of a thinker who can also lead.

To be successful, it is important to have a great knowledge of your particular subject. To be a boss or leader you must be asking the inquiry questions that lead to the deeper understanding. Being able to answer the *inner* questions sets you apart from the experts who are doing and not leading. Curiosity bubbles up from your inner core.

**Daily Application:** Take some time and honor your knowledge base. Acknowledge the curiosity you had in order to amass your amazing knowledge base. Notice where you excel and lead. Journal how you use inquisitiveness to move you toward life mastery.

**Personal Reflections:** _____
_____
_____
_____
_____

## Day 283
# SELF-WORTH

*Doing for others what they should do for themselves, may be the kindest way to destroy their self-worth.*

~ Dave Kauffman \*\*

Learned helplessness is rampant. Too often, doing for others those things they could be doing for themselves is regarded as being helpful yet it is not helpful. In fact, it is hurtful. Essentially, what the person internalizes is that somehow, they are not enough so others have to do it for them. This creates many problems across our society. If someone asks for your assistance, by all means support them and assist. This does not mean do it for them. There is a big difference.

I know people who do their children's homework for them while pretending they are helping. These parents are sending an unconscious message to the child that they are unable. The child's self-worth will suffer.

You may think you are doing a good thing by covering for someone. This actually fuels self-doubt and a sense of not being enough. I believe that allowing others to do what is right for them and being available if needed is a much more healthy and productive stance. Let's build each other up rather than destroy self-worth.

**Daily Application:** Take time today to check your inner motives before doing something for someone else. Is there a way you can assist rather than do for them? How can you help them build confidence in themselves by your support? Now go do it.

**Personal Reflections:** _____
_____
_____
_____
_____
_____

Day 284
# SYMPHONY

*No one can whistle a symphony. It takes the whole orchestra to play it.*
*~ H. E. Luccock*

I love symphonies and the amazing energy of a full orchestra. There is such depth and variety that come together to create amazing music. I love the varied instruments coming together for the power, deep and rich sound. I think this is living life fully, enjoying the range, tempo, pitch and quiet of the transitions. Awesome I say.

When you control your experience or live life without the full use of your inner orchestra, things can become dull. Half measures do nothing for you. They actually make your life more challenging by creating an illusion of progress when in fact that is not the case. You are in control of your life and how much of you comes alive each day. Live with your entire symphony playing each part with precision. You will enjoy a much richer and deeper meaning to your life.

**Daily Application:** Take a few deep breaths and relax your jaw and shoulders. Imagine your day ahead and begin to see all the opportunity for vibrancy and richness. Now, check-in within and begin to allow that amazing energy to come forward. Create the music of your dreams.

**Personal Reflections:** _____
_____
_____
_____
_____

## Day 285
## OPEN-MINDED

*Life is only as hard as we make it based on our own individual, narrow minded perceptions. Free your mind and give yourself the chance of a lifetime!*

~ Lori Givens **

Being open-minded is one of the key components for a happy, successful life. When you are closed off from new ideas and inspirations, no matter the cause, you become like the Dead Sea. I usually refer to this malady as *the sleep walkers*. These people are moving about, much like robots, yet their minds are not alive and free.

We see the world through our own autobiography and we see what we are able to see based upon our perceptions, beliefs and motives. Are you paying attention to your own perceptions? Are you able and willing to challenge yourself to open new doors of perception?

Being open-minded requires a level of hope and faith in you and the world. Being open-minded helps you correct errors you have previously made on your journey. This is a key component for a visionary leader.

**Daily Application:** Make a note of the places in your life that are challenging or troubling. Write what you believe about these circumstances. Be open and ask another trusted person for their ideas. Without judgment or explanation, write their ideas down. Thank them. Then reread the feedback and ask yourself about the possibilities that they suggested. Try one and be open.

**Personal Reflections:** _____
_____
_____
_____
_____
_____

## Day 286
# DESTINATION

*Direction determines destination*
*~ Jim Rohn*

We all have destinations waiting for us to arrive. Yet we cannot arrive without first taking the initial step. By stepping forward, you begin to see the vast array of opportunities along your path. When you do not take that step, the opportunities remain just out of view. Because you cannot see them when you are at a standstill does not mean they are not there. It means that you are not moving so the landscape cannot open as you travel.

One of my sailing friends was talking about sailing into the horizon. That is a step. The horizon keeps moving and along the way are a multitude of opportunities. On this boat delivery, they had many chances to enjoy various experiences from catching a large tuna to using new sails and baking bread with the generator running at sea. Keep taking those steps!

Are you going to take the step that will reveal opportunities? Those who seize opportunities and are moving forward tend to enjoy a more rich, happy and successful life. Are you in?

**Daily Application:** Pay attention to the steps you take today toward your destination. Notice all the opportunities awaiting and choose which ones to take. Make it a great day.

**Personal Reflections:** _____
_____
_____
_____
_____
_____

## Day 287
# WANT

*Choices: The power we have to create the life we want.*
~ Carole R. Gill **

We all know there is a vast difference between wants and needs. We all have an idea of the life we want. Not everyone is fully aware of the power in the choices they make. Every choice in thought, word and action impacts your life's journey and what comes into your life. Your choices are what make up your life. They have creative power. Use this power wisely.

Your choices have great power. You can create great experiences or you can manifest your biggest fears based on the choices you make moment to moment. Your choices hold the power for your happiness and success. Choose wisely.

When you have a clear idea of what you want, you can align your choices toward that clarity. Herein lies your ultimate power of creation!

**Daily Application:** Pay attention to the choices you make today; the minor and major ones alike. Notice the power they possess in the events of your life. Journal some of your choices and insights.

**Personal Reflections:** _____
_____
_____
_____
_____
_____

## Day 288
# LEADERSHIP

*A leader is best when people barely know he exists, when his work is done, his aim fulfilled, they will say: we did it ourselves.*

~ Lao-tzu

Leadership is an art and a skill. The way you lead will impact the results you attain, no matter the project. Lao-tzu's idea about leadership is very appealing to those who are not ego driven and wanting personal credit for the team's efforts. Are you a leader that leads with a quiet authority, strong and capable yet not loud and dictatorial? Maybe you have experienced leaders who rule by force or fear. I have worked with and for those types. It was not fun. Though I did my job and did it well, I was never really satisfied or happy.

When you are living in your personal flow, you are the leader. This transcends any position or official authority. In any group of people, when a challenge emerges to deal with, you will find the leaders because the others naturally are drawn to them. Often, they are not the ones with the leadership title. Service oriented leaders tend to be the ones who become obvious over time and through thick and thin.

**Daily Application:** Journal today about your personal leadership beliefs and style. Are you a leader who leads with a quiet authority and gets the job done with the most harmony and focus? Are there any areas you would like to change? Today, notice various leadership styles and notice what is attractive to you.

**Personal Reflections:** _____
_____
_____
_____
_____
_____

## Day 289
# MOTIVATION

*Motivation will almost always beat mere talent.*
~ Norman R. Augustine

How motivated are you today? For me, motivation comes and goes at times and can be dependent upon the projects at hand. Some days I am highly motivated to do laundry and clean and other days, not so much. Motivation takes us a great distance in life. I have hired truly motivated people many times over the years and they have more often exceeded what their talent may have appeared. Motivated people, in my experience, tend to be more teachable and open to learning and progressing. Some people with expertise and talent can get stuck in a rut and miss opportunities and solutions that a motivated person may solve more easily.

Motivation is directly related to interest and desire. Being unmotivated is not a sign that something is wrong, it means that there is no real interest. Until you develop the discipline to do what is necessary even when you don't want to, you may look like an unmotivated person when really you are allowing your interest level to dictate your actions.

**Daily Application:** What motivates you? Reflect today on how your motivation changes or remains consistent throughout the day. How do your skills and talents impact your motivation? Notice this in others as well and journal your observations.

**Personal Reflections:** _____
_____
_____
_____
_____
_____

## Day 290
# KNOWLEDGE

*Discussion is an exchange of knowledge; argument an exchange of ignorance.*

~ Robert Quillen

Have you ever been in a discussion that may have looked like an argument to others? How do you determine the difference? For me, a discussion is an exchange of knowledge and points of view may vary yet the people involved listen, ask questions and dialogue about the topic. Arguments, for me, is when an agenda is being pushed.

I think Robert is saying that there is a big difference and that the arguments you are in tell on your level of ignorance. Are you willing to discuss varied points of view without pushing your agenda? This is the sign of a knowledgeable person that has their pride and ego in check. Just because you know something doesn't give you license to impose your knowledge on others. It does give you the opportunity to teach by your example how to use knowledge effectively. Remember, people know your real knowledge by your words and actions.

**Daily Application:** Listen to your many discussions today. Pay attention to the interactions of others. Are you seeing more knowledge or ignorance? How can you use your knowledge to promote discussion rather than arguments? Journal your thoughts.

**Personal Reflections:** _____
_____
_____
_____
_____
_____

## Day 291
# ENCOURAGEMENT

*Correction does much but encouragement does more.*
*~ Johann Wolfgang von Goethe*

This quote hits home. In my work, there are many opportunities for some form of correction that I offer my clients and co-workers. There are even more chances to share encouragement. Encouraging what is working is very powerful. You most likely respond better to encouragement than correction. When you grow your skills and natural assets and knowledge, then your success is assured. Your unique talents and gifts make you uniquely qualified for your success.

Rather than trying to learn and do what is not natural, expand and grow what is your passion. Stay aware of others who have complementary skills and visions. This is where great collaborations can occur. You are meant to live in the flow of your specific gifts and talents. When we all stay in our personal flow, the pieces come together for a greater whole.

**Daily Application:** Spend about 20 minutes in quiet time then make the decision to be encouraging to yourself and others today. Offer support and enthusiasm. Use encouragement to guide. Notice how your day unfolds. Journal your experience in the evening.

**Personal Reflections:** _____
_____
_____
_____
_____
_____

## Day 292
# UNDERSTANDING

*Your pain is the breaking of the shell that encloses your understanding.*
~ Kahlil Gibran

When you understand, you become calm. When you are anxious, angry or fearful, you are lacking understanding. Understanding is mental, emotional and spiritual in nature. There are different levels of understanding and each is part of your equilibrium.

Notice when you are not understanding and you are upset or confused. If you are sensitive, your emotions and sensitivities can take over which creates additional challenges. If you have someone in your life with these sensitivities, realize the understanding is essential for calm and balance to be present. The questions must be answered and support given.

Understanding is vital for you to thrive. Different people will understand you differently. You will understand life's events and circumstances on different levels. When you begin to feel anxious, take a few moments to seek understanding within the situation. Understanding may not come in one day. Seek it still.

**Daily Application:** In your quiet time this morning, take the time to be open to where understanding can help calm any area of your life. Maybe the understanding is in a belief system or something subtle. Pay attention to your responses when your understanding is not complete. Seek understanding and journal your progress.

**Personal Reflections:** _____
_____
_____
_____
_____
_____

## Day 293
# LOYALTY

*Love and loyalty runs deeper than blood.*
~ Richelle Mead

Blood is thicker than water yet love and loyalty run deeper. Loyalty is an interesting topic. Healthy loyalty can be powerful and awesome. Misplaced loyalty can cause turmoil, chaos and even harm. Loyal friends are a real treasure. If you are an inherently loyal person, I'll bet that you have been taken advantage of at times. I once worked with a person who was skilled at exploiting others' loyalty to use them then when she was done, cast them aside. The loyal people, and there were many, left harmed. As long as the person was loyal and not causing any waves, things were good. It this situation, the employer used the sense of loyalty to manipulate and control.

Healthy loyalty and love, does run deeper than blood. In my work with many people over decades. This has held true in many cases. Loyalty without good boundaries or some level of neediness attached can pose challenges in any relationship. Be sure your loyalty is healthy and not misplaced.

**Daily Application:** Spend quiet time today and reflect on your loyalty. To what and whom are you loyal? Who is loyal to you? Spend time in gratitude for healthy connections. Take a few deep breaths and relax. Journal your ideas.

**Personal Reflections:** _____
_____
_____
_____
_____
_____

## Day 294
# SPORTS

*I may win and I may lose but I will never be defeated.*
*~ Emmitt Smith*

Sports is an area that many bright and sensitive people excel. It takes a keen sensitivity on many levels to succeed in sports. Winning or losing the particular game is only a part for a successful athlete. There is so much more, like training, discipline and focus on desired results with massive action. As Emmitt says, win or lose, he is not defeated. To be defeated means that you are giving up. In sports, a defeatist attitude will not prevail.

In life, as well, being defeatist and seeing a loss of a segment in life as a defeat can cause great problems. Also, only focusing on wins and going from one win to the next win also causes problems. In life, as in sports, it is your attitude and your focus that create overall success. With the right attitude, you will never be defeated.

**Daily Application:** What is your focus today? Are your actions putting you in position to win? Journal the ways you are disciplining yourself for success. Use the sports mentality to propel you in life. Share your results.

**Personal Reflections:** _____
_____
_____
_____
_____
_____

## Day 295
# SEA

*We must free ourselves of the hope that the sea will ever rest. We must learn to sail in high winds.*

~ Aristotle Onassis

This is a true statement. The sea never rests, the waves are always hitting the shore. Some days seem calmer than others yet the sea is never at rest. We must free our thinking of the idea that things will stop for our convenience. Rather, being prepared for high winds is where the challenge lies.

As I have sailed throughout my life, I had to be prepared for the high winds. The crew that does not pay attention to weather changes or high winds on the way, often gets caught off guard and then struggles. Learning to sail in the high winds is about preparation and skill. It also means not to take things for granted.

The sea teaches a multitude of life lessons every day. We must be free of the hope that things will be different. It is best to learn to use the high winds to propel you forward.

**Daily Application:** Are you hoping that things will be calm? Take a few minutes and go within and check your hopes and dreams. Are you wanting the sea to rest? Are you learning to sail in high winds? Journal your ideas.

**Personal Reflections:** _____
_____
_____
_____
_____
_____

## Day 296
# LUCK

*Luck favors the prepared person.*
*~ Dave Moore* **

Luck has many meanings to different people. For me, LUCK means: Living Under Correct Knowledge. It is not something that is random or by chance. When I am lucky, it is because I am living under the spiritual laws and therefore things are aligned in my favor. There is no chance to it. When you are in alignment with the higher spiritual principles, you are putting yourself in position to receive. You must be prepared on all levels.

I think Dave has a great point here. Being prepared is vital on all levels when you want to be lucky. As a professional athlete, Dave lived this version of luck through his entire athletic career. I venture that he continues this mindset in his business and family as well. When others would say he was lucky, the truth was he worked diligently with focus and prepared himself. There is behind the scenes preparedness happening even when you cannot see it.

Luck, then, favors those who are aligned and preparing themselves in whatever manner is necessary. It is not happenstance as many might think.

**Daily Application:** Ponder any areas of your life that you would like to feel lucky. Now, create a plan to be prepared and aligned in order to put yourself in position to be lucky. Journal your vision and your plan to be prepared.

**Personal Reflections:** _____
_____
_____
_____
_____

## Day 297
# RELIGION

*We have just enough religion to make us hate, but not enough to make us love one another.*

*~ Jonathan Swift*

Religion is a charged word and much gets blamed on those representing religion. I think the issue of caring and loving one another transcends religion and blaming religion for the hate is a convenient way to shift responsibility for our personal words and actions. The religious wars of all kinds only fuel the hatred. Maybe a spiritually based solution could help elevate the love one another consciousness.

When you right fight, you are often acting from an underlying fear even if you are not aware of the fear. Religion is meant to bring people together in community. Just because someone has a different view does not make them your enemy. Difference and diversity is healthy as long as the boundaries are healthy and respectful.

Let's use religion to move toward love, kindness and compassion which includes healthy respect and boundaries.

**Daily Application:** Taking quiet time, ponder your connection to the idea of religion. Are your beliefs and connection serving your highest good? Journal your thoughts, ideas and emotions. Make peace with yourself and others so love can enter more fully.

**Personal Reflections:** _____
_____
_____
_____
_____
_____

## Day 298
# VENTURE

*The vision must be followed by the venture. It is not enough to stare up the steps; we must step up the stairs.*

~ Vance Havner

I love this quote. Do you have a vision for your life? It can be found within your heart's desires. Having a vision is great and it is a prerequisite to focused action toward your goal. To take on your vision with a sense of adventure creates the venture. When you block your vision from emerging, it keeps trying to come forth. In fact, it won't leave you alone. Look at your life. If there is a heart's desire that you are ignoring for any reason, see how it keeps making itself known to you so you will do something. The doing something to follow the vision is taking the steps of the venture.

Taking the steps is important. We live in an on-demand world yet this area of life still requires us to take action that is derived from the vision and focused on moving up the steps. What steps are you taking? Are they focused toward the realization of your vision?

**Daily Application:** During your quiet time and then throughout the day, check in on your venture. Are you stepping up your stairs? Are you allowing distractions? Are you wanting to go up someone else's stairs? Journal specific actions that take you up your stairs. Now, get stepping!

**Personal Reflections:** _____
_____
_____
_____
_____
_____

## Day 299
# BELIEF

*Belief is the magic key that unlocks your dreams.*
*~ Orrin Woodward*

Belief and having belief makes your dreams come alive. The difference between those with belief and those without belief is forward thinking and action. Take a moment and reflect on your dreams for your life. Notice how the areas where belief is alive, there is a sense of excitement and action. This is the magic that I think of as I read this quote. When you have a dream that you do not yet have belief in, it can seem far away or even depressing because your self-talk doesn't yet have the uplifting and magical belief language.

Belief is the difference between living your dreams and making excuses for not living your dreams. Belief transcends your fears and helps you move toward your vision in spite of your best self-sabotage moments. Those people you admire for following their dreams believed in them even when the nay-sayers were loud.

**Daily Application:** In your quiet time today, check in with your belief in your dreams. Are you experiencing the magic in your belief? Do you need a booster of belief? Journal about your dreams and your inner belief. Now, celebrate and remain focused.

**Personal Reflections:** _____
_____
_____
_____
_____

## Day 300
# WORLD

*Change your thoughts and you change your world.*
~ Norman Vincent Peale

Yes. You are a creative being and your thoughts change things. I learned many years ago, if you don't like your life, change your thoughts. Thoughts are things and have creative power. What you think about and speak, you are creating in your world. All your thoughts and words are creative equally. So, watch those commercial thoughts (I call them); those thoughts that are creating things and experiences that you do not intend for yourself.

Saying one positive affirmation while secretly thinking thoughts of unworthiness and fear can create a real mixed bag of results. All your thoughts are creative, even the ones you are not paying attention to at the moment. You can create the world you imagine and you must align your thinking and words.

Pay attention to your thinking. Are all the thoughts you have bringing you what you truly desire? Change your thoughts and you change your world, clearly stated yet not easy to do all the time. Therein lies our practice.

**Daily Application:** Spend time today really looking within to feel what you desire for your world. Now, align your thoughts. Write down what comes to mind and create simple phrases and commands that can keep you on track. Use them when you are distracted. Journal your experience.

**Personal Reflections:** _____
_____
_____
_____
_____
_____

## Day 301
# BRILLIANCE

*We are as brilliant as a billion shining stars.*
*~ Michelle S. Royal* **

When do you feel brilliant? Your inner brilliance radiates from you when you open your channels and allow your magnificence to come out and play! Think about the amazing light that is within you for a minute. Even in your struggles and darker days, that light is still shining brightly.

What are you doing with your brilliance? Are you hiding under the stress and strains of life or are you in denial that it exists or are you allowing your beauty to shine? As a visionary, your light and vision are necessary for the progress and healing of our world. Your light is a bit brighter and with a different hue than others.

I can feel and sense the brilliance in others who are visionaries on a mission. Maybe they can feel and sense my light as well. We are meant to come together and support and encourage one another to let our light shine. My support for your brilliance is unwavering and focused on the higher good for you and others. Shine on!

**Daily Application:** During your quiet time, take a few deep breaths. Relax and get in touch with your inner light. Focus on your brilliance and the avenues it wants to emerge. Now, do some fire breathing and fan the flames! Your brilliance is grand indeed.

**Personal Reflections:** _____
_____
_____
_____
_____

# Day 302
# POETRY

*The poetry of the earth is never dead.*
*~ John Keats*

Our Earth is poetry in motion. The flow and grace and intensity can be found everywhere. Notice how she is self correcting and has a rhythm of beauty. Sometimes she is fierce and sometimes quiet and gentle; all in the seasons and all in her prefect time.

That is how I read good poetry, enjoying the rhythm and the message of grace and poise. Our Mother Earth has been existing in perfect poetry and beauty for many years. She is wiser than the wisest human. She speaks to us in poetry. Are you listening?

Spring, summer, autumn and winter are poetry and beauty in motion. The earth is alive and vibrant as she heals and supports and moves through space. How are you poetry in motion in your life? How do you honor and revere Mother Earth?

**Daily Application:** Spend some time in nature. Enjoy the power and beauty. See the poetry. Write your feelings and thoughts and share your ideas. Dedicate some time to the care of Mother Earth and invite others to join you.

**Personal Reflections:** _____
_____
_____
_____
_____

## Day 303
# INQUISITIVENESS

*I have no particular talent. I am extremely inquisitive.*
~ Albert Einstein

Being inquisitive is a great gift. It seems that many talented people do not see their talents as readily as others. I'll bet you have talents and skills that you do not notice in yourself that others notice. Is inquisitiveness one of them? I have many gifted clients that are very inquisitive and they ask questions and explore nearly all the time. Inquisitive people are not only asking questions and exploring, they are also open to the information they are receiving.

My friend is inquisitive. He is always checking things out and learning new things. Every time we speak, he has some new information and insight to share. I love our conversations. His excitement inspires my inquisitiveness. It is a beautiful dialogue and dance.

Ask questions and check out subjects you find interesting. Take your questions to the next level and keep growing in your insights, awareness and knowledge. Remember to share. That's what Einstein did, right?

**Daily Application:** What are you exploring today? Maybe it is a new idea or some point of curiosity. Ponder your deeper thoughts and ideas. Invest in exploring today. Share your results in your journal and to a human if you wish.

**Personal Reflections:** _____
_____
_____
_____
_____
_____

## Day 304
## SOUL

*The soul always knows what to do to heal itself. The challenge is to silence the mind.*

*~ Carolyn Myss*

Your soul knows. Your inner, higher guidance is always whispering information, solutions and actions to take. Are you listening? When I teach meditation in its many forms, I always meet the struggle of quieting the mind. This takes practice and investment. There is so much noise clutter both inside your head and outside in the world that hearing your soul's whisper may be challenging. Initially, you may want to simply allow for small spaces to develop in your thoughts. Then move to more inner quiet. It is a process.

Listening to your soul is vital to your success. Notice how many successful people have a quiet type practice, whether it is yoga, meditation, hiking, bicycling or swimming. The common denominator is a dedicated time for inner quiet.

**Daily Application:** Be still and quiet often today. Allow your mind to quiet as much as possible. Spend time reflecting on your health and ask your soul for guidance. Listen and document your results.

**Personal Reflections:** _____

## Day 305
# KNOWING

*The only true wisdom is in knowing you know nothing.*
*~ Socrates*

Socrates challenges us to have a deeper knowing than the content that is found in our heads. A knowing is different than knowing something. For me, a knowing is a more existential and spiritual term for having a hunch or just knowing something to be true from the spaces in my inner wisdom. This is different than knowing something which implies content, intellectual information and linear knowledge.

Wisdom comes as a result of paying attention to lessons being learned and transforming and expanding your consciousness. Wisdom is the ability to evaluate, discern and apply what you know. The discernment requires an inner connection that is spiritual.

Your true wisdom comes in knowing that the mystery and the unknown is so vast that to pretend to know would be foolish. I have always heard that the more you know the more you know you don't know. There is always more. This is what is fun for me!

**Daily Application:** Ponder your inner wisdom. Be still and quiet for some time. Reflect on the vastness of your intuition and your knowledge base. Journal your awareness and insights.

**Personal Reflections:** _____
_____
_____
_____
_____
_____

## Day 306
# PROCRASTINATION

*Life is wasted in procrastination.*
~Epicurus

Procrastination is more common than you might think. It comes from several different sources and can be a real challenge. Procrastination can come from fear. Fear of not being worthy or fear of not getting it right are two of the biggest culprits. When you are procrastinating, you are letting fear stop your progress and connection to others. Essentially, you are wasting opportunity and possibility which is your life.

Procrastination is an issue that many people face regularly. Let's begin to take some action to reclaim more of our lives by focusing and acting more consistently. Notice how I said "our"? Maybe we all can support one another in moving toward a fuller expression of our visions when we support one another in taking proper action. I will support you.

**Daily Application:** Ponder those things that you have put on the back burner. Are you procrastinating? Are you making good excuses? How can you move forward by taking a few small actions today! Journal your ideas, take the actions and celebrate afterwards.

**Personal Reflections:** _____
_____
_____
_____
_____
_____

## Day 307
# HOPE

*Hope is being able to see that there is light despite all the darkness.*
~ Desmond Tutu

You are an amazing gift of light to the world. Your brightness is striking. When you enter the room, others experience hope. Hope is your bright light beaming and shedding light for others. This world can be dark at times and it is your hopeful light that can inspire someone to shine their light brightly.

Hope shows up after being opened to the beauty and possibilities that are presented to you by the Universe. Hope springs from the depth of your being as you connect to the awe-inspiring power that surrounds you.

The light is from you and me. Others are touched by this powerful light. That's why as visionaries, we may have to deal with resistance from the darkness. The push back is real yet we are called to keep shining and get brighter still. Be sure to remain connected with others who get you. It is a noble calling. I have hope.

**Daily Application:** Be still and connect to your inner knowingness and guidance. How can you shine brightly today? Share your hope frequently. Journal and document your experience.

**Personal Reflections:** _____
_____
_____
_____
_____
_____

## Day 308
# TEAMWORK

*The truth is that teamwork is at the heart of great achievement.*
*~ John C. Maxwell*

The "me" mentality is ineffective and simply doesn't work in the long run. Maybe for a short sprint, but no further. No matter your project, vision or focus, teamwork is the necessary ingredient for great achievement.

Many entrepreneurs seem to want to do things themselves. Too much of solo pushing makes for a tired and burned out person who could become bitter and resentful at the very thing they once loved. Even people who have one-person businesses need a team to move forward. Each person doing what they do best! Having others to share ideas with and create strategies for your vision is crucial for your happiness and joy!

I had a client who was trying to do everything alone and when we got some help for him in the right places, his business soared. His family life became better too! There are cascading benefits to focusing on your gifts and talents while having others focus on theirs.

**Daily Application:** Take a few deep breaths. Look at your life from a high perspective. Is there anything that you could get assistance with that could make everything better for all? Visualize and plan. Be open to opportunities to act on this idea.

**Personal Reflections:** _____
_____
_____
_____
_____

## Day 309
# CHARACTER

*Great minds discuss ideas; average minds discuss events; small minds discuss people.*

~ Eleanor Roosevelt

I have heard it said that gossip and talking about others is not only small minded but on the same frequency as murder. Wow. This seems harsh until you examine the message. What you say, you cannot unsay. What you hear you cannot unhear, right? Your character is revealed by what you are discussing. This is both listening and speaking.

When someone goes to speak, I often say to myself "You are telling on yourself." This means that I am clear that what someone says is about them, not anything else. So, using offensive language says something about you, right? Talking over people or being self-centered becomes obvious by how someone speaks. It is part of their character.

Make an inner commitment to discuss ideas. Keep building your character by associating with great minds. You are a great mind so shine your light and attract the others. You will do this by sharing your ideas and listening to other people's ideas.

**Daily Application:** Take time to honesty evaluate your speech and the things you listen to on a regular basis. Take some deep breaths and relax your mind and body. Ponder your choices and choose actions to build character by discussing ideas! Journal your ideas and decisions.

**Personal Reflections:** _____
_____
_____
_____
_____
_____

## Day 310
## FORCE

*Perpetual optimism is a force multiplier.*
~ Colin Powell

Force is a mighty strength. It can help plow through difficult obstacles. Force is used in many situations for the good yet some may want to cause harm. Here, let's talk about the force of optimism. When you are perpetually optimistic, it becomes a formidable force of its own. Think about it, consistently optimistic people have an amazing force that cuts through stuff with an ease that is wonderful to experience. Optimism seems to add to the force and creates new outcomes that may not have been seen previously.

A couple that I know demonstrated this idea of optimism being a force multiplier. Both of them are so optimistic. In fact, they say that this is why they found each other attractive. What I notice about their professional and personal lives is that any challenge is met with a strong, aligned optimism that seems to take care of the problem without much difficulty.

Being optimistic with alignment is mighty and it multiplies your strength in all situations. Who do you know that is optimistic in a perpetual manner?

**Daily Application:** What is your strength. Is optimism a part of your mighty energy?

**Personal Reflections:** _____
_____
_____
_____
_____
_____

## Day 311
# ABILITY

*Ability will never catch up with the demand for it.*
~ Malcolm S. Forbes

You are so talented and able. I'll bet you are someone who others look up to and say that they wish they could be as talented as you. Even with all your ability, there is still a demand for more. The world is ever expanding and the demand for more and more advanced ability keeps expanding as well.

Do you have a practice of regular reading or content learning every day? How about a regular practice of going within and accessing your inner guidance and knowing? How do you expand your ability on a regular basis? These are paramount questions for visionary leaders. We are charged with carrying the torch of knowledge, skill and ability. Leaders are always growing.

No matter how much learning and skill building you do, there will always be more demand and more need in the world. This is due to the expansion. You must also learn to pace yourself and trust that ability, demand and your roles will keep evolving and becoming more obvious every day. Support improved ability for yourself and others.

**Daily Application:** In your quiet time, ponder the demands for your abilities. Plan your course of action and how you wish to proceed. Now expand to the greater arenas of your life and journal your awareness and ideas.

**Personal Reflections:** _____
_____
_____
_____
_____
_____

## Day 312
# POLITENESS

*Rudeness is the weak man's imitation of strength.*
~Eric Hoffer

How polite are you? Being polite places you in the seat of authority in any situation. When someone is rude or emotionally out of control, they are showing their inner weakness. Being respectful and considerate starts within. You must first be polite and well mannered at home before you can demonstrate it in public. When you are stressed or under pressure, any rudeness may surface. To remain in your authority and therefore strong, being civil and respectful of yourself and others is a must.

When someone is rude, they are pretending to be strong. Under any rudeness or emotional outbursts is a weakness that is fueling the problems. Strong people can be seen being courteous and civil, even in challenging situations. There are healthy boundaries that strong people are good at enforcing.

Being polite is a desirable way to approach life. When you need to speak up or have to set firm boundaries, stooping to a rude level may not be your best action. Discern before acting or speaking and stay true to your inner beliefs.

**Daily Application:** Take some time for quiet throughout the day. Notice the energy difference from polite to rude in people you are around. Decide how you want to approach your life and the people in your sphere of influence. Act accordingly. Journal as you are led.

**Personal Reflections:** _____
_____
_____
_____
_____

## Day 313
# DISCOVERY

*The sure way to create new ventures of discovery is to keep an open mind.*
~ Charles Kettering

Be open. Be willing. It is your open mind that leads you toward amazing truths and awareness. Truly, you are on an adventure that has great discoveries on every corner. When I hear the word discover, I always think of a surprise just around the bend or hidden in an exciting place. The idea of discovery gets my curiosity and my thinking moving in great ways.

Visionaries love to create. You are able to imagine great ventures and discoveries and you are able to create amazing things from the visions in your mind. All this is discovery. You are discovering inside and in your physical world. Others get to discover along with you too.

What new things are percolating just under your surface? Go within and discover them and then share your magnificent discoveries!

**Daily Application:** Ponder your recent discoveries. Share some inspiration with others with an open mind. Explore your inner ideas with curiosity. Be still and journal your thoughts.

**Personal Reflections:** _____
_____
_____
_____
_____
_____

## Day 314
# MASTERY

*Mastering others is strength. Mastering yourself is true power.*
*~ Lao-tzu*

Self-mastery is a noble and powerful strength. We live in a culture that is so externally focused that they actually think strength is based on control of others. The real power and authentic strength starts within and then moves out. Master your inner landscape and world and the outer one comes right along.

We all have struggles managing our emotions at times. We either shut down or become overly emotional. Self-mastery is not as easy as it may sound. It takes dedication and consistent focus. The idea of mastering yourself goes back centuries and has been pursued by many notable and noble people in history. I believe that visionary leaders are uniquely positioned to develop great mastery and thereby be great beneficial influences in our world.

Let's live with authentic power rather than mere strength and force.

**Daily Application:** Spend your quiet time in nature or another relaxing place that varies from your norm. Notice your inner mastery when making a shift or change in venue. Ponder these ideas and choose your path moving forward. Strength or power? Journal your ideas.

**Personal Reflections:** _____

# Day 315
# THINKING

*We are shaped by our thoughts. We become what we think.*
*~ Gautama Buddha*

Thoughts are things. We are hearing more frequently these days this concept of our thoughts creating our lives. I find it noteworthy that Buddha was teaching this idea long ago. I believe it is true that we are shaped by our thoughts. Working with others and myself over many years, this seems to be evident in many ways. I believe that this Truth is part of the nature of our Universe.

Successful and happy people tend to use this Truth whether they are aware of it or not. You are in charge of your life much more than you may realize or fully understand. Just like gravity, you may not fully understand it yet it still exists and impacts your life continuously. Pay attention to your thoughts and watch how they create you.

**Daily Application:** Spend time today really paying attention to your thinking; both your primary thoughts and the secondary thoughts. Notice how your thinking colors and changes your perception and your world. Use your thoughts for your benefit today.

**Personal Reflections:** _____
_____
_____
_____
_____
_____

## Day 316
# SECRET

*Keep looking up... that's the secret of life.*

*~ Snoopy*

There is a secret to life. Keep looking up. Up toward the bright side. Up toward better days. Up toward the sun. There are many ways to look up. Looking up toward brighter days is a powerful way to live in hope. Snoopy was a great support for Charlie Brown. He kept the characteristic response of a lovable canine friend. Look at the fun or good and you possess the secret to life.

I have family and friends that live by this philosophy. Keep looking up. It is the secret to living a long and happy life. I came home a while ago somewhat stressed from the long day and the bad traffic. I was tired and probably somewhat heavy in my energy. I was greeted at the door by my lovable canine, tail wagging and toy in mouth. I immediately smiled and hugged her. We looked up and the secret to feeling great again came rushing back. She is the perfect reminder.

Looking up also activates your visual centers and takes you out of your kinesthetic center, thereby lifting your spirits. So, looking up has many uses both metaphorical and physical. Take it from Snoopy!

**Daily Application:** Take a few deep breaths and drop your shoulders. Loosen your jaw and look up. Notice your feelings change and a smile emerge. There is no accident. Keep looking up and the optimistic side of life will shine through. You hold the secret.

**Personal Reflections:** _____

_____
_____
_____
_____
_____

## Day 317
# EMPATHY

*Empathy is like giving someone a psychological hug.*
*~ Lawrence J. Bookbinder*

We all need hugs. The right hug with love and compassion can change lives. Empathy is a warm, loving hug. Having empathy means that you identify and feel with someone. There is an inherent level of understanding. Think of time you have felt understood. That feeling is usually warm and soft, like a great hug. That is empathy.

Earlier today, I had the privilege to meet with a new client. He was referred to me because most other mentors don't understand him and he was struggling with fears and anxiety. After our talk, he left with a smile and a spring in his step. When he shared that he was so happy that I understood him and he could relax, that was him receiving my empathy, my psychological hug so to speak. When someone is empathetic with you, can you receive it?

**Daily Application:** Notice how you respond when someone offers you empathy. How do you show empathy? Now, reflect on this and notice any inner resistance. Breathe deeply and free yourself from that static. Give yourself some empathy.

**Personal Reflections:** _____
_____
_____
_____
_____
_____

## Day 318
# VIBRANCY

*A vibrant inner life is far more powerful than a busy outer one.*
*~ David Romanelli*

Our lives are constantly being bombarded with stimulus trying to grab our attention. Some people are even addicted to being busy and moving all the time. Being busy can be a distracting drug. It zaps your energy and mental clarity and alertness. When I become busy for a long period, I notice my energy and vitality dropping. Being distracted by the outside world is not always in our best interest.

To be vibrant is all about depth, richness and a sense of aliveness that is above the norm. My inner life today is vibrant and it is what sustains me. Here is where my authentic power and energy are stored and ready to move! People notice when I am more vibrant than other days when they comment about my energy and my smile. I'll bet we could see this in you too.

Taking good care of your inner life is vital to your well-being and it far outweighs being focused on the external busyness of life. Go within.

**Daily Application:** Take some time apart for a while today. Nurture your inner world and add some color and texture. Spend enough time that you can feel your energy brightening. Now enter the rest of your day with a focus on maintaining your inner vibrancy. Journal your results.

**Personal Reflections:** _____
_____
_____
_____
_____
_____

## Day 319
# DISTANCE

*Only those who will risk going too far can possibly find out how far one can go.*
~ T.S. Eliot

I am willing to go the distance. I think this is in my nature somehow. Are you compelled to go the distance and take calculated risks? One of my colleagues takes lots of risks and once in a while, she goes a bit too far. She can share about the breaking points and when she knew she went too far and then how she recovered. She then goes the distance again and is willing to take risks based on her vision and drive to be of service. Her work and focus is admirable.

Are you one who stretches and risks or are you more conservative and not a risk taker? Most calculated risks can serve your progress and stretch you beyond your current ideas of how far you can go. Have you ever taken a risk and thought you wouldn't make it and you did make it just fine? I have.

Humans mostly underestimate how far they can go. A mother stopping harm from coming to her baby will go far beyond what she thinks. You, too, will risk beyond what you think and you will learn just what you can do under different circumstances.

**Daily Application:** What risks are you taking? Are you going the distance in bringing your vision into the world? Ponder just what keeps you going and what risks you are taking to go the distance. Journal some of your thoughts. Honor your focus and drive.

**Personal Reflections:** _____
_____
_____
_____
_____

## Day 320
# UNITY

*Talent perceives differences, genius unity.*

~ William Butler Yeats

We are all part of the one greater whole. We are all intrinsically connected. We all have many talents. They are often very different. When we come together, we are using our genius and therefore we are living in the one larger whole. I am an emotionally and spiritually intense person. I also have an intellect and athletic nature. My friend who is in the Air Force is very different than me. He has little emotional and spiritual intensity and he has high intensities in the other areas. We are very different. We both know and we honor the differences in our intensities and talents.

Unity is a coming together on the higher plane of awareness while understanding and experiencing the oneness of our connection to all that is. Genius tops talent in every situation because genius sees the connections while talent remains focused on the differences. The whole is greater than the sum of the parts.

**Daily Application:** Do some stretching and breathing to open your heart and spine. Breathe deeply and relax your mind. Connect to your inner genius and relax into the unity in spirit. Slow down and enjoy, then journal or draw your experience.

**Personal Reflections:** _____
_____
_____
_____
_____
_____

## Day 321
# EXPERIENCE

*Experience is the name everyone gives to their mistakes.*
*~ Oscar Wilde*

I have experience. You have experience. We have all made mistakes. Most of our mistakes are mis-takes. We were wanting to do well and the scene did not turn out the way we would like. You have a choice in how you view your mistakes. Seeing your mistakes as opportunity to gain experience can be very helpful. Using mistakes as an excuse and then calling them experience as a way to deflect responsibility can be problematic.

Oscar's intention is not completely clear is this quote. I choose to see this as a reminder to not cop out; rather gain as much experience from my mistakes as possible. I have personally been able to make gains in my life by taking my mistakes and learning from the experience.

Remember, every experience is valuable and not all experiences are mistakes.

**Daily Application:** Take a few minutes today and reflect on the ways you use this statement with regard to mistakes you may make. Do you assign the same meaning to others? Journal your thoughts and check to see how they align with your vision.

**Personal Reflections:** _____

_____
_____
_____
_____
_____

## Day 322
# CONFIDENCE

*If you have no confidence in self, you are twice defeated in the race of life.*
~ Marcus Garvey

Confidence in you is vital for your happiness and well-being. Confidence means you can trust yourself and you have an inner conviction. Without this inner assurance and belief, you are running an all uphill race. You will become exhausted and eventually slow down or stop.

Do you have confidence in yourself? Do you appreciate and respect your inner qualities and gifts? I believe that the more you appreciate your own abilities, the more confidence you have in yourself. This appreciation and belief are what create success and happiness.

I have confidence in myself. I deliver what I promise to the best of my ability. I am not perfect. Confidence is more about the credence and conviction that I have in my focus, talents and abilities. My confidence helps me succeed and serve others well.

**Daily Application:** In quiet today, breathe into your inner confidence. Are there any weak spots or questions? Focus on strengthening and building your inner confidence. Breathe and sit in stillness, creating your inner view. See yourself leaving defeat in the dust!

**Personal Reflections:** _____
_____
_____
_____
_____
_____

## Day 323
# ART

*In every work of art, the artist himself is present.*
~ Christian Morgenstern

Your life is a masterpiece. Are you signing autographs yet? With everything you think, do and say, you are creating the amazing masterpiece that is your life. Carole King called it a tapestry. Sometimes your art is in textiles and another time watercolors or oil paint and yet another time in the theatre or in your writing. In every scenario, you are the artist and you remain present within the art. This is the beauty. You get to know the artist through their work.

People get to know you through your art. In whatever way your art shows up, it is art just the same. Musicians are known for their art and painters for theirs. What is your art? I have a client who is known for her smiles and jovial attitude even in challenges. This is her art. She struggles to see herself as an artist when I can see it so clearly. I think it is her definition of what constitutes art.

Your life is a living work of art. What are you creating?

**Daily Application:** You are interwoven in your own work of art. If you create art outside of yourself, you are present within the piece. Your life is a living, breathing masterpiece in the making. Be present in this creation. Breathe a bit today and spend some quiet time in creating mode. Go create!

**Personal Reflections:** _____
_____
_____
_____
_____
_____

# Day 324
# RESENTMENT

*You can resent your bald spot or be glad you have a head.*
*~ Paul Pearsall*

Resentment is a word that has a strong emotional charge for many people. Resentment means to re-feel a bitter type of indignation. This can be common when you don't get what you want. Do you quietly resent things in your life? It there a low-grade bitterness growing because things aren't the way you imagined? Resentment steals your joy and happiness. You end up angry and alone. Resentment is toxic.

The alternative is gratitude. Being grateful for what you do have and that you are alive is a great start. As in the quote, you have a choice in each moment, resentment or gratitude. Several of my friends can sometimes express resentment when things are not turning out as they would like. They call me Pollyanna when I speak to gratitude. I simply know that when I let bitterness and resentment color my daily life, I end up sad and upset. So, I focus toward gratitude. Sometimes I have to consciously change my mind and other times it is much easier. What about you?

**Daily Application:** Take a few long, deep breaths. Is there any bitterness or resentment in your emotions? Do you feel saddened somehow? What is there to be grateful for today in your life? Can you replace your bitterness with gratitude, just for today? Journal you progress and your ideas.

**Personal Reflections:** _____
_____
_____
_____
_____
_____

## Day 325
# INERTIA

*Life leaps like a geyser for those who drill through the rock of inertia.*
*~ Alexis Carrel*

When you are in motion, it is easier to remain in motion. When you are not moving, getting going seems really difficult at times, right? Doing nothing makes it easier to do nothing. I have heard it said that if you want something done, ask a busy person. This makes total sense to me. Once moving, keeping going is much easier.

When you awaken and get going, life jumps up and greets you. When you drag yourself out of bed and sit, it is harder to get going. It makes the beauty of life seem elusive somehow. When I changed from dragging myself out of bed to jumping out of bed and doing something, my entire world changed. My attitude lightened and opportunities showed up all around me. Once I broke through the inertia, I was off and running!

When you are wanting more opportunity and happiness, get up and greet the day by getting going. I think that is why so many motivational speakers say to get up and make your bed right away and get going. Your movement favors you with an advantageous outcome.

**Daily Application:** Set your intention to get going and keep moving. This does not mean to exhaustion like a machine. It means on purpose with a focus, remembering that part of moving includes the rests and spaces for creativity. Journal some of your amazing ideas. Take action.

**Personal Reflections:** _____
_____
_____
_____
_____

# Day 326
# SUFFERING

*Suffering is part of our training program for becoming wise.*
~ Ram Dass

Life is messy. It is not all peaches and cream. Wisdom has a price tag and suffering often is part of the price. When I ask people about the events and happenings that have really impacted their life, they always share a story of deep pain that includes some level of suffering they have walked through. They all say they are better and wiser because of the event. I think this is because the depth of pain breaks open the inner walls and out of the mess is the beauty that has been trying to be freed all along.

You have the ability to transform and grow by walking through your pain and moving past the story and into a place of wisdom. Holding onto the suffering like a badge does not serve you. Within any suffering are the seeds of hope. Allow those seeds to grow.

**Daily Application:** Ponder today your victories over suffering in your lifetime. Ponder today the wisdom you now possess that previously did not exist. Take some time to offer your wisdom and encourage another.

**Personal Reflections:** _____
_____
_____
_____
_____
_____

## Day 327
# STRESS

*Stress is caused by being here and wanting to be there.*
~ Eckhart Tolle

Are you living in the past or the future and not being fully present today? Some people even spend more time in their imagination about how things should be than they do on actually doing them. All these separations cause stress and ultimately pain. Like I have heard, over and over, if you don't like something in your life, make a change, you are not a stature or a tree. Eckhart Tolle speaks about being in the now moment. After all, whether we believe it or not, we are living in an eternal now moment.

You can create stress for yourself by wanting and wishing you were somewhere different. You can become open and receptive to your current life. Being willing to be receptive to the moments as they move along creates a flow for you. Let's live in the flow!

**Daily Application:** Take some time in quiet, breathing deeply and allowing the stress in your body to begin to melt away. Focusing on your breath, relax. When you are ready, move into the day and keep breathing with full deep breaths!

**Personal Reflections:** _____
_____
_____
_____
_____
_____

## Day 328
## MANAGEMENT

*Management is not a science, it is an art.*
~ Michael Eisner

Management involves people most often. We are all amazing and fascinating creatures and thus do not follow straight forward linear logic. Management is more of an art form than a linear, rational science. I always smile when I hear some of my linear clients talk about their struggles when managing because what is eluding them is the human connection part.

Interesting how often people are promoted for excelling in linear, problem solving skills yet when it comes to management, they need more people skills than linear skills. I am sure you know exactly what I am talking about. You have probably been on one or both sides of this situation.

When you are being a great manager, you are involved with the people first, this is an art. People have emotions and ideas and histories. Some are sensitive while some overthink while some need reassurance. To focus on the people and the tasks simultaneously and being able to place the right people on the right assignment, now that's the skill that awesome managers have mastered.

**Daily Application:** Take some time apart today and ponder your unique management art. How do you engage and inspire others? What do you call your art form? Journal some of your ideas.

**Personal Reflections:** _____
_____
_____
_____
_____
_____

## Day 329
## PACIFISM

*There are causes worth dying for but none worth killing for.*
~ Albert Camus

Settling disputes peacefully is wonderful. Pacifism is a paradigm that does not condone violence under any circumstance. Some people feel so strongly that they will not engage in any fight because of the violence. Peaceful demonstrations are part of the ways they get the attention of others.

This does not mean the person is weak. In fact, the person must be strong to decline falling into the heated energies of anger, hatred and fear. To choose not to fight is much harder at times than fighting. I know people who think that pacifism means being weak. I do not agree. Inner strength is required to take a stand without violence.

What are your thoughts? Do you agree with Albert or not? This is a day to ponder your own inner beliefs and how you are living them.

**Daily Application:** In quiet, contemplate your beliefs around violence and confrontation. Remember this is not a right/wrong dialogue. As you become clearer about your inner beliefs about these matters, you are able to discern better decisions and actions for your welfare. Journal your ideas.

**Personal Reflections:** _____
_____
_____
_____
_____
_____

## Day 330
## VACATION

*Every time you make someone laugh, you've given them a small vacation.*
~ Joan Rivers

I love this! Think about it, when you are laughing, you are somehow taking a break. In my work, my greatest joy is being with someone when they smile for the first time after a long difficult period of their lives. Hearing them laugh makes my heart sing and then I laugh with them. In that moment, we are on vacation from the stuff of life. That relief makes all the difference.

Joan Rivers made us laugh. I think this is one of the many draws toward comedians and funny videos. We get a break for a minute from whatever is going on. How do you create laughter for yourself and others? Do you use your humor to make others laugh and have a mini-vacation?

I even have vacation friends. These are friends that bring me such joy that I laugh often and have the chance to forget the day. Just a few hours with them and I am renewed and refreshed. I love my mini-vacations with my vacation friends!

**Daily Application:** Take a mini-vacation today in the form of laughter. Create humor for another and laugh together. Be sure not to laugh at the expense of another. Now set you intention, mark your calendar for laughter each day!

**Personal Reflections:** _____
_____
_____
_____
_____
_____

## Day 331
# CONTEMPLATION

*The contemplation of beauty causes the soul to grow wings.*

~ Plato

Contemplation is a favorite of mine. Looking within and contemplating adds depth, insight and power to my life. Through contemplation, I soar and am alive in possibilities. Reflecting on my goals and vision gets me ultra-focused. I like what Plato says because sometimes it does seem as if I am flying. My path seems so effortless while I am in my contemplative space.

Contemplate the possible consequences of your vision and actions. Realize that there may be unintended consequences to your actions. Use your gift of inner inspection to help you discern your highest road.

When do you contemplate? Some use contemplation as a form of prayer. Other use contemplation in their studies. In these cases, the inner self has more freedom to soar. However, some use contemplation to avoid action and this can be a great stall tactic that can yield frustration or irritation. Be aware of your motives and the timing of your action. Use the power of contemplation to serve you rather than fuel doubt.

**Daily Application:** Spend your quiet time today in contemplation. Pay attention to your inner dialogue. Notice your inner messages as your mind quiets. Remain in contemplation for at least 20 minutes and then journal your insights.

**Personal Reflections:** _____
_____
_____
_____
_____

Day 332
# CITIZENSHIP

*I am not an Athenian or a Greek, but a citizen of the world.*
~ Socrates

Socrates had an idea about citizenship. He was taking a stand that citizenship was geography independent. He was declaring that he is a citizen of the world. I believe he was asserting that some of the divisions among people were unnecessary when you realize that you are a citizen of the world. Since citizenship refers to being a member of a community, why couldn't it be the world? What is the need for so much division?

Fear attracts separateness and division. Then comes the conquering and demise of the beauty of a larger citizenry. Socrates also spoke about being an educated citizen. When you experience yourself part of the larger group, your choices become much more plentiful.

Are you a citizen of the world? How do you describe your connection to the larger community? How expansive is your perspective?

**Daily Application:** Ponder how you relate to your citizenship. Breathe deeply and allow your inner vision to expand farther and notice your emotional experience. Release fears and resistance. As you expand, take a breath and notice all your insights. Draw or journal your experience.

**Personal Reflections:** _____
_____
_____
_____
_____
_____

## Day 333
## POVERTY

*Poverty was the greatest motivating factor in my life.*
*~ Jimmy Dean*

Poverty comes in many forms. There is poverty in finances and money. Poverty in relationships, ideas and action abound. There is also poverty mentality. This mentality is one of the most powerful restrictors of happiness that I have seen. Poverty mentality is the belief that there is not enough and there won't be enough to go around. It is an extension from the Great Depression and other recessions along the way. Poverty mentality keeps your good away from you.

Being poor in mind and spirit creates poverty in the physical. If you secretly believe you are not enough or worthy enough to receive the good life, you will sabotage it every time. Poverty leaves as you come into who you are meant to be living your vision. Yes, poverty is a strong motivator. No one likes to be or feel poor, right?

**Daily Application:** Ponder your flow of abundance in your life. Notice the blocks. These are the places where poverty of some type has lodged itself. Take the time to kick out those low beliefs and thoughts. Replace them with beliefs of being a blessing. You will then be blessed. Journal your ideas. Create an abundance affirmation.

**Personal Reflections:** _____
_____
_____
_____
_____
_____

Day 334
# IDEAS

*The difficulty lies not so much in developing new ideas as in escaping from old ones.*

~ John Maynard Keynes

You have ideas in abundance. The ones who are outside of the box are great. I am a visionary leader who has no real box. A client once told me that when it comes to pushing the envelope, I have no envelope to push. I think he was sharing a truth that at the time I thought was funny yet did not fully see. Escaping the old ideas takes free thinking, paradigm shifting and expansive understanding. It is difficult. I was working with an artist on some art for advertising a few years ago. She was a great artist. Once she came up with an idea, all her subsequent versions were along the same lines. She struggled with escaping her old ideas. This happens to all of us from time to time.

     I practice taking in varied information in varied formats to keep my thinking and brain pliable and open. I am predictably unpredictable which allows for more new ideas and less restriction from old ideas. Do you have a plan and strategy for escaping the old and bringing in the new?

**Daily Application:** Take some quiet time in nature or another different place. Breathing deeply and reflecting on your vision that started with an idea. Ponder any places that expansion could enhance or support your heart's desire. Write and/or draw your ideas and their relationship to one another. Escape from what is limiting you from within!

**Personal Reflections:** _____

_____
_____
_____
_____
_____

## Day 335
## RESPONSIBILITY

*The attitude we hold towards ourselves can either heal or keep us separate. Changing our mental habit patterns is our individual responsibility.*
~ Ruth Toledo Altschuler **


Each one of us is responsible for our own thoughts, words and actions. Your life is a perfect reflection of all your experiences, beliefs and actions. The good news is that any changes you want to make can be made by taking responsibility for where you are now and then being personally responsible for your changes. All your actions and attitudes either support your goal or distance you from the goal. There is no middle road.

By changing your mental habits and self-talk, you begin to change the trajectory of your path. Over time, your new results create a new history. You are always creating so you can change your mind at any time! By being responsible you succeed and are free to live your vision.

Changing mental patterns and habits is not always easy. Focus and determination are essential elements. Focus your mind on healing any separation. Take responsibility for what is happening between your ears! No one makes you think anything. You are the thinker behind the thoughts.


**Daily Application:** Take the time to pay close attention to your thinking and your attitude. Are you being supported? Notice how your thinking is reflected in your life experience. Ponder any adjustments you wish to make. Begin now. Journal your commitment.


**Personal Reflections:** _____

_____

_____

_____

_____

_____

## Day 336
## SOCIAL INTELLIGENCE

*You can't take the "high road" on a high horse.*
*~ Matt Kahn*

This quote says so much. Authenticity is one of the most respected traits and for good reason. When you are real, you are using your social intelligence to connect with others in the right and perfect manner for the circumstance. Being socially intelligent is the trait of someone who is doing what is right for the sake of doing the right thing. Socially intelligent people also take the "high road" as not to engage with toxic, destructive people and situations.

Pride enters your life on a high horse. It offers the illusion of being better when really underneath you are experiencing fears of not being good enough. That high horse actually pushes others away and creates discord. It is not socially intelligent. If you want to influence or lead others, taking the high road is much more powerful because you are not turning people off along the way.

Social intelligence is becoming more challenging to find in people. When some people only engage with others electronically, their social intelligence is impaired. It creates a false high horse and perpetuates separation which undermines self-esteem and confidence. Take the high road of kind connection and you are richly rewarded beyond your imagination.

**Daily Application:** Ponder your level of authenticity. How do you experience your own social intelligence? Are changes in order? Journal your ideas.

**Personal Reflections:** _____
_____
_____
_____
_____
_____

## Day 337
# REPUTATION

*You can't build a reputation on what you are going to do.*
*~ Henry Ford*

I have a few clients who give themselves credit for doing things on their to do lists because it is on the list and not actually completed. We work frequently on the idea that knowing you have to do it and doing it are two different things entirely. Henry Ford had a point.

Your reputation is what others think about you and therefore can trust about you. If you are a talker and not a doer, then that is what they will think about you. Leaders are typically action takers so they build that reputation regardless of circumstance.

Taking action on your ideas builds a reputation just like any other consistent behavior or way of interacting. One of my clients has a loud voice volume. She laughs so loud that it can be offensive. She was unaware that many of her family and friends distanced themselves because of her voice volume. She was not angry, just loud. This has caused her much heartache as it created a reputation she did not want.

**Daily Application:** Ponder what your reputation is among your peers. Are you happy with how you are showing up in the world? Take some quiet time to reflect and commit to any changes you may want to make. Honor what is working.

**Personal Reflections:** _____
_____
_____
_____
_____
_____

## Day 338
# GROWTH

*The key to growth is the introduction of higher dimensions of consciousness into our awareness.*

~ Lao-tzu

Growth and personal development are common topics in today's world. Webinars, books, podcasts and more are ways to obtain the information you may want. I believe that Lao-tzu had the right idea. Without higher dimensions of consciousness being allowed into your awareness, actual personal growth cannot occur. New information that does not elevate your consciousness is nice, yet it does not yield authentic growth.

Growth on a personal level has many facets. Your inner luster and your higher awareness will yield a feeling of being lighter somehow. You are elevated from the mire and static of the everyday mundane existence. You must however, be willing to explore higher dimensions and to seek the currently unknown for growth to take root deep within your being.

As you become curious about your personal growth, introduce yourself to higher dimensions. Seek to learn and integrate new and you will feel new.

**Daily Application:** In your quiet time, ask the question: "What higher knowledge will help expand my consciousness today?" Listen for that inner prompting to learn something new and practice the idea. Write your awareness and ideas. Keep going each day.

**Personal Reflections:** _____
_____
_____
_____
_____
_____

## Day 339
# RESULTS

*Your positive action combined with positive thinking results in success.*
*~ Shiv Khera*

What results are you seeking? For many on a transformation or healing path, they have an idea of what they are seeking. I always say that nothing turns out the way you imagine, so create and vision from within and always hold room for something different, more or better. It always works this way, with focus and action, your results will transcend your initial vision.

Positive action and positive thinking mean that you are aligned and focused toward your inner vision and heart's desire. Taking action toward your goals is a positive action while being distracted and taking ransom action is considered to take you away from your goals. Successful people pay attention to make sure that their actions and thinking align with their stated vision and goals. This is how you become successful in any and all life areas.

**Daily Application:** Take some quiet time and ponder your personal operational definition and criteria for success and what results you are seeking. Write your ideas down and check in with them throughout the day to see how your ideas are lining up to your actions. Be willing to be aligned by making changes.

**Personal Reflections:** _____
_____
_____
_____
_____
_____

## Day 340
# TEMPO

*If you can't play it, it's not meant to be played.*
*~ Paul ILL \*\**

There is a tempo to the flow of life. Each one of us has our unique tempo. There is a rhythm and a groove that is always playing. The question is whether you are in tune and keeping the tempo. When you are not up to playing a certain melody for your life, it is not meant for you. There is no right or wrong, there is what works best for you and serves the higher good.

Many musicians are tuned in to the tempo and rhythm of the music they are playing. If they cannot get the groove to work, then wait they must for the inspiration to reignite and they can then move forward. When the playing is overly difficult and can't be done at any point, it is not meant to be performed at that time.

You cannot play all the songs. You can play your songs well and the others may take time and stretching. You may never be meant to play the other tempos. I work with a musician who is best categorized as a country/ballad musician. She struggles when others ask her to play a jazz piece or a rock piece. She may be able to stretch but she will not be fully comfortable. She is meant to play country ballads.

**Daily Application:** What is your tempo and rhythm? Sit quietly and allow your inner song to be heard. Go forward and play your song. Enjoy your personal tempo. Draw your experience of playing your own song.

**Personal Reflections:** _____

_____
_____
_____
_____

## Day 341
# REBIRTH

*A rebirth out of spiritual adversity causes us to become new creatures.*
~ James E. Faust

How many rebirths have you had? I have had many and I venture to believe I will have more. Spiritual adversity comes in many forms. It surrounds who you are and what you are bringing to the world, your sense of purpose, living your heart's desire and connection to who you are, really. As we are invited by life to grow and expand, there are many deaths and rebirths along the way.

One epiphany can change everything in your life and turn it upside down. Going from believing you are inherently bad to believing you are a blessing can cause a death of the old and a rebirth.

We are new creatures as we grow and expand and shed the old. Sometimes it takes adversity to get you out of your comfort zone so you can see a higher truth about you. This can be painful, scary and exhilarating all at the same time. Being born again as we grow is normal. What was true in your early years is most likely not true now. It is ok. This is the process.

**Daily Application:** We experience many rebirths are we grow spiritually. Ponder your personal journey of your connection to who you are and your purpose. Now, honor your path and all your rebirths.

**Personal Reflections:** _____
_____
_____
_____
_____
_____

## Day 342
# WORLD PEACE

*What can you do to promote world peace? Go home and love your family.*
*~ Mother Teresa*

World peace seems so big, right? Some would say it is impossible so they do not even consider the possibility. Some blame others for the lack of world peace and never look at themselves. Some think that giving love to others without looking at themselves will bring he peace. Mother Teresa suggests that peace begins at home and emanates from there. The peace must first be at home and then it spreads.

Again, we are being instructed that our world is best when we act from the inside out. As long as we are focused on others, progress is hindered. We are living in an ever-expanding Universe. Beginning at home is critical for success. Love your family of which you are a member. Looking to others to blame or to do this for you simply will not work.

World peace begins at home with each of us. As human beings, we are called to shine our lights and to begin within ourselves and our homes. Then we come together for an even greater good.

**Daily Application:** Ponder world peace. Allow your heart to emanate the love that is you. Love yourself and your family and friends. Share with healthy boundaries. Write a love letter that inspires your inner peace to come forth.

**Personal Reflections:** _____
_____
_____
_____
_____
_____

## Day 343
# LOGIC

*A mind all logic is like a knife all blade. It makes the hand bleed that uses it.*
~ Rabindranath Tagore

When you live from the neck up, you are causing harm to yourself. We are beings that have many diverse facets that are meant to come together for the greater whole. Your thoughts and intellect are beautifully complemented by the power of your emotions, the vibrancy of your spiritual connection, the inspiring social connection and the amazing functioning of your physical body. Living from logic only cuts apart all the other amazing parts of you.

I know many people who are afraid of their emotions. They end up erupting and causing great pain because they were never taught about the amazing power of all of them. I think it is tragic to live in one small aspect of yourself. It is time to awaken and appreciate all of who you are. Logic is one great piece. It is not the whole. It is time to stop the bleeding.

**Daily Application:** Be still and quiet for a minute. Can you feel your heart beating? How about breathing, can you feel the air coming and going? Logic doesn't control these things. It is time to stop taking them for granted. Ponder your awesomeness and release your reliance on logic alone. Journal your ideas.

**Personal Reflections:** _____
_____
_____
_____
_____
_____

## Day 344
# EXUBERANCE

*Spring is nature's way of saying "Let's Party!".*
~ Robin Williams

Exuberance is such a great word. It sounds as fun as the meaning. It is alive and vibrant. Spring is alive and vibrant. Everything is coming back to life in full color. I resonate with this quote of having a great celebration. Our Earth has glorious seasons and they unfold right on time, without human orchestration! Spring is the party season for nature.

When you do feel your exuberance? Early morning, later afternoon or in the middle of the night? When do you come out of hibernation and spring to full lively adventure? When you are exuberant, you are more cheerful and uplifted. You may even appear younger than your age because of your radiance.

How do you come alive in the spring? It is a time of creativity and movement. Now is the time to awaken and spring forth. There are many springs each year in relation to your many projects. Each time you are coming alive with something new, spring has sprung! Go for it.

**Daily Application:** Ponder your spring times as a leader with vision. How often are you teaming with new life and vibrancy each year? Share your exuberance with others as you bring to life your vision.

**Personal Reflections:** _____
_____
_____
_____
_____
_____

## Day 345
# FAILURE

*You want to know the difference between a master and a beginner? The master has failed more times than the beginner has ever tried.*

~ Yoda

Everyone has a different definition of failure. Some say that that there is no failure, only lessons. Some say that failure gives you lessons that lead to wisdom. Some take failure so seriously that they become depressed or go into denial about the actual events. Failure is a charged word in our culture.

      A failure is simply an event and it is not a statement about who you are. You cannot be a failure. You can experience events that you label a failure but you are not an inherent failure. This is not possible.

      I had an event venue fall through with a short time to schedule another venue. At first, my thinking was all about the problems and disappointment. It could have been seen as a failure. Instead of allowing it to define me or stop me, I sought another venue. I actually found one that was much better with more pleasant staff and accommodations for less. So, the initial problem that appeared to be a failure, was turned into a success by my actions focused consistently toward my goal.

**Daily Application:** Take a few long, slow deep breaths. Focus your attention inward. Check in on your definition of failure. Is it serving you? Journal your ideas about failure being an event and unhook yourself from using the idea of failure as part of who you are.

**Personal Reflections:** _____
_____
_____
_____
_____
_____

## Day 346
# AWARENESS

*It's not about perfection. It's about awareness, and acceptance. It's about living the full expression of humanity that you are, in all of your glory, all of your foolishness, and all of your complexity, with honesty and compassion.*

~ Sharon Rosen \*\* (from her book Crazy World, Peaceful Heart)

Awareness is the first step in making any sort of change, improvement or transformation. When you are aware of your current state of affairs and you are also aware of your vision or ideas, then you are uniquely poised to move forward with great satisfaction. Being human and moving through life can be tricky at times. Things can become complex and messy yet with compassion, everything works out.

When you have an inner awareness of your inner landscape including beliefs, thoughts, ideas and focus, you are able to plan accordingly as you move forward. When your inner awareness is defocused, or you are not aware of your inner awareness, you can become easily distracted from your goals and heart's desires.

**Daily Application:** Spend some time in quiet reflection. Open your awareness to your inner world and your outer environment. Use your inner rhythm to inspire your focus. Practice surrendering to the beauty of your life. Share. Journal your awareness's and inspirations.

**Personal Reflections:** _____
_____
_____
_____
_____
_____

## Day 347
# CLOSENESS

*Friend, our closeness is this: Anywhere you put your foot, feel me in the firmness under you.*

~ Rumi

What an amazing visual of friendship. It speaks to the loyalty and strength of being a friend. Are you able to receive such support from your friends? Many visionary leaders have challenges with being supported by others. Visionaries are often the one doing the support. Are you able to receive support from your friends? How close are you really? Are your closest friends aware of how you are feeling and what excites or scares you? Can you receive their support?

Imagine that your friend was that firmness, do you put your full weight in your steps? Is it often difficult to receive support, even from our closest friends? You may feel unworthy or fearful that it will back fire. We all need friends who are our inner circle and are able to be that firm strength in our messy moments. The beautiful power of Rumi brings such power and connection to the real closeness of friends.

**Daily Application:** In your quiet time today, ponder your relationship with your closest friends. Can you feel their firmness supporting your walk? Are you able to receive their support on your journey? Draw or journal your ideas about allowing the closeness to develop and be firmer still. Smile and honor your friends.

**Personal Reflections:** _____
_____
_____
_____
_____
_____

## Day 348
# CAPABILITIES

*What makes you altogether more beautiful is that despite facing problems bigger than your current capabilities, you have not given up.*
~ Brendon Burchard

Being a capable person is inspiring. No matter the insurmountable odds, you have prevailed because you have not given up! You are fully equipped and capable. There is no accident. In every area of our lives there are challenges and this is simply part of being alive. Leaders have an inherent ability to attend to challenges and obstacles with some focus that others do not fully possess or maybe even understand.

As you grow and develop, your capabilities expand and they keep expanding as long as you are focused on growing, evolving and transforming as a person. One of my artist clients is developing new techniques. She is working diligently to add to the things she is capable of in her work. One of my athlete clients is gaining new skills as well so he can advance his skill level in his sport. He is capable as he learns and grows despite not currently being able to play in the next bracket.

**Daily Application:** What are some of the challenges that you have faced that you were not sure you could handle? You handled the situation in what ways as you look back. Being capable is a fantastic and beautiful aspect of you. Today, celebrate your ability to keep moving forward and expanding.

**Personal Reflections:** _____

_____

_____

_____

_____

_____

## Day 349
# EXTRA-ORDINARY

*Be extra-ordinary and take risks: risk taking is the friction before the flame that ignites an idea, unites a plan, and can impact the world.*
~ Sheryl Nicholson, CSP **

I read a lot of books, listen to many different podcasts and speak with a myriad of people. The common denominator that underpins success and happiness is taking healthy risks. To be extra-ordinary it means you must be willing to take the risk to follow your vision no matter what others may say. Your vision and calling is yours alone. Many well-meaning people may try to dissuade you and your job is to listen humbly and continue on your path no matter what. Follow your inner voice and allow your vision to emerge. You then, become extra-ordinary!

You are here to make a difference. You have a gift to offer. Now is the time to step up and be that extra-ordinary person who follows their inner guidance and lives the vision. The world is waiting for your unique talents and gifts to be presented and freely given.

**Daily Application:** Meditate today on your inner flame and that inner voice that is encouraging you forward with your vision. What risks help ignite your action plan? Journal your plan and go ahead and jump!

**Personal Reflections:** _____

_____
_____
_____
_____
_____

## Day 350
# CLARITY

*Confusion is the first step toward clarity.*
~ Syd Field

Confusion used to really annoy me. When I was confused, I would get frustrated and sometimes would simply change what I was doing. I love being clear and having clarity in my decisions and actions. Confusion can be a real irritation for many people. Clarity is expected by ourselves and our culture at large.

Confusion and mystery or uncertainty are different things. Mystery and uncertainty and being OK with these requires a spiritual connection and a feeling of being safe in the Universe. Mystery means that humans cannot possibly know what is happening in the unknown realms. Confusion to me is trying to understand things in the human realm that is not apparent and thus trying to figure it our creates confusion. Without this confusion, new mental clarity and understanding cannot surface. You can be clear while also having mystery and uncertainty.

When I am unclear and confused when approaching a project or challenge. I tend to get excited as I become open to the possibilities for clarity as I move forward in my understanding and knowledge. How about you?

**Daily Application:** Ponder your personal process of going from confusion to clarity. Are you a talker, a reader, a researcher, a listener or any combination? How do you handle confusion and what are ways you can grow to excitement for your journey? Journal some of your thoughts.

**Personal Reflections:** _____
_____
_____
_____
_____
_____

## Day 351
# INTENTION

*Giving never happens by accident. It's always intentional.*

~ Amy Grant

Your intentions show your determination. If you are going to give, you must do so with intention. Giving takes planning, even if briefly. What you intend will create your life. Giving requires first learning how to receive. To receive you must be open and willing in a humble way. Your intentions come to light as you do your business. Whatever you are determined to do comes to light more rapidly than a mere good idea. The difference is determination.

Intention is a creative power and it creates your world. Whatever you intend has the formative power of creation. Be aware of what you are intending because you hold more power than you may realize.

What are your intentions? Are they intentions of giving and service? Notice your intentions and your reaction to the word. Many people think this is a negative word when in fact it is a neutral word that speaks to determination. Intend to give freely of your time and talent.

**Daily Application:** Notice your intentions. What is your emotional response to the word today? Note any static of defensiveness. Journal your intentions for the day. Notice the place where you are giving.

**Personal Reflections:** _____
_____
_____
_____
_____
_____

## Day 352
# LISTENING

*The practice of active listening is a superpower that can move mountains and change the universe.*

~ Raymond Hinst **

Actively listening to another is scarce today yet it is one of most powerful rapport building actions. Most people are simply waiting for the speaker to stop long enough for them to answer. What is often called a conversation is more like sequential monologues. Active listening is much like a superpower yet everyone has the innate ability yet so few ever use their superpower.

Building a relationship with someone, whether a co-worker or someone you see periodically, takes investment in the person and the connection. I enjoy my shopping experiences more when the people actively listen and we can connect on some level. I enjoy social events more when I leave having connected to others. Whenever you feel that connection, active listening was used. It is a superpower and you have it in your arsenal.

**Daily Application:** Listen today. Really listen to your inner dialogue, your words and other people's communication. Use your superpower to move those mountains of challenges and questions. Focus on building connection that support all concerned.

**Personal Reflections:** _____

## Day 353
# INTENSITY

*Long term consistency trumps short-term intensity.*

~ Bruce Lee

The tortoise beats the hare and long term consistent focused action beats the flash in the pan all day long. Kaizen involves daily small actions and progress on you journey toward a larger goal. Intensity is amazing and if it is allowed to burn unbridled, it dissipates and eventually stops your forward momentum.

Begin to think generationally rather than short term. You can then use your intensity and passion in ways that serve your greater good. Think of the martial artists, they do not burn extra intense energy. They are focused and deliberate. This longer-term focus will be victorious because there will be energy left after the intensity flash is over. Which works best for you? Are you running a marathon or a sprint? Choose your strategy wisely.

**Daily Application:** In your quiet time, honor your intensity and the energy it gives you. Ponder how you might use it with focus for your long-term consistency. Share your plan with a trusted other and ask them to remind you when you are off track. Celebrate you!

**Personal Reflections:** _____
_____
_____
_____
_____
_____

## Day 354
# MENTORING

*The greatest good you can do for another is not just to share your riches but to reveal to them their own.*

~ Benjamin Disraeli

A good mentor asks great questions that allow the mentee to uncover their personal answers from within. Where a therapist or counselor looks for what is not working in order to fix it and a coach focuses on a particular goal, a mentor has both the experience and knowledge to ask effective questions that lead to the solutions and answers. The mentee has the opportunity to uncover their inner riches.

Helping someone reveal their own truth is one of my greatest joys and honors I experience frequently. It is one thing to share what I may know and it is so much greater and more powerful to be the catalyst in another's self-discovery where their personal riches are revealed.

**Daily Application:** Become still. Is there someone whom you can mentor by helping them reveal their own riches simply by being in interaction with you? Seek opportunity to be that beneficial presence and be awed at the power of your mentoring.

**Personal Reflections:** _____
_____
_____
_____
_____
_____

## Day 355
# CHANGE

*Very often a change of self is needed more than a change of scene.*
~ A.C. Benson

Do you want change? What are you willing to do for the change to occur? What are you no longer willing to do? The only constant in the world is change. Nature is always changing as each day, night and season unfold. When you are in nature, it is often easy to be in the change than when you are focused on your goals or your personal life. Many of my clients come to me wanting change. Many aren't sure about the effort needed to make the change.

       Change can be an asset as you grow and evolve. Change offers you the opportunity to remain free from being stuck and it allows you to create the life you imagine. If you are struggling with change, practice seeing change as an ally rather than an enemy. See change ushering in the new and give yourself permission to release what is no longer serving you.

**Daily Application:** In your quiet time, note some area that you desire change in your life. Now journal the change you desire and follow with your willingness to be in the flow of the change. Exhale and release resistance and inhale to welcome the new.

**Personal Reflections:** _____
_____
_____
_____
_____
_____

## Day 356
# COMPASSION

*Compassionate action involves working with ourselves as much as working with others.*

~Pema Chodron

Being compassionate with yourself for the grand adventure of being human with all the messiness and blunders is where real compassion begins. Then, as you are compassionate with yourself, you can be compassionate with others. You become gentler with yourself when you live by these higher principles.

Being hard on yourself and expecting unrealistic production lacks compassion. You are not a machine and expecting machine-like behavior is not serving you or your highest good. When you are realistic and caring for you, your efforts toward others becomes more real and authentic. Enjoy your inner journey as you work with others.

Sharing care, sensitivity and warmth toward yourself enhances your ability and effectiveness with others. Work with yourself to be ever vigilant about self-compassion as you walk your journey into your vision.

**Daily Application:** Spend your quiet time opening your heart to compassion. Compassion for all sentient beings. Notice any unforgiveness in your heart and allow it to be washed clean by compassion. Write some of your insights. Spend today sharing your compassion with others.

**Personal Reflections:** _____
_____
_____
_____
_____
_____

## Day 357
# SILENCE

*Silence is the sleep that nourishes wisdom.*
*~ Francis Bacon*

For some, being silent is difficult if not nearly impossible. Yet silence is where your wisdom grows. It is in silence that your inspired ideas surface and direct you toward living you vision more fully. Silence is even more challenging to find in everyday life. I notice ever increasing noise levels as the city I live in is growing. There are days I ponder moving to get some peace and quiet.

How is your level of inner silence? Inner silence and quiet is tricky to attain if your fear or grief levels are high. I have a client who told me that he has trouble being in silence because he can't handle the thoughts running through his mind. He told me he must always keep some type of background noise going in order to function. Apparently, the background noise distracts him from the lack of inner silence. His greater wisdom will elude him and he will remain feeling sad and unfulfilled as long as he runs from himself.

You can become silent within. It is possible to maintain silence while the world swirls around. This is a practice that is worth its weight in wisdom.

**Daily Application:** Take some time in silence. Notice your response to the silence. Any discomfort or desire to be distracted by electronics or noise is a wall between you and your wisdom. Breathe deeply and allow your emotions to surface and be revealed. Journal your experience.

**Personal Reflections:** _____
_____
_____
_____
_____

## Day 358
# PERMISSION

*You don't need permission to chase your dreams. Go execute!*
~ Gary Vaynerchuk

Permission is an interesting word. You don't need anyone else's permission to follow your heart and create your amazing life. You do need you own internal permission to follow your vision and move forward. Where Gary suggests you chase your dreams, I might also add that you must be open and willing to allow your true calling to emerge so you know what you are going after in the first place.

I gave myself permission to follow my dreams and allow my heart's desire to emerge. You know it is your heart's desire because it is for the good of all. I have permission to go for it and create opportunities for expansion and growth and transformation. I was once told by a client that my work is one of restoration – helping people restore their lives. I had to give myself permission to step forward in order to seize the dream. Giving yourself permission internally, gives you the authority to execute your dreams.

**Daily Application:** You are on your path to serve others. You do not need permission to go for your vision and create the dream you imagine. Journal today about your vision and how you are executing the attainment of your dreams.

**Personal Reflections:** _____

_____

_____

_____

_____

_____

## Day 359
# ASPIRATION

*Our aspirations are our possibilities.*

*~ Robert Browning*

If you can dream it you can do it. Your aspirations are your possible results. An aspiration is something you are hoping for. The things that come to your mind are within your possibilities or they wouldn't be coming to your mind.

What do you think about and dream about? I think about more transformation and higher awareness for people. Less pain and fear and more joy and harmony. I believe these things are my possibilities. I strive toward them each day and my hope is alive.

My clients have hopes. I think everyone has hopes, whether they admit it or not. No one wakes up every day wanting to be miserable. Knowing that your hopes are possible with focused effort. Are you willing to go for it?

**Daily Application:** Check with your aspirations. What are some of the first steps toward achievement of your dreams? Journal in quiet your plan of action. Post it where you can see it regularly so you don't lose focus.

**Personal Reflections:** _____
_____
_____
_____
_____
_____

## Day 360
# HEALING POWER

*Music has healing power. It has the ability to take people out of themselves for a few hours.*

~ Elton John

You are fully equipped to heal. To heal means to reconnect to your source. All dis-ease is a disconnection from source that first was spiritual, then emotional and is now physical. Knowing that the healing powers are within you is a great treasure that can be brought forward. Many people, sadly, do not ever travel inward to discover the hidden healing power within. I love that idea of tapping the magic and zooming inward.

When I tapped into the healing magic within, my entire life changed. As I teach clients and friends ways to go within and free the inner healing powers, they also end up making great strides toward their health. Zoom inward, not just a saunter but a zoom! Move it and free your inner potential.

I am sure you have heard of so many non-verbal healing type activities. When this healing power re-emerges, great transformations are evident. What have you been open to that gets you going within?

**Daily Application:** Reflect on your understanding of ways to heal that are independent of current allopathic intervention medicine. How are you willing to zoom within and tap your amazing inner resources? Make a commitment to try something new and share your experience.

**Personal Reflections:** _____
_____
_____
_____
_____

## Day 361
# THOROUGHNESS

*Employ every economy consistent with thoroughness, accuracy and reliability.*

~ Arthur C. Nielsen

Being thorough is very important to your success. Many a mistake is made by taking a cursory look at something and missing important details. It is vital to carefully manage your resources such that you are reliable and accurate in your dealings. Being reliable is a key complement to being thorough. As leaders, we are called to be as Arthur describes. Being thorough adds to your credibility and confidence.

My newest client is very thorough. She investigates as many avenues as possible on a subject. She told me that she loves being accurate in what she shares with others so she investigates most things. Her stumbling block is in consistency. She can either move much too fast and do too much of be off the grid so to speak. We are working on consistency and focus so that being thorough serves her highest vision.

**Daily Application:** Spend time in quiet today and notice how you invest your daily energy toward your vision. Are you paying attention or is there a lot of wasted time and energy? How can you become more focused and consistent in your work? Now, create a phrase to keep you focused and use it. Journal as you wish.

**Personal Reflections:** _____
_____
_____
_____
_____
_____

## Day 362
# INTUITION

*Intuition is seeing with the soul.*

~ Dean Koontz

Intuition is amazing and profound. Many of the greatest inventors, artists, thinkers and change makers use their intuition whether they mention it or not. Using that inner sense that just knows while focusing on your goal can be a great asset. Intuition means that you are able to connect what is not only intellectual. It is an energy connection that transcends knowledge and logic.

With intuition, you can see and know things from a profound level; the level of your soul. These deep connections offer you multifaceted information and guidance that is comprehensive and often outside of what your intellect can imagine.

In your growth and transformation, your intuition is a part of you that you may want to develop by working with this aspect of yourself.

**Daily Application:** How have you been transformed as a result of deep personal connection? What is your personal use of intuition? Spend some of your quiet time pondering these ideas. Move into your day and notice the power of your fascinating life through your intuitive eyes.

**Personal Reflections:** _____

_____
_____
_____
_____
_____

## Day 363
# MIND

*Intuition does not come to an unprepared mind.*
~ Albert Einstein

Each one of us has intuition and some of us acknowledge it and use it more than others. Have you ever had a gut feeling and not followed it? When this happens, you may regret not listening to your own inner wisdom. You create a multitude of opportunities when you take your intuition and you pay attention and take action that is aligned.

In a world of excuse and blame, you are able to create options and opportunities that many miss because they refuse to pay attention and take action. When you bring your mind and intuition into a harmonious relationship, you become aware of amazing opportunities that abound. This is not accidental or luck. Choosing to marry these qualities is a way of life. Be prepared to say yes to the opportunities that show up.

**Daily Application:** Today, take a broader view of how marrying your inner qualities can bring about increased opportunities and understanding. Pay attention to how you can use your gifts together for a greater good. Journal your ideas and awareness.

**Personal Reflections:** _____
_____
_____
_____
_____
_____

## Day 364
# BREAKTHROUGH

*All personal breakthroughs begin with a change of beliefs.*
~ Anthony Robbins

Many of your beliefs are instilled in you before you were five years old. As an adult, to make powerful and lasting changes, those outdated beliefs must be replaced with a belief that serves your highest good. The most powerful personal breakthrough is when you go from a limiting belief to an empowering belief. The change to competence from unknowing is a game changer.

I have completed a couple of fire walks. The first one was so profound that it is with me many years later. That experience changed many of my belief systems and rid me of profound anxiety. I had a breakthrough.

I'll bet you have had many breakthroughs in your life. All of them leading you toward more freedom and personal power. Breakthroughs are a result of a belief change that often comes as a result of challenges. Your challenges and frustrations point to the areas that a belief change is needed for your breakthrough to happen and propel you forward.

**Daily Application:** In your quiet time today, ponder your beliefs. Are there any you would like to change? Ponder any breakthroughs you may want. Ask to see the beliefs that need to change. Go within and listen then journal your insights. Then take action.

**Personal Reflections:** _____
_____
_____
_____
_____
_____

## Day 365
# FORGIVENESS

*True Forgiveness is when you can say... Thank you for that experience.*
*~ Carl Jung*

Forgiveness is about compassion. Forgiveness comes when you are able to have a compassionate heart for you and others for the great adventure of being human. No doubt you have suffered some pains and betrayals and have also caused pain. There comes a time when forgiveness is the only viable answer. You can forgive someone from a distance.

Saying thank you for the experience doesn't necessarily mean that you must engage with the person. You can have forgiveness in your heart, be grateful for the experience and keep moving forward on your road. Forgive yourself. Forgive others. Keep clear boundaries as not to expose yourself further to harm.

Forgiveness sets you free from the bondage. You do not need the other person to free yourself from the pain. Make the decision to forgive and set yourself free.

**Daily Application:** Everyone has something to forgive. Spend some quiet time pondering where unforgiveness lives in you. Meditate on compassion and forgiveness, springing yourself from the trap of pain. Journal as you are led. Offer gratitude for the experience.

**Personal Reflections:** _____
_____
_____
_____
_____
_____

## Day 366
# SYNCHRONICITY

*I am open to the guidance of synchronicity, and do not let expectations hinder my path.*

~ Dalai Lama

When things come together, they come together, and things change. The synchronicity at this very moment is that I was preparing to write this reading and my phone rang. It was an amazing woman I haven't spoken with recently. She and I spoke and the synchronicity of our coming together was amazing. We knew that there are no accidents and we reconnected in a synchronous way as I was getting ready to write on the subject!

Paying attention to the sequence of events and being willing to go with the flow offers you great advantage. Having limiting expectations can hinder your progress. I am always looking for the synchronicities and it is good.

Expectations on some level can create rigid responses to life and become obstacles to your awareness of synchronicities. If I expect you to always be on time and you are late, I have limited emotional and mental responses available to me because of my expectation. By preferring your timeliness, I give myself freedom of response if any. Allowing for synchronicity and releasing limiting expectations, you are free.

**Daily Application:** Spend time in quiet. Relax and look at your life in your mind's eye. Now listen to your inner voice that is guiding you. Follow your message. Write down the message.

**Personal Reflections:** _____
_____
_____
_____
_____

# Complete!

You have successfully completed 366 days of growth, inspiration and transformation.

*Take some time to honor your dedication and commitment.*
*Share your experience.*

*How do you feel? Let me know when you have completed this journey.*
*dianne@visionsapplied.com*

*Journal your ideas, inspiration and progress. Honor your journey and your commitment.*

## HOPE REALIZED

## Remember:
### If your life is worth living, it is worth recording.

## Contributors

No work is completed in solitude. In my professional world, there are many who come together to support one another. Several of my contemporaries have been included among the historical greats because great wisdom emanates through these thought leaders today. I trust you will be inspired by their wisdom. The following colleagues, who are known to me personally, have contributed quotes for this book. I have included below information about these leaders and the day numbers on which they are featured. Enjoy their ideas and check in to see what they are up to these days.

They are listed here in alphabetical order by first name.

**Carole R. Gill**                    **Day 94 and 115 and 287**

Carole takes a dynamic approach that uses current "best practices" in leadership to teach individuals to become more effective leaders, communicators, collaborators and team builders. Her areas of expertise include leadership development, executive coaching, employee engagement, building emotional intelligence competencies, as well as organizational and team development. Visit: www.CaroleGill.com

**Cynthia Citron**                    **Day 86 and 200**

Cynthia Citron, MA, MBA, LMHC, CRC, BCN is the CEO of Reboot, a science-based brain and mental health company, dedicated to optimizing brain and mind functionality in the areas of Attention, Motivation, Multitasking, Anxiety, Mood, Sleep and more. Visit: Rebootlivebetter.com

**Dave Kauffman**                    **Day 59 and 283**

Dave is a Strategic Advisor, Keynote Speaker, Author and Trainer. Dave helps business owners find freedom in their company, so they can spend more time with their family and friends. Dave is an expert in Peak Performance and is a Master trainer of the DISC Model of human behavior. He is also handpicked by the Zig Ziglar family to carry on the legacy of American Legend… Zig Ziglar. Visit: www.Empoweringsmallbiz.com

**Dave Moore**　　　　　　　　**Day 83 and 146 and 296**

Dave played in the NFL for 15 years under 2 Hall of Fame head coaches. Currently serves as the color analyst for the Buccaneer Radio network broadcasting the Tampa Bay Buccaneer football games. Dave owns an Independent Insurance Agency "Moore Resources" writing Property & Casualty insurance products. Website: www.DaveMooreInsurance.com

**Don Ollsin**　　　　　　　　**Day 142 and 227**

Don is a Master Herbalist, Herbal Elder and Mentor. He lives on a gulf island in the coast salish sea with his partner Sandy in their strawbale home. Visit: www.grassrootsherbalism.com

**fiZ Anthony**　　　　　　　　**Day 125**

fiZ is a "Hit" Singer/Songwriter whose music has been on the Billboard Charts. He is the author of Ignite the Rock-Star Within a book that helps people get clear on their "Life Purpose". fiZ has been awarded for his humanitarian work with Physically Challenged Children. fiZ has a company called Signature Songs, as he injects his infectious HIT Songwriting Style to help Speakers, Entrepreneurs, Authors and Companies "Ignite Their Brand" by taking their Message/Mission Statement and helping them create a "Signature Song". Visit: www.signaturesongsbyfiZ.com or www.fiZ4ever.com.

**Gabriel Aluisy**　　　　　　　　**Day 158**

Gabriel is the founder of The Private Club Agency, a Tampa, Florida based design, marketing and consulting firm focused on membership marketing and retention strategy at private clubs. He is the author of The Definitive Guide to Membership Marketing and the bestselling book Moving Targets: Creating Engaging Brands in an On-Demand World. Each week, Aluisy hosts the Private Club Radio Show, the industry's first and only podcast dedicated to private club education. Visit: www.aluisy.com

### George Kao — Day 160

George is one of the most authentic & generous business & marketing coaches online. He has coached hundreds of clients since 2009, and now offers his comprehensive content for free on his website. Visit: www.GeorgeKao.com

### Jennifer Kaye — Day 244

Jennifer Kaye is a well-known and respected leader in the field of intuition. Over the past twenty-five years, she has built a reliable and elegant platform of information and experience with tools and techniques that educate her clients so that they can gain self-confidence, hope, clarity, and ultimately healing from the inside out. Visit: www.jkdickinsonauthor.com

### Judi Snyder, CeFT — Day 252

Judi and her husband Jeff are independent financial professionals who specialize in educating clients on "The Best Investment You've Never Hear Of". Judi is fiercely committed to teaching the secrets of "Work Optional Wealth". Visit: www.JPSnyder.com

### Kenny Loggins — Day 48

Kenny is an American singer-songwriter and guitarist. His remarkable four-decade plus career has brought him from the top of the charts to the toast of the Grammys. He's had smash hits on Hollywood's favorite soundtracks, rocked worldwide stages, and found his way into children's hearts while bringing his soulful, beautiful voice to platinum albums of a stunning variety of genres. His gift for crafting deeply emotional music is unparalleled. Visit: www.kennyloggins.com

### Lori Givens — Day 285

Lori has been teaching yoga for over 14 years, she has trained thousands of yogis and yoginis across the globe in the Bikram tradition. She was featured for her success in yoga in two issues of Oprah's "O" Magazine and has continued her yoga journey into the corporate world as a corporate coach and trainer, spreading mindfulness and meditation. Visit: www.LoriGivensYoga.com

### Michelle S. Royal — Day 265 and 301

Michelle is an innovator, entrepreneur and artist. She is the founder of RIDG, a group of creative consultants who work exclusively with executives of large companies equipping them with unique team management tools. She lives in St. Petersburg, FL with her partner, Peter, and their three dogs. Visit: www.ridg.com

### Paul ILL — Day 340

Paul is a musician, songwriter, author and mental health professional. As a studio musician, he has sold over 24 million records, and more than 4.5 million as a songwriter. He is the author of the internationally published "Studio Musician's Handbook" and is an MFT student/Trainee. He is a graduate of Berklee College of Music and is a former United States Air Force Officer. Visit: www.disreputablefewmusic.com

### Raymond Hinst — Day 76 and 174 and 352

Raymond is a graduate of the FSU Film school. He is a filmmaker, author, and the fourth-generation proprietor of one of the largest and oldest bookstores in America, Haslam's Book Store in Saint Petersburg, FL. Visit: www.haslams.com

### Ruth Toledo Altschuler — Day 107 and 335

Ruth is an experienced Flower Essence Practitioner and Educator. Her work is based on three decades of a solid practice with results in Brazil and now brings her inspiration and knowledge to English speaking audiences. Visit www.essencementoring.com

### Sandy Freschi — Day 157 and 224

Sandy Freschi is a Human Design Blueprint Specialist who helps people reconnect with their unique strengths and gifts. Sandy believes that each person is endowed with the wisdom they need to live the highest version of life. She strives to help people unlock their personal truth and live it powerfully in each and every day. Visit: www.sandyfreschi.com

**Sharon Rosen**  **Day 58 and 68 and 346**

Sharon Rosen is an author, mindful living guide, energy healer, and teacher who loves helping other people relax, release, and embody self-love and compassion. Her home on the web is www.heartofselfcare.com


**Sheryl Nicholson, CSP**  **Day 114 and 349**

Sheryl is an International Speaker, Author, Podcaster and I love to do something creative every day.  So right now, Sheryl is working on creating painted fish from royal palm fronds.  What Fun! Visit: www.Sheryl.com

# About the Author

Nationally known speaker Dianne A. Allen, MA takes her raw experience, education and information and presents a daily strategy for personal transformation and development. She works as a mentor, author, speaker, podcaster and life catalyst for bright and sensitive people. She creates exciting and diverse avenues to opening and expanding possibilities of personal and business growth. If you want to be free of what holds you back, Dianne has a way of offering that needed push of inspiration to get your moving for your highest good. With over 3 decades of working with personal and business development, Dianne is committed to presenting ideas and strategies in understandable and empowering ways. Dianne has taken her dedication to a daily practice of meditation and writing and created *Hope Realized* as a guide and strategy for creating the life you deserve through personal development, growth and education.

Dianne has been featured on CNN, CBS, Fox and local news outlets. She has also been featured on radio and podcasts. Along with speaking at state and national conferences, Dianne presents retreats, workshops and conferences on a regular basis. For more event and webinar information, visit www.visionsapplied.com

## Dianne's Earlier Books

- How to Quit Anything in 5 Simple Steps
- The Loneliness Cure – A Guide to Contentment
- 7 Simple Steps to Get Back on Track and Live the Life You Envision
- Daily Meditations for Visionary Leaders
- Midlife Suicide – Points to Consider

## Dianne's Podcasts:

- ***Someone Gets Me***

  Subscribe today on iTunes or Stitcher or listen at www.someonegetsme.com

- ***Meditations for Visionary Leaders***

  Subscribe today on SoundCloud or iTunes or listen at www.visionsapplied.com/podcast

HOPE REALIZED

www.ingramcontent.com/pod-product-compliance
Lightning Source LLC
Chambersburg PA
CBHW070418010526
44118CB00014B/1804